Apache Mahout: Beyond MapReduce

Distributed Algorithm Design

Dmitriy Lyubimov
Andrew Palumbo

Dmitriy Lyubimov, Andrew Palumbo

Apache Mahout: Beyond MapReduce

Distributed Algorithm Design

First Edition

ISBN-13: 978-1523775781

ISBN-10: 1523775785

Library of Congress Control Number: 2016902011

BISAC: Computers / Mathematical & Statistical Software

7" x 10" (17.78 x 25.4 cm) paperback

Attributions.

LaTeX styling in this book is derived from work by Mathias Legrand and Velimir Gayevskiy (http://latextemplates.com) with permission of Velimir Gayevskiy.

Preface

Target Audience.

This book is for machine learning practitioners, algorithm designers, applied researchers, and anyone who likes to experiment with bits and pieces of "mathematically infused" algorithms.

It is of course mainly for people who would like to learn about the new Mahout Samsara environment in particular.

The audience could further be divided into two categories: users of Mahout's off-the-shelf capabilities, and people who would like to use Mahout to design their own solutions (algorithm designers). The first edition of this book targets mostly the latter, that is the people who would like to develop their own machine learning solutions with the help of Mahout Samsara.

Some material assumes an undergraduate level understanding of linear algebra, calculus, and on occasion multivariate calculus. The examples are given in Scala and assume familiarity with basic Scala terminology and a minimal notion of functional programming.

What is different?

First, at the time of this writing, much of the prior printed matter on Mahout is focused on the Apache Hadoop MapReduce-based capabilities of Mahout.

As of Mahout 0.10.0 all the MapReduce algorithms officially entered their end-of-life phase. They were sweepingly deprecated, and the project has not been accepting any new MapReduce algorithms since. Strictly speaking, the announcement of the MapReduce end-of-life in Mahout came even earlier, in the first half of 2014, as a news post on the

Mahout web site and the Jira issue MAHOUT-1510[1].

In place of Hadoop MapReduce, Mahout has been focusing on implementing a flexible and backend-agnostic machine learning environment. Mahout is targeting Apache Spark and Apache Flink as the main execution backends, and there is also support for Mahout on the H2O engine. The new programming API is completely based on a Scala DSL, which is mostly an algebraic DSL. Mahout Samsara is the code name for the aggregate of all these new features working together from the 0.10.0 release on.[2]

To the best of our knowledge, at the time of this writing this is the only book that is devoted solely and in depth to Mahout Samsara.

Second, much of the previous printed matter on Mahout targets the aspect of off-the-shelf usage of Mahout algorithms. While this book has some end-to-end off-the-shelf tutorials too, its main target is machine learning algorithm design using the Mahout Samsara environment.

Third, this book is also different from many traditional books on Machine Learning in that it (almost) never re-traces any mathematical inference of the end-game math formulations. There are no lemmas, theorems or proofs supporting the mathematical outcomes of the methods we consider. This is not the focus of this book. Instead, we give references describing the algorithms. These references provide all the necessary details we omit. We then focus on turning the mathematical description of a method into program code.

The philosophy of the book.

In many ways in this book we try to do the same thing that a lot of computer science books do: we teach design principles and hands-on coding of algorithms. Except instead of coding algorithms expressed in pseudocode, we actually code mathematical formulas. Formulas are also just a form of an algorithm. The main difference is merely the algorithm notation. For that reason, this book has some amount of mathematical equations, simply because we have to outline the final formulation of the methodology we code, before we show how to code it. As it has been previously said, we do not go into details of the method inference though.

The skills taught in this book allow the reader to implement a significant variety of existing Machine Learning approaches on his or her own, so that he or she is not bound by the algorithm's off-the-shelf availability. Implementing a machine learning algorithm is still largely an art rather than a recipe. Nevertheless, we aspire to demonstrate that with Samsara, the ease and maintainability of such an effort approaches the ease and maintainability of using numerical-friendly platforms such as MATLAB or R. One often-used measure of such performance is the number of lines in a program. Most, if not all, code examples in this book should not exceed a single page (assuming all comments and line skips are removed).

We also provide help with math notational fluency. By math fluency we mean the ability to parse mathematical expressions and see coding patterns in them.

---

[1]Some of the first elements of the Mahout Samsara Scala DSL bindings were present as early as the Mahout 0.9 release.

[2]Chapter 1 focuses on the definition of Mahout Samsara in more detail.

For computer science people who perhaps feel a bit intimidated by math notations, we have just one piece of advice – for the purposes of practical applications remember this: a math formula is just *an algorithm*; math notation is just *pseudocode*. If you spend a few minutes going over the notation conventions in § A.2, you will be able to read the pseudocode in this book, and after that, you will know the drill.

At times for a practitioner it is pragmatic to accept that "that is how the math works out," to be able to map it to code, and to debug and experiment quickly, rather than to track all origins of the final formulation. As long as an engineer is able to parse and codify the math notations, in-depth understanding of the theory and method inference may be pragmatically less important.

We aspire to achieve these goals by providing various hands-on patterns of translating simple formulations into distributed Samsara code, as well as more involved examples where these patterns connect into larger, coherent algorithm code. Like many texts in Computer Science, we employ the "learning by example" approach.

Thus, while learning the mathematical details of the method described by the BFGS example in chapter 3 is educational, the main purpose of that description is not to teach the BFGS underpinnings, but rather to illustrate a variety of hands-on techniques while treating potentially *any* algebraic approach in the context of the in-memory Mahout Samsara DSL (also known as "Scala Bindings").

To recap, in this book we do the following:

- We take off-the-shelf math, for which we provide in-depth references.
- We provide math notation explanations for the final method formulation.
- We explain math-to-code mapping patterns.
- We give tips for working with distributed and non-distributed math.
- We also give basic design narration about the behind-the-scenes architecture of the Mahout Samsara framework.
- We give one end-to-end extended classification tutorial.
- Finally, in the appendices we provide a reference for the R-like Mahout DSL.

The example code in this book can be found at: https://github.com/andrewpalumbo/mahout-samsara-book.

Acknowledgments.

We would like to thank Andrew Musselman, Gene Linetsky, Nathan Halko, Suneel Marthi and Tony Jebara (in alphabetical order) who provided preprint reviews, corrections, insights and ideas for this book.

We extend our cordial thanks to Nathan Halko who helped the Mahout team with the MapReduce version of Stochastic SVD and everyone involved with him in the random projection study [Halko et al., 2011]. We would like to thank Sebastian Schelter for his extensive help with and support of the early Mahout Samsara ideas; Anand Avati for his extensive and incredibly talented contribution to the physical layer translation for the H2O backend; Alexey Grigorev, Kostas Tzoumas, and Stephan Ewen for their ongoing effort to provide physical translation for the Apache Flink backend in Mahout.

We would like to thank our families for the much needed support on their behalf and tolerating the long hours we have to put towards this book's completion.

And of course we would like to thank all the contributors to Mahout – past and present.

Disclosures.

In this book, when we say "Mahout" or "Mahout Samsara," we refer to the Apache Mahout project, release 0.10.0 or later. Parts of this book are updated for Apache Mahout releases 0.11.0 and 0.10.2 and may not be backwards compatible with earlier releases.

When we say "Flink," we refer to the Apache Flink project.

When we say "Spark," we refer to the Apache Spark project, release 1.2.x or later. When we say "GraphX" or "MLlib," we refer to respective subcomponents of the Apache Spark project.

Some parts of this book further develop concepts contained in the working notes that were licensed by the authors to the Apache Software Foundation under a non-exclusive Apache ICLA.

Some examples contain code based on the code that had been previously licensed by the book authors to the Apache Software Foundation under a non-exclusive Apache ICLA.

Athough the authors have taken every effort in preparation of this book, there is no warranty, express or implied, on the information offered in this book. Neither the authors nor the publisher will be held liable for any damages caused or alleged to be caused by the information contained in this book.

See also "Attributions" on the copyright page.

SF BAY AREA   *Dmitriy Lyubimov*
NEW YORK   *Andrew Palumbo*

May, 2015

Contents

Appendix

First steps

Meet Mahout 0.10+ ("Samsara")

Mahout 0.10.x+ releases, also known as code name "Mahout Samsara," are a new genera-tion of Mahout releases that presents a major re-thinking of the philosophy of the previous Mahout releases.

First, to state the obvious, Mahout has abandoned MapReduce-based algorithms. The Mahout team still supports them (and they are now moved to mahout-mr artifact). But the Mahout project management committee ("PMC") does not accept any new MapReduce algorithms.

Second, Mahout shifts the focus from being a collection of things to being a pro-gramming environment, in particular a Scala-based programming environment.

Third, Mahout supports different distributed engines, also known as "backs." As it stands, Samsara runs on Spark and H2O, but work is under way for an Apache Flink translation as well.

We will now try to emphasize some of the key philosophical points of this work.

Mahout exists to help people create their own math, as opposed to just plugging in an off-the-shelf black-box solution.

Indeed, having fairly well-adjusted and complicated black box solutions is a good thing. People have spent quite a bit of time researching and optimizing them.

The problem is, very often off-the-shelf offerings are just not enough. We want to customize and build our own models, our own features, and our own specific rules and ensembles. We want to do it *quickly* and we want to try it *now*.

Let us look at a couple of intentionally simple examples.

Suppose we want to compute the column-wise variances of a matrix. For that we are going to the use simple formula:

$$\text{var}(x) = \mathbb{E}\left(x^2\right) - \left[\mathbb{E}(x)\right]^2$$

applied column-wise on a big, distributed matrix **X**. Here is how it is going to look in the new Mahout environment:

```
val mu = X colMeans
val variance = (X ^ 2 colMeans) -= mu ^ 2
```

That is it. All in a fully distributed fashion. On Apache Spark or H2O or, soon, Apache Flink.

Let us take on a little bit more complicated case. What if we want to compute an n-dimensional column-wise covariance matrix of the dataset **X**?

Assuming that

$$x_i \triangleq \mathbf{X}_{i*},$$

i.e., that every row is a point in the dataset, we can use a multivariate generalization of the previous formula:

$$\text{cov}(\mathbf{X}) = \mathbb{E}\left(\boldsymbol{x}\boldsymbol{x}^\top\right) - \boldsymbol{\mu}\boldsymbol{\mu}^\top,$$

where

$$\boldsymbol{\mu} = \mathbb{E}(\boldsymbol{x}).$$

Here is the Mahout code for that formula:

```
val mu = X.colMeans()
val mxCov = (X.t %*% X).collect /= X.nrow -= (mu cross mu)
```

This is a so called "thin" procedure, i.e., one that assumes that while the $m \times n$ input matrix **X** is too big to be an in-core matrix, the $n \times n$ covariance matrix will fit into memory in one chunk. In other words, it assumes $n \ll m$. The code for a "wide" distributed covariance computation needs a couple more lines but is just as readable.

So, what is the difference between Mahout 0.10+ and MLlib?

Well, what is the difference between R and an R package? What is the difference between Julia and libSVM?

The answer is that Mahout strives to be a *math platform* first, and a *collection of solutions* second. In that sense GraphX, for example, is just as dissimilar from MLlib: it is a *platform* for Graph algorithms first, and everything else second.

The bottom line is that Mahout strives to help you create your own math at scale.

Mahout wants to simplify dialect learning.

There are programming environments such as Python, R, MATLAB, and others that have passed the test of time for the purposes of numerical algorithm design in terms of their language dialects.

The Mahout team is building the environment dialect in the image of R. The new Mahout is a Scala-based beast, and all algebraic expressions are now in Scala with an R-like Scala DSL layered on top.

Initially, Samsara had a DSL (enabled via a separate import) for MATLAB-like dialect as well, but unfortunately Scala operator support posed issues implementing the entire MATLAB operator set verbatim. As a result, this work received much less attention. Instead, we focused on the R side of things.

The goal is for the Mahout DSL to be easily readable by R programmers. E.g., A %*% B is matrix multiplication, A * B is the element-wise Hadamard product, methods like colMeans, colSums follow R naming.

Among other things, arguably, math written in an R-like fashion is easier to understand and maintain than the same things written in other basic procedural or functional environments.

Mahout Samsara is backend-agnostic.

Indeed, Mahout is not positioning itself as Spark-specific. You can think of it that way if you use Spark, but if you use H2O, you could think of it as H2O-specifc (or, hopefully, "Apache Flink-specific" in the future) just as easily.

Neither of the above examples contain a single Spark (or H2O) imported dependency. They are written once but run on any of supported backs.

Not every algorithm can be written with this set of backend-independent techniques of course – there is more on that below. But quite a few can – and the majority can leverage at least some of these techniques as the backbone. For example, imagine that the dataset **X** above is a result of an embarrassingly parallel statistical Monte Carlo technique (which is also backend-independent), and just like that perhaps we get a backend-agnostic Gibbs sampler.

Mahout is an add-on to backend functionality.

Mahout is not taking away any capabilities of the backend. Instead, one can think of it as an "add-on" over, e.g., Spark and all its technologies. The same is true for H2O.

In truth, algebra and statistics alone are not enough to make ends meet. Access to the Spark RDD API, streaming, functional programming, external libraries, and many other wonderful things is desirable. In the case of Apache Spark one can embed algebraic pipelines by importing Spark-specific capabilities. Import MLlib or GraphX and all the goodies are available. Import DataFrame (or SchemaRDD) and use the language-integrated QL, and so on.

But if we want to draw any parallels, MLlib is "off-the-shelf code." Mahout 0.10+ is about that, too; but we hope that it is more about "off-the-shelf math" rather than code. In other words, Mahout 0.10+ is for people who like to experiment and research at scale using known mathematical constructs, execute more control over an algorithm, and pay much less attention to the specifics of distributed engines, and potentially would like to share the outcomes across different operational backends.

Algebraic Optimizer Stack.

The Mahout environment is more than just a Scala DSL. Behind the scenes, there is an algebraic optimizer that creates logical and physical execution plans. The whole process is not unlike the processes happening in a relational database optimizer or in Apache Hive.

For example, the Samsara optimizer understands that a thing like

```
dlog(X * X + 1).t %*% dlog(X * X + 1)
```

is in fact (in simplified physical operator pseudo code)

```
self_square(X.map(x => log(x * x + 1))).
```

Off-the-shelf methods.

Of course, in Mahout 0.10+, we want to provide an off-the-shelf code experience too. But even use of off-the-shelf methods should be easily composable via the programming environment and scripting. Using an environment that is intentionally standardized on a limited number of tensor types makes gluing things together easier.

2

Setting things up

This chapter discusses how to set up Mahout Samsara. It also shows how to run Mahout scripts using the Mahout shell for Spark, as well as how to start writing Scala programs and tests using the Mahout Scala API.

2.1 Compiling from source

Prerequisites: Git, Apache Maven, Java, Scala. This example also assumes an Ubuntu OS.

The Scala version needs to be compatible with the Apache Spark release.

The following example assumes Scala 2.10.4 and Apache Spark 1.2.1.

We will work with an Apache Spark backend in this example, so we will need Apache Spark downloaded and extracted into a local folder as pointed to by the SPARK_HOME environment variable. The major version of the Mahout Spark dependency must be in sync with the major version of the local installation of Spark.

Spark version compatibility:

At the time of this writing, Mahout 0.10.x targets Spark 1.2.x, and Mahout 0.11.x targets Spark 1.3+.

Cloning the repository.

```
git clone https://github.com/apache/mahout mahout-src
```

```
Cloning into 'mahout-src'...
remote: Counting objects: 91272, done.
remote: Compressing objects: 100% (20/20), done.
remote: Total 91272 (delta 4), reused 0 (delta 0), pack-reused

  91252

Receiving objects: 100% (91272/91272), 46.46 MiB | 5.16 MiB/s,

  done.

Resolving deltas: 100% (51708/51708), done.
Checking connectivity... done.
```

Picking up a release.

Let us see what releases we got:

```
cd mahout-src/
git tag -l
```

```
mahout-0.1
mahout-0.10.0
mahout-0.10.1
mahout-0.2
mahout-0.3
mahout-0.4
mahout-0.5
```

```
mahout-0.5-RC-1
mahout-0.5-RC1
mahout-0.6
mahout-0.7
mahout-0.8
mahout-0.9
mahout-collection-codegen-plugin-1.0
mahout-collections-1.0
```

We are going to pick the latest release at the time of writing this section, which is 'mahout-0.10.1'.

Create a local branch synchronized to the release tag:

```
git checkout -b mahout-0.10.1 mahout-0.10.1
```

```
Switched to a new branch 'mahout-0.10.1'
```

Now we can compile the release. We usually set a shell alias for compilation, but in this case let us proceed with the full command line:

```
mvn clean && mvn install -DskipTests=true
```

Hopefully, our compilation completes without error and we end up with a status declaring success for all modules:

```
[INFO] Reactor Summary:
[INFO]
[INFO] Mahout Build Tools ................................ SUCCESS [  2.810 s]
[INFO] Apache Mahout ..................................... SUCCESS [  0.067 s]
[INFO] Mahout Math ....................................... SUCCESS [ 14.929 s]
[INFO] Mahout HDFS ....................................... SUCCESS [  3.555 s]
[INFO] Mahout Map-Reduce ................................. SUCCESS [ 21.059 s]
[INFO] Mahout Integration ................................ SUCCESS [  3.810 s]
[INFO] Mahout Examples ................................... SUCCESS [ 18.204 s]
[INFO] Mahout Math Scala bindings ........................ SUCCESS [ 58.620 s]
[INFO] Mahout H2O backend ................................ SUCCESS [ 24.473 s]
[INFO] Mahout Spark bindings ............................. SUCCESS [ 55.177 s]
[INFO] Mahout Spark bindings shell ....................... SUCCESS [  9.088 s]
[INFO] Mahout Release Package ............................ SUCCESS [  1.046 s]
[INFO] ------------------------------------------------------------------------
[INFO] BUILD SUCCESS
[INFO] ------------------------------------------------------------------------
[INFO] Total time: 03:33 min
[INFO] Finished at: 2015-07-02T21:07:08-07:00
[INFO] Final Memory: 73M/795M
[INFO] ------------------------------------------------------------------------
```

In case we want to compile the *HEAD* of a branch or the master branch, rather than a branch at a release tag, the procedure is similar except for the branch checkout line. Then we would need to specify the branch of interest in the form of <git remote>/<branch name>:

```
git checkout -b master origin/master
```

2.2 Running the Mahout Spark shell

Perhaps the simplest way to check things out is running something in the Mahout shell. To kick the tires, there is a tutorial published here: http://mahout.apache.org/users/spark-bindings/play-with-shell.html.

There are a few things that we may need to do in order to run the Spark shell with Mahout.

Set up the following enviornment variables:

- SPARK_HOME containing the path to an Apache Spark distribution of a proper version. This is a required setting.
- MAHOUT_OPTS containing additional options as needed. This setting is optional, and mostly intended to tune up the Spark parameters such as executor memory and block cache size. One can use "-D<property>=<value>" format.
- MASTER containing the Spark master URL, such as "spark://localhost:7077". This setting is optional. If it is not set, then a "local" Spark master URL is assumed.

We have an option to either configure those on a permanent basis, or just supply them inline when launching the Mahout shell. We will be using the latter approach, for better illustration and reproducibility.

Do not override the *spark.serializer* property. Apache Mahout on Spark requires the use of the Kryo serializer and will set it automatically so. A user setting, if any, will be ignored.

You may want to adjust the parameters of the Kryo serializer such as the Kryo buffer size, as needed.

Assuming all of the above is complete, we now can try to run the Mahout shell for Spark. The following will start the Mahout shell with a "local" Spark master and default configuration:

```
SPARK_HOME=~/tools/spark bin/mahout spark-shell
```

To run the shell against a remote Spark cluster in standalone mode or any other non-local master, we can use the following command:

```
MASTER=spark://remote-host:7077 SPARK_HOME=~/tools/spark

 bin/mahout spark-shell
```

We can also run in local multithreaded mode. E.g., to enable 8 threads in the local executor process we can use the following command:

```
MASTER=local[8] SPARK_HOME=~/tools/spark bin/mahout spark-shell
```

Assuming everything is fine, we will now have a Mahout shell running:

```
          -                 -
 _ __ ___    __ _| |__    ___  _   _| |_
| '_ ` _ \ / _` | '_ \ / _ \| | | | __|
| | | | | | (_| | | | | | (_) | |_| | |_
|_| |_| |_|\__,_|_| |_|\___/ \__,_|\__|   version 0.10.0

Using Scala version 2.10.4 (Java HotSpot(TM) 64-Bit Server VM,

  Java 1.7.0_51)

Type in expressions to have them evaluated.
Type :help for more information.
Created spark context..
Mahout distributed context is available as "implicit val sdc".
mahout>
```

The Mahout shell has already added imports per §§ B.1, C.1 and C.13.1.

It also has initialized a Mahout context and assigned it to an implicit variable sdc. So we are ready to go.

Now we can try something just to make sure it works. The following creates a random 5000 × 5000 matrix:

```
mahout> val mxA = Matrices.symmetricUniformView(5000, 5000, 1234)
```

```
mxA: org.apache.mahout.math.Matrix =
{
  0 =>    {0:0.4586377101191827,1:0.07261898163580698,2:-0.4120814898385057,

  3:-0.34642075708405595,4:0.13562878996026145,5:0.45784520525982153,
  6:-0.4706505546910752,7:-0.23016615311845348,8:0.21877862831669628,
  9:0.479636479803259,10:0.19463854560108987,11:-0.22143915316681387,
  12:0.2097891013284503,13:-0.19744761560808702,14:-0.4407562546938582,
  15:0.3862335162012072,16:0.14407519172762487,17:0.04194022497803126,
  18:0.10862031391251574,19:-0.32684877921184075 ... }

  1 =>    {0:0.48977896201757654,1:0.2695201068510176,2:0.2035624121801051,

  3:0.24936953161203088,4:-0.47270888285344,5:0.06258489700284349,
  6:0.49054005184097776,7:-0.18983013078048971,8:0.2565323032908135,
  9:-0.09123189392334696,10:0.3342825154746871,11:-0.015098754906761836,
  12:0.27954086668921596...
```

Next, for example if we want to compute the row-wise sums of the matrix:

```
mahout> mxA rowSums
```

```
warning: there were 1 feature warning(s); re-run with -feature for details
res2: org.apache.mahout.math.Vector = {

  0:-16.911353545163376,1:-9.328607253897887,2:-0.9022006322434142,
  3:-11.379344287283237,4:10.411525568084947,5:-28.712167983430355,
  6:-12.969264999322888,7:-14.64031679074268,8:-30.720517068387412,
  9:-23.22425369388522,10:-22.161706888225407,11:4.772496332091681,
```

```
12:-9.060065202760626,13:11.562883581995248,14:-0.29272459239141413,
15:-7.636569776657746,16:-12.18039811638719,17:-2.6923715992174957,
18:26.83481240763156,19:12.054353280744268,20:-4.981047775343252,
21:3.1502971709356715,22:-9.419045942578768,23:-21.19686552923006,
24:3.510200582956171,25:35.19528637991668,26:12.616172798031199,
27:-4.191721641713555,28:25.523833687339835,29:19.502674040710776,
30:23.824906163653832,31:-7.682365447133579,32:-7.824953868277797,
33:-53.14074199115451,34:16.62522828...
```

```
mahout>
```

   Mahout truncates the printout of big vectors and matrices.

Writing Mahout shell scripts is also easy with the help of an integrated development environment (IDE) such as IntelliJ IDEA.

We usually use the *.mscala* extension for Mahout-scala scripts. The file extension can be added to the "Scala" editor extension in IntelliJ IDEA in order to enable the IntelliJ Scala plugin features.

See *simple.mscala* in the source code for an example of how to load and run Mahout shell scripts.

2.3 Using Mahout in a Spark application

Setting up an IntelliJ project.

Shell scripting is one way to deploy math jobs, but perhaps even more frequently used is to use Samsara APIs in an application that is statically compiled and run.

Here we briefly describe how to set up a Mahout standalone application using IntelliJ IDEA.

It is possible to set up a non-Maven project, but since Mahout uses Maven as its build tool, we will use Maven for the sample application for consistency. Setting up a Maven project is trivial using the "new project" wizard (Fig. 2.1 to 2.2).

Since we are using Mahout 0.10.2, JDK 1.7 and Scala 2.10.4 are used.

Setting up dependencies.

First, since we are building a Scala application, we are going to need the Scala library. We add the following under the Maven "dependencies" tag to the pom.xml file:

pom.xml

```
<dependency>
  <groupId>org.scala-lang</groupId>
  <artifactId>scala-library</artifactId>
  <version>2.10.4</version>
</dependency>
```

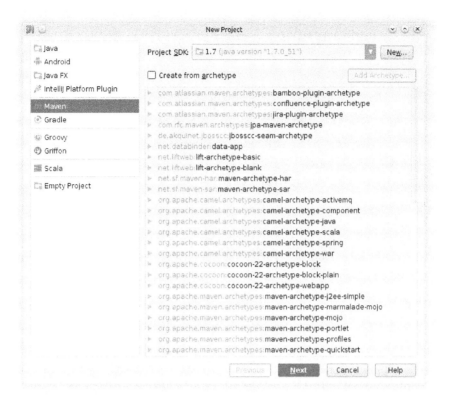

Figure 2.1: Create a new maven project (1 of 3).

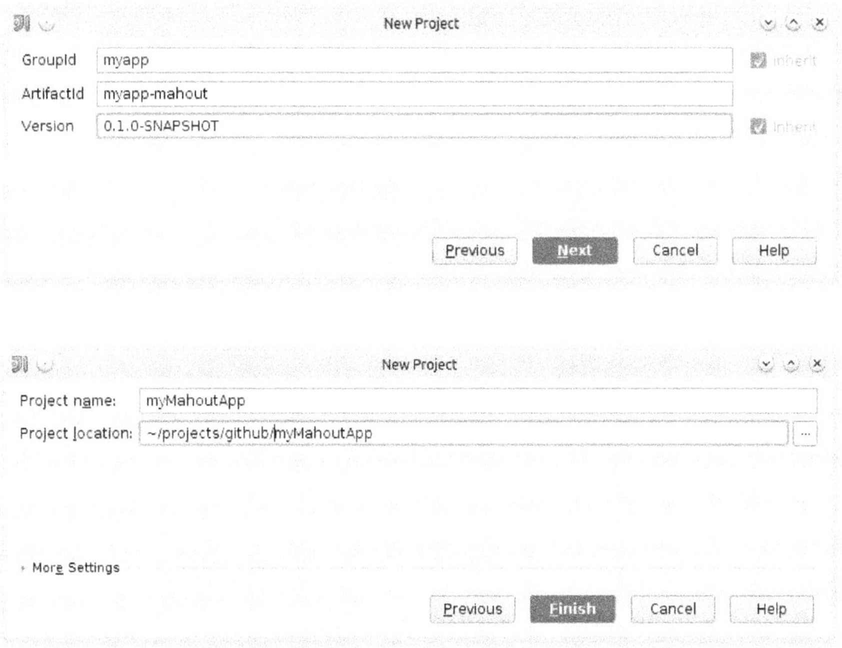

Figure 2.2: Project attributes (2, 3 of 3).

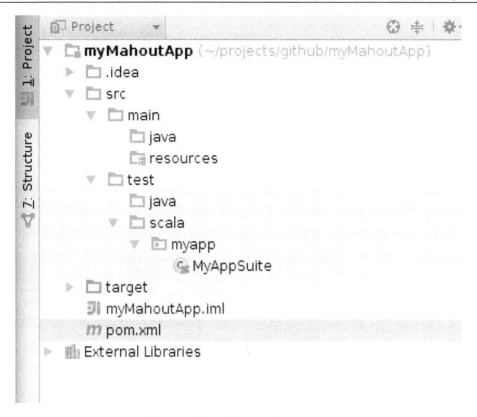

Figure 2.3: myMahoutApp layout

Also, if you would like to enable Scala compilation with Maven, the following plugin is needed under the build/plugins definitions:

pom.xml

```
<plugin>
  <groupId>net.alchim31.maven</groupId>
  <artifactId>scala-maven-plugin</artifactId>
  <version>3.2.1</version>
</plugin>
```

Adding this will tell IntelliJ IDEA to use the Scala plugin. Sometimes IntelliJ does not auto detect a Scala application after a Maven re-import; if this happens, the Scala environment can be added in the module settings. You may also need to manually add src/main/scala and src/test/scala folders as the source root folders.

Next, we will need to add Mahout dependencies. The Mahout Scala API dependency is "mahout-math-scala" (both for distributed and in-core computations).

Since we are going to use Spark for the purpose of this example as our Mahout backend, we will also need the "mahout-spark" dependency. This dependency contains Samsara Spark-specific physical plan operators.

pom.xml

```xml
<dependency>
  <groupId>org.apache.mahout</groupId>
  <artifactId>mahout-math-scala_2.10</artifactId>
  <version>0.10.2</version>
</dependency>
<dependency>
  <groupId>org.apache.mahout</groupId>
  <artifactId>mahout-spark_2.10</artifactId>
  <version>0.10.2</version>
</dependency>
```

Finally, for our tests, we are going to need three more dependencies.

The first dependency is "scalatest". *Scalatest* (http://scalatest.org) is a very popular unit test framework for Scala.

The other two dependencies are test artifacts from the "mahout-math-scala" and "mahout-spark" modules. We are going to use Mahout unit test classes, as it will help us with things like setting up a local Spark context with all its Mahout-specific parameters. These artifacts bear "tests" classifiers.

pom.xml

```xml
<dependency>
  <groupId>org.scalatest</groupId>
  <artifactId>scalatest_2.10</artifactId>
  <version>2.2.4</version>
  <scope>test</scope>
</dependency>
<dependency>
  <groupId>org.apache.mahout</groupId>
  <artifactId>mahout-math-scala_2.10</artifactId>
  <version>0.10.2</version>
  <classifier>tests</classifier>
  <scope>test</scope>
</dependency>
<dependency>
  <groupId>org.apache.mahout</groupId>
  <artifactId>mahout-spark_2.10</artifactId>
  <version>0.10.2</version>
  <classifier>tests</classifier>
  <scope>test</scope>
</dependency>
```

Finally, to tell Maven to run Scala tests, we need to disable the Maven surefire plugin and enable the Scalatest plugin:

pom.xml

```xml
<!-- disable surefire -->
<plugin>
  <groupId>org.apache.maven.plugins</groupId>
  <artifactId>maven-surefire-plugin</artifactId>
  <configuration>
    <skipTests>true</skipTests>
  </configuration>
</plugin>
<!-- enable scalatest -->
<plugin>
  <groupId>org.scalatest</groupId>
  <artifactId>scalatest-maven-plugin</artifactId>
  <version>1.0</version>
  <executions>
    <execution>
      <id>test</id>
      <goals>
        <goal>test</goal>
      </goals>
    </execution>
  </executions>
</plugin>
```

2.4 Kicking the tires with a unit test: fitting a ridge regression

Next, we are going to set up a simple test class.

The test class is called "MyAppSuite" and it is located in the "myapp" Scala package in the test/scala directory as shown in Fig. 2.3.

The imports used are shown in example 2.1, which are regular imports for Mahout distributed and in-core algebra, plus some extra things.

The test class declaration (example 2.2) uses the Mahout test framework. This framework sets up an implicit Mahout context for Spark. FunSuite and Matchers are components of the scalatest framework, but DistributedSparkSuite is the trait that sets up Spark contexts. By default the test sets up a local Spark context; but it does pay attention to the *MASTER* environment variable. It is therefore possible to run Mahout Spark-based distributed unit tests against remote clusters, if so desired.

■ **Example 2.1 Test imports.**

```
import org.apache.log4j.Level
import org.scalatest.{Matchers, FunSuite}
import org.apache.mahout.logging._
import org.apache.mahout.math._
import org.apache.mahout.math.scalabindings._
import drm._
import RLikeDrmOps._
import RLikeOps._
import org.apache.mahout.sparkbindings.test.
  DistributedSparkSuite
import scala.util.Random
```

■ **Example 2.2 Test class declaration.**

```
class MyAppSuite extends FunSuite with DistributedSparkSuite

 with Matchers {

  private final implicit val log =

 getLog(classOf[MyAppSuite])

 ...
```

■ **Example 2.3 Distributed ridge regression.**

```scala
/** Distributed ridge. */
def dridge(drmX: DrmLike[Int], y: Vector, lambda: Double):

 Vector = {


  require(drmX.nrow == y.length,

 "Target and dataset have different point count.")

  // Add bias term.
  val drmXB = (1 cbind drmX).checkpoint()

  // A = X'X + lambda*I
  val mxA: Matrix = drmXB.t %*% drmXB
  mxA.diagv += lambda

  // b = X'y
  val b = (drmXB.t %*% y).collect(::, 0)

  // Solve A*beta = b for beta.
  solve(mxA, b)
}
```

■ **Example 2.4 Simulating regression data with a small noise.**

```
/** Simulate regression data. Note, data dim =

 beta.length - 1 due to bias. */

def simData(beta: Vector, m: Int, noiseSigma:Double = 0.04) = {
  val n = beta.length
  val mxData =

 Matrices.symmetricUniformView(m, n, 1234) cloned


  // Bias always 1
  mxData(::, 0) = 1
  val y = mxData %*% beta

  // Perturb y with a little noise for
  // things to be not so perfect.
  y := { v ⇒ v + noiseSigma * Random.nextGaussian() }

  // Return simulated X and y.
  mxData(::, 1 until n) → y
}
```

■ **Example 2.5 Simple OLS test.**

```
test("ols") {
  setLogLevel(Level.TRACE)

  // Simulated beta.
  val betaSim = dvec(3, 25, 10, -4)

  // Simulated data with little noise added.
  val (mxX, y) = simData(betaSim, 250)

  // Run distributed ridge
  val drmX = drmParallelize(mxX, numPartitions = 2)
  val fittedBeta = dridge(drmX, y, 0)
  trace(s"fittedBeta:$fittedBeta")
  (betaSim - fittedBeta).norm(1) should be < 1e-2
}
```

Fitting a ridge regression.

In this example we are going to consider fitting a ridge regression, which is a regularized version of Ordinary Least Squares, or OLS. OLS is described in the shell tutorial mentioned previously in § 2.2; for ridge regression explanation see, for example, [Murphy, 2012] p. 226, or others.

The analytical solution for ridge regression is

$$\beta = \left(\mathbf{X}^\top \mathbf{X} + \lambda \mathbf{I} \right)^{-1} \mathbf{X}^\top y. \tag{2.1}$$

We will not go into much detail of the math in this section, since our main goal is to show an example of a Mahout applicaton running on Spark, and a test.

For the sake of clarification of input matrix construction, matrix $\mathbf{X}$ is induced by the dataset

$$\mathcal{D} = \{ \boldsymbol{x}_i : i = 1, 2...m \}$$

such that $\mathbf{X}_{i*} = \boldsymbol{x}_i$. Vector $\boldsymbol{y}$ is a vector of observed target variable values (m in total) such that for all i y_i is an observation of target variable corresponding to input point $\boldsymbol{x}_i$. The assumptions are that the dimensionality of input n is low, and that $n \ll m$.

The parameter λ is called the "regularization rate."

The procedure is "thin" in that it assumes that while $\mathbf{X} \in \mathbb{R}^{m \times n}$ could be a tall but thin distributed matrix, and operations $\mathbf{X}^\top \mathbf{X}$ and $\mathbf{X}^\top \boldsymbol{y}$ require distributed computations, the intermediate products of $n \times n$ geometry can easily fit into the memory of the driver application.

The implementation of the analytical ridge regression formula (2.1) as a thin distributed procedure `dridge()` is given in example 2.3. Matrix inversion never happens in this implementation; instead, a linear system $\mathbf{Ax} = \mathbf{b}$ is solved. Here, $\mathbf{A} \triangleq \mathbf{X}^\top \mathbf{X} + \lambda \mathbf{I}$ and $\mathbf{b} \triangleq \mathbf{X}^\top \boldsymbol{y}$.

Moving on. The dataset simulation procedure `simData()` (example 2.4) is designed for the purpose of the test. It generates random input $\mathbf{X}_{sim}$ and observed targets $\tilde{y} = \mathbf{X}_{sim}\beta_{sim} + \text{small noise}$. Note that the dimensionality of β is $n + 1$ since regression computes an additional bias term coefficient.

Finally, the test itself is given in example 2.5. To keep things simple, we build an OLS test ($\lambda = 0$), since the optimal fitting of the regularization rate λ would require building a cross-validation routine, which is significantly more code than we want to show here.

The logic is as follows. First, we arbitrarily choose a "control" regression solution β_{sim} and generate simulated data for it $\{\mathbf{X}_{sim}, \tilde{y}\}$. Then we fit a ridge regression to the simulated data and assert that the obtained solution does not differ much from the parameters of the simulation: $\beta \approx \beta_{sim}$.

For the purpose of data simulation, the arbitrarily chosen "ground truth" is taken as $\beta_{sim} = \begin{pmatrix} 3 & 25 & 10 & -4 \end{pmatrix}^\top$.

Here is the trace output from the executed test:

```
TRACE MyAppSuite: fittedBeta:{0:2.999461136442734,
1:24.999014192539708,2:9.996450220755309,3:-4.003128071537974}
```

As we see, the inferred regression coefficients are very close to the simulation "ground truth" and the test passes.

We will continue the regression example in § 4.15. Then, we will consider how to perform regression slope testing with help of Mahout distributed algebra.

As we see, test-driven development of applications using Mahout math is quite easy. Even though it requires a few additional steps compared to running things in the Mahout shell, the steps are simple and constitute a one-time investment.

Coding with Mahout

Part II contains recipes and tricks for coding in-core and distributed algebra. It goes over some patterns and practices of such programming.

It gives a few examples of assembling such patterns in slightly more complicated constructs based on simple formulas. However, these examples only serve the purpose of explaining coding patterns and are not necessarily complete algorithms. Complete algorithms are the subject of part III.

The layout of this part is as follows. Chapter 3 discusses the DSL of Mahout in-core algebra and examples of its application. Chapter 4 discusses Mahout distributed algebra and examples of combined applications of the Mahout in-core and distributed algebra APIs.

3

In-core Algebra

This chapter provides a quick hands-on tutorial on Mahout's in-core algebra capabilities and demonstrates most of the frequently used algebra coding patterns.

The term "in-core" is a historical synonym of "in-memory," and refers to algorithms running in RAM only.

This is in contrast to "sequential" algorithms that can act on sequential, streaming data, perhaps doing multiple passes. As such, sequential algorithms do not have to keep all data in memory. Even so, sequential algorithms are limited to sequential data access.

Yet another type of algorithm is a "distributed" algorithm. This type of an algorithm is the focus of this book. Distributed algorithms rely on message passing between several working processes. This inevitably creates some data input and output (I/O), so even if the data itself may fit into the RAM of multiple machines, we cannot say that distributed algorithms possess all properties of "in-core" algorithms.

Mahout mainly deals with two types of computations: in-core algorithms (single node) and distributed algorithms. Although Mahout has several sequential algorithms, they are not truly integrated with the Scala-based environment, and therefore we will not consider the sequential algorithms at this time.

All the examples in this chapter assume the necessary package imports per § B.1.

Not all details will be explained although many nuances should be approachable by R programmers without further explanation given the R-like nature of the DSL.

Instead, this chapter focuses on giving tips, techniques and examples. It takes a closer look at particularly important capabilities and features and provides guidance for some recommended coding practices.

While reading this chapter, should some capability need clarification, please refer to the Mahout in-core algebra reference given in appendix B for further details.

3.1 Tensor types

The two most important interfaces to know for in-core algebra are `org.apache.mahout.-math.Matrix` and `org.apache.mahout.math.Vector`. Those interfaces represent the in-core API for double precision matrices and vectors. At present, all implementations of Mahout matrices and vectors are Java-based.

From here on we will use the `typewriter font` for the class and package names. For brevity we may use class names without their package names. In this chapter we will mostly refer to classes of the `org.apache.mahout.math` package.

Vector implementations.

Mahout has three vector implementations. The dense vector implementation, `DenseVector`, is backed by an array of `Doubles`. The two sparse vector implementations are `RandomAccessSparseVector` and `SequentialAccessSparseVector`.

The `RandomAccessSparseVector` is backed by the open hash map collection. The `SequentialAccessSparseVector` is backed by arrays of non-zero element indices and values. The difference between these vectors stems from the characteristics of their backing structures: a random access vector is fast for accessing individual elements by an ordinal index, and only okay for the speed of a sequential iteration. A sequential vector is fast for the speed of a sequential access, but is significantly worse for random access patterns.

In-core matrix types.

Mahout has quite a few in-core matrix implementations. A lot of them, such as the triangular or the symmetric matrices, imply a specialized use case. We, however, will only look at four matrix implementation classes as the mainstream means of building the in-core algorithms.

"Dense matrix".

The `DenseMatrix` implementation is backed by rows of `DenseVectors`. As its name implies, it is intended for storing dense matrix data.

"Sparse Row matrix".

The `SparseRowMatrix` implementation is backed by rows of sparse vectors. The construction may perform either *shallow* or non-shallow (deep cloning) data initialization. In case of a shallow initialization, the implementation does not particularly care about vector types (it could be even a mix of any of the three vector implementations, as far as we can tell). However, in a scenario of non-shallow initialization, a choice needs to be made whether to use random access or sequential vectors as the vectors backing the matrix rows. Note that if a sparse row matrix is initialized with sequential vectors, the column-wise iterator will be particularly, and even dramatically, slow. Some standard operators such as matrix multiplication mitigate these problems automatically thanks to the matrix *flavors* (§ 3.6).

All rows in a `SparseRowMatrix` must exist (even if they have zero non-default elements) and are hanging off an array of references.

"Sparse matrix".

SparseMatrix is very similar to SparseRowMatrix. In fact, it is also backed by rows of sparse vectors, so perhaps naming is a little bit unfortunate, since it does not demonstrate the actual difference between these classes.

The real difference between SparseMatrix and SparseRowMatrix is that in a SparseMatrix row vectors are hanging off a hash map rather than an array. This means that the rows with zero non-default elements do not have to be present at all. Therefore, this matrix should be preferred for very sparse structures with a significant number of empty rows. If this condition is not met, SparseRowMatrix should be preferred instead, as the row iterator of the SparseMatrix (which is in essence a hash map iterator) will be somewhat slower than that of the SparseRowMatrix.

All the three types of the matrices mentioned above have row-major packing. Mahout also has the SparseColumnMatrix class, but it is not used, is deprecated, and will likely be removed in the future. So there are actually no column-major matrix implementations in Mahout. However, they are not needed. Any row-major matrix for all intents and purposes becomes a column-major matrix after applying the transposition decorator:

```
// mxA is now column-major
val mxA = new SparseRowMatrix(m, n).t
```

Diagonal matrix.

The DiagonalMatrix is another very useful type which is usually constructed by means of diag, diagv or eye DSL shortcuts. It is backed by a single vector representing the matrix diagonal. Operators like matrix-matrix multiplication and serialization take these peculiarities under advisement when optimizing in-core operations.

Here is an example of creating a 10 by 10 identity matrix, which is a special case of a diagonal matrix:

```
// 10 x 10 identity matrix
val mxI = eye(10)
```

3.2 Matrix views

Matrix views are implementations of the Matrix trait that do not have actual data container structures. They are either:

(1) Decorators over another matrix; or
(2) Functional views that are capable of producing matrix element on demand, idempotently with respect to the element location.

3.2.1 Transposed Matrix View

One of the most important matrix views is transposed matrix view. Technically, it is a modifying view; i.e., a matrix *decorated* via the view is completely symmetric in all respects concerning functionality without any nontrivial performance penalty to worry

---

■ **Example 3.1 Matrix and Vector blocking.**

```
mxA(Range, Range) ⇒ Matrix // a view
mxA(Range, Int)   ⇒ Vector // a column
mxA(Int, Range)   ⇒ Vector // a row
mxA(Int, Int)     ⇒ Double // matrix element
v(Range)          ⇒ Vector // a vector view
v(Int)            ⇒ Double // vector element
```

---

about.

Although it is possible, we probably never want to explicitly create a transposed view. It is implicitly handled by the transposition operation:

```
val mxAt = mxA.t
```

In this example, mxA.t is assigned a newly created transposed view **iff** mxA is *not* a transposed view itself. Otherwise, if mxA is already a transposed view, it is stripped off of the decorator and the decorated matrix itself is returned:

```
mxA.t.t eq mxA // true
```

3.2.2 Block views

Just like the transposed view, block view is a *decorator* over another matrix. Two Range arguments in the Scala "magic" apply() method on a matrix induce a matrix block view:

```
val blockA = mxA(0 until 3, 5 until 10)
```

The matrix/vector blocking mechanism in the Mahout DSL is different from the one found in R, and in some ways it is also limited compared to R's blocking. Valid combinations of sub-blocking and resulting types are shown in example 3.1.

Similarly to a matrix view, a single Range argument to a vector's Scala "magic" apply() induces a vector view.

The limitations, as compared to R, are:

(1) Negative indexes to cut out elements or blocks are not supported;
(2) Arbitrary indexing sequence overlays are not supported;
(3) Filtering boolean sequence overlays are not supported.

Another important difference, compared to R, is that all tensor-type ordinal indices in Mahout are 0-based. For example, the following R code assigning a new value to the first row of a matrix:

```
m[1,] <- c(1, 2, 3)
```

■ **Example 3.2 Iterate over in-core matrix.**

```
val mxA = dense((1, 2, 3), (4, 5, 6))
// Row-wise iteration
for (row ← mxA) row += 1.0
// Column-wise iteration
for (col ← mxA.t) col += 1.0
```

in Samsara would look like:

```
mxM(0, ::) = (1, 2, 3)
```

3.2.3 Functional matrix views

In the mahout-math module (the Java side of the *mahout-math* library) there is the concept of a "functional view". The Java side has a type, `IntIntFunction`. An argument of that functional type could be provided to construct a (dense) matrix read-only view via `Matrices.functionalMatrixView(m, n, gf, denseLike)`. The 'gf' function is expected to be idempotent, meaning it will always return the same matrix element for the same element location. Specializations of functional views are used for the following random matrices views:

$U(0, 1)$ **random matrix view.**
```
val inCoreA = Matrices.uniformView(m, n, seed)
```

$U(-1, 1)$ **random matrix view.**
```
val inCoreA = Matrices.symmetricUniformView(m, n, seed)
```

Univariate $\mathcal{N}(0, 1)$ **matrix view.**
```
val inCoreA = Matrices.gaussianView(m, n, seed)
```

3.3 Iterating over tensors

3.3.1 Row-wise or column-wise iterations

The simplest way to iterate over an in-core matrix is to iterate row-wise or column wise.

If we see the following error:

```
Error:(16, 16) value foreach is not a member of org.-
apache.mahout.math.DenseMatrix
```

we must make sure the following import is present:

```
import scala.collection.JavaConversions._
```

In example 3.2 we used Scala *for-comprehensions* to iterate over a matrix. A matrix is therefore *Iterable* over *rows*, and a transposed view of the matrix (mxA.t) is *Iterable* over *columns*.

Traversal order.

It is important to mention that *order of iterations over columns or rows is not guaranteed*. The iterator contract is such that matrices are not necessarily traversed top down, or in any other particular predefined order. That's why matrices are *Iterable* over rows, but not over a *sequence* of rows. Row or column ordinal indices in traversals can be obtained via row.index (col.index), where row (col) is the iterator variable.

If we want to obtain a list of rows (columns) *in-order* and have it *indexed* for fast sequential access, code like the following may be used instead of naive iterator conversion:

```
// mxA is of type o.a.m.math.Matrix:
val rows = Array.tabulate(mxA.nrow){ i ⇒ mxA(i, ::) }
val cols = Array.tabulate(mxA.ncol){ i ⇒ mxA(::, i) }
```

Vectors cache norms.

Why would one want to stash matrix rows as in the last example? One reason might be because vectors *cache their norms*. If an algorithm requires access to the same row multiple times and uses its norm, it might be worth pre-stacking them into an *IndexedSeq*. This programming pattern occurs quite often in geometry-influenced algorithms.

Another reason is that, unless the matrix implementation is backed by row(column) vectors, matrix blocking operation will return a *vector view* object which is created every time a row is requested. Modern JVMs are pretty good at creating many small objects fast; but it is probably still not worth doing if an algorithm performs massive passes over the same set of vectors.

Completeness of traversal guarantees.

Even though the order of traversal is not defined, *the column/row iteration is contractually guaranteed to visit all rows*.

However, in the case of sparse matrices (o.a.m.math.SparseMatrix in particular), it may be beneficial to skip over completely empty rows.

If an algorithm benefits from iterating over non-empty rows only, the iterateNon-Empty method could be used as shown below:

```
for (row ← mxA.iterateNonEmpty)

// ...
```

Modifications to row or column vectors inside iterations modify the matrix itself.

Performance considerations of iterating over columns or rows.

Iterating over rows or columns is natural but may be subject to performance penalties. For example, if the underlying matrix is really column-major packed with `SparseSequentialAccessVectors`, then row-wise iteration is going to be extremely slow because of the high cost of random access in column vectors.

Check the *flavor* of a matrix (§ 3.6) to verify the best iteration direction, or – better yet – use operations of functional assignment `:=<func>` or `::=<func>` that automatically select the best iteration strategy.

3.3.2 Iterating over vector

Mahout supports both dense and sparse vectors. Therefore, there are vector iteration patterns for all elements as well as non-zero elements:

```
// all elements
for (el ← vec.all) el := 5.0
// non-zero elements only
for (el ← vec.nonZeros) el := el + 5.0
```

The *el* variable in the example is of type Vector.Element. It has methods index(), get(), and set(). However, the DSL may allow the omission of get() and set() invocations in many cases, as shown above.

Just like with matrix iterators, *vector iterators are not guaranteed to return elements in order*. Concrete implementations `DenseVector` and `SequentialSparseVector` do return elements in order but this behavior is not considered to be a documented behavior of either implementations or the `org.apache.mahout.math.Vector` trait.

3.4 Assignments

3.4.1 Assignment operators ':=' and '::='

In Mahout there are two assignment operators, ' `:=` ' and ' `::=` '. The first form will assign right hand side expression to every element of the matrix:

```
// Assign 5.0 to every element of matrix A
mxA := 5.0
```

If matrix A is sparse, it keeps around non-zero elements only. If our assignment does not have any effect on zero elements, we may choose to ignore them:

```
// Element-wise sqrt(A)
mxA ::= sqrt _
```

The right hand side can be a scalar or matrix expression, or a functional expression.

The difference therefore is that the ':=' operator performs assignments to all elements, and the '::=' operator may (but not necessarily must) omit assignments to most (but not necessarily all) current zero elements inside the matrix.

3.4.2 "Magic" Scala assignment '=' vs. ':='

The "Magic" Scala 'update' syntax, where defined, is equivalent to the ':=' operator, i.e., a dense assignment *by value*. Note that the Scala regular assignment '=' may mean an assignment by reference for reference types, an assignment by value for value types, or a "magic" (update(...)) assignment, which modifies the left-hand side either partially or completely[1]. Therefore, the definition of the '=' operator may not necessarily always be consistent in terms of disambiguation between by-reference and by-value assignments.

Mahout always treats the ':=' operator and the "magic" (update(...)) assignment '=' as having by-value, deep-copy semantics. For clarity, even though both Scala "magic" '=' and Mahout ':=' have by-value semantics, it is recommended to use the ':=' operator rather than the "magic" '=', because the '=' operator sometimes also has a by-reference semantics. Here are some examples:

```
// By-reference, Scala-defined
mxA = mxB

// By-value, Mahout-defined
mxA := mxB

// By-value, Scala "magic" update()
mxA(0 until 5, ::) = mxB

// By-value, Mahout-defined
mxA(0 until 5, ::) := mxB
```

Note that to a certain degree this problem exists in Scala prior to any Mahout DSL interpretations of assignment: even in pure Scala code, the assignment operator has by-value semantics with value types and by-reference semantics with reference types. Since Scala allows new definitions of both value and reference types, the treatment of this assignment semantics ambiguity in Scala is less trivial than it may seem at first glance.

Another difference between '=' and ':=' ('::=') is that the ':=' ('::=') operators evaluate to their left-hand side. This is consistent with the C interpretation of assignment. On the other hand, standard Scala assignments evaluate to Unit. For example:

---

[1] See [Odersky et al., 2004], § 6.15, "Assignments."

```
// mxB is a deep clone of mxC;
// mxA and mxB hold the same reference:
val mxA = mxB := mxC

// ...which is really:
val mxA = (mxB := mxC)
```

Here, mxB := mxC performs by-value assignment of mxC to mxB and evaluates to the reference of mxB which is subsequently assigned to mxA by reference.

3.4.3 Associativity of assignment operators

For those of you who are familiar with the Scala notion of operation associativity, the following will hardly be anything new.

In Scala, every operator is a function call.

That is, for any binary operator (i.e., an operator taking exactly two arguments) the notation

```
a op b
```

or

```
a :op b
```

in Scala really means just calling a function

```
a.op(b)
```

or

```
a.:op(b)
```

On the other hand, the notation

```
a op: b
```

in Scala means calling function associated with the right hand side of the operation:

```
b.op:(a)
```

This is all standard Scala.

In Mahout, however, this has interesting implication for in-place element-wise assignments.

For example,

```
mxA -= mxB
```

or the somewhat more cumbersome

```
mxA :-= mxB
```

both mean exactly what we would intuitively expect:

$$\mathbf{A} \leftarrow \mathbf{A} - \mathbf{B}.$$

A slightly less intuitive case is the following:

```
mxA -=: mxB
```

In Mahout it means in-place operation:

$$\mathbf{B} \leftarrow \mathbf{A} - \mathbf{B}.$$

That is, right-hand associativity in Mahout assignments means a flip of the assignment target (but not the meaning of the operation): 'mxA -=: mxB' still means $\mathbf{A} - \mathbf{B}$, although it is assigned to the right-hand-side variable $\mathbf{B}$.

The rationale behind this is to enable in-place assignments on the right-hand-side of non-commutative operations. Indeed, for a commutative operation such as addition, 'mxA +=: mxB' is really the same as 'mxB += mxA'. Thus commutative operations do not have a need for a special right-associative assignment operators. However, for a non-commutative operation such as subtraction, 'mxA -= mxB' is obviously not the same as 'mxB -= mxA'.

 Mahout does not have right-associative forms '=:' or '=::'. Right-hand associativity is only implemented for in-place element-wise assignments.

3.4.4 Using functional in-place assignments

Functional in-place assignments are also an iteration. The direction of iteration in this case is automatically selected to be optimal with respect to the underlying data structure. Example 3.3 shows in-place assignments with a function.

There are two benefits of using functional assignments:

(1) They are in-place, which means no intermediate result formation.
(2) Unlike row-wise or column-wise traversal, the operator chooses the best performing direction of traversal automatically.

3.5 Avoiding forming intermediate results

Let us consider a simple computation $\mathbf{c} \leftarrow 5.0 - \mathbf{c} + \mathbf{a} \circ \mathbf{b}$. Verbatim translation of the computation is given in example 3.4[2].

The efficiency of this code is not necessarily optimal, since in reality it forms 3 intermediate vectors before final result is achieved: $\mathbf{x}' = \mathbf{a} \circ \mathbf{b}$; $\mathbf{x}'' = 5.0 - \mathbf{c}$; $\mathbf{x}''' = \mathbf{x}'' + \mathbf{x}'$. Finally, $\mathbf{c} \leftarrow \mathbf{x}'''$.

---

[2]We denote element-wise vector multiplication and matrix Hadamard product as $\mathbf{A} \circ \mathbf{B}$.

■ Example 3.3 Functional in-place assignments.

```
// matrix functional in-place assignments
mxA := { x ⇒ x + 1.0 }
mxA ::= { x ⇒ x + 1.0 }
mxA := { (row, col, x) ⇒ x + 1.0 }
mxA ::= { (row, col, x) ⇒ x + 1.0 }
// vector functional in-place assignments
aVec := { x ⇒ x + 1.0 }
aVec ::= { x ⇒ x + 1.0 }
aVec := { (idx, x) ⇒ x + 1.0 }
aVec ::= { (idx, x) ⇒ x + 1.0 }
// Short form
mxA ::= math.abs _
```

■ Example 3.4 In-core computation forming intermediate results.

```
cVec := 5.0 - cVec + aVec * bVec
```

■ Example 3.5 In-core computation, in-place where possible.

```
cVec = (5.0 -=: cVec) += aVec * bVec
```

It is possible to get rid of some of intermediate results by using in-place variants of the operators.

In example 3.5 only one intermediate operator is formed. It is possible to execute this expression without any intermediate results at all if either aVec or bVec could bear side-effect modification, by replacing '*' with '*='.

Similarly, functions like mlog(x) and vlog(x) (matrix and vector element-wise log) create a new intermediate result. If it is otherwise okay to perform in-place evaluation, it would be preferred on the grounds of avoiding intermediate result allocation. In this case, functional assignment is the in-place form of log(x) evaluation:

```
cVec := log _
```

A special form is the in-place operation of $\mathbf{b} \leftarrow \mathbf{a} - \mathbf{b}$, which is carried out via right-associativity of assignment:

```
aVec -=: bVec
```

The above means "perform a - b in-place on b". Similarly, 1/x in-place inversion will look like:

```
1 /=: xVec
```

Finally, for completeness, forms like '`1 +=: xVec`' are also supported, although it is the same as '`xVec += 1`' due to commutativity of addition.

The matrix multiplication operator '`%*%`' does not have an in-place form.

Bottom line.

In-place operations are good. In-place functional assignments are even better. Try to use them whenever computation can tolerate side effects.

3.6 Matrix *flavors*

Every (or almost every) JVM-backed matrix has a structure *flavor* attached to it. This is a general hint about matrix structure (sparse, dense, row/column-major, backed by a vector, or not having a clear row/column structure). This information allows certain operators to use optimal matrix traversal patterns that avoid extra object view allocations and perhaps speed up computation.

Such operators currently are matrix multiplication '`%*%`' as well as assignment operators '`:=`', '`::=`'. In particular, matrix multiplication is capable of optimizing based on row/column major order, diagonal matrices, or self-squared expressions of the type $\mathbf{X}^\top\mathbf{X}$ and $\mathbf{X}\mathbf{X}^\top$.

Element-wise operations are optimized in most if not all cases.

As of Mahout 0.10.2, every matrix supports the `Matrix.getFlavor` method, which returns a `MatrixFlavor` trait.

The most important hints are whether a matrix is dense (`o.a.m.math.MatrixFlavor.isDense`) and the internal structure traversal hint (`o.a.m.math.MatrixFlavor.-getStructure`).

Matrix structure hints are defined in `o.a.m.math.flavor.TraversingStructureEnum`. The most significant hints for the purpose of efficient traversal are:

- ROWWISE, COLWISE. These hints imply that matrix rows(columns) are backed by vectors. This also means that a vector slice in the proper direction will not be a vector view (§ 3.2.2) but rather, in most cases, the actual backing vector. Thus, the slice operation can be expected not to create intermediate wrapper objects. This also means better CPU cache efficiency since proper traversal access order will imply getting elements which are close or even contiguous in memory. In particular, non-transposed `DenseMatrix` and `SparseRowMatrix` report ROWWISE structure hints.
- SPARSEROWWISE, SPARSECOLWISE. These hints are like hints in the previous category, except they also imply that a matrix may not necessarily contain all backing

■ **Example 3.6 Matrix traversal.**

```
def matrixTraversal(mxA: Matrix, f: MatrixSlice ⇒ Unit) = {
  mxA.getFlavor.getStructure match {
    case ROWWISE ⇒ for (row ← mxA) f(row)
    case COLWISE ⇒ for (col ← mxA.t) f(col)
    case SPARSEROWWISE ⇒

  for (row ← mxA.iterateNonEmpty()) f(row)

    case SPARSECOLWISE ⇒

  for (col ← mxA.t.iterateNonEmpty()) f(col)

    . . . . . . . .
  }
}
```

row (column) vectors and that non-empty vector iterator (§ 3.3.1) will be effective. In particular, `SparseMatrix` reports `SPARSEROWWISE`.

For example, if we wanted to apply some function f over the non-empty matrix slices of a matrix, perhaps it might look like example 3.6.

3.7 Parallelizing in-core algorithms

All the recipes we have given so far for in-core math are unfortunately Java-only and single-threaded. As it stands, this is probably the weakest spot of the current Mahout generation: the performance of in-memory standard computations such as matrix-matrix multiplication or solving linear systems is not spectacular by modern standards. Mahout in-memory JVM operations historically are based on the Colt single-threaded JVM matrix library, and hence inherited most of its performance weaknesses. Single threaded, Java-only matrix-matrix multiplication is one of them[3].

That does not mean that customized multicore parallelizations of algorithms are not possible.

However, current in-core Mahout math is not really primed for multicore use. Most of the time, the programmer must be conscious of possible race conditions.

That, in turn, means that the programmer must be aware of the underlying data structure.

Most, if not all, of the vector and matrix implementations will generally allow concurrent read only access without race conditions. It is hard for the authors to verify this across the entire mahout in-memory math code base. However, the general pattern for the in-memory data structures backing tensor types is to perform stateless read access

---

[3]In practice it is actually fairly easy to hack mahout-math solvers to use faster libraries as needed in order to be pragmatically more useful than the current public version at the time of this writing.

> ■ **Example 3.7 Parallel computation of colMeans, rowMeans using Mahout shell for Spark.**
> ```
> mahout> val mxA = dense ((1,2,3),(4,5,6))
> mxA: org.apache.mahout.math.DenseMatrix =
> {
>   0 =>    {0:1.0,1:2.0,2:3.0}
>   1 =>    {0:4.0,1:5.0,2:6.0}
> }
> mahout> for (row ← mxA par) yield row.mean
> res0: scala.collection.parallel.ParIterable[Double] =
>
>  ParArray(2.0, 5.0)
>
> mahout> for (col ← mxA.t par) yield col.mean
> res1: scala.collection.parallel.ParIterable[Double] =
>
>  ParArray(2.5, 3.5, 4.5)
>
> mahout>
> ```

along with a stateful iterator implementation. This means concurrent reads should be liberally allowed (as long as they do not share same iterator instances).

Far fewer implementations would allow concurrent modifications. The best strategy for concurrent modifications is not to modify the same data structure concurrently.

For example, if a matrix rows are backed by `RandomAccessSparseVector`, it is not safe to modify the same row concurrently even at different indexes, since it is backed by a hash table structure, which does not support concurrent modifications.

Similarly, it should not be okay to modify a `SequentialAccessSparseVector` by inserting more elements even at different offsets, since mutation of the structure is not atomic.

At the time of this writing, there is no clean API that would allow us to be certain of underlying data structure guarantees while being completely agnostic of the actual implemented class. We have to be aware of the underlying data structures. Typically, we know it is safe to use separate vectors, or vector views across dense matrices for the purposes of concurrent modification.

In the future, the matrix flavor could probably provide more help in determining thread-safe parallel matrix iteration and modification. Also additional operators (e.g., parallel functional assignment) could be developed to advance in-core parallelism goals.

However, since most computations on Samsara are intended for a cluster backend task environment, tasks should normally assume that only one core is available, and the need for parallelism of in-core operations therefore should be less important. If backend tasks create more than one thread of CPU-bound computations, that would not necessarily be prudent. Running too many threads may create more problems for CPU

■ **Example 3.8 Creating even split ranges.**

```
def createSplits(nrow: Int, nsplits: Int):
  TraversableOnce[Range] = {

  val step = nrow / nsplits
  val slack = nrow % nsplits

  // Ranges.
  // 'slack' ranges 'step+1 wide' each
  ((0 until slack * (step + 1) by (step + 1)) ++

    // And the remainder is 'step' wide
    (slack * (step + 1) to nrow by step))
    .sliding(2).map(s ⇒ s(0) until s(1))
}
```

cache performance as well as additional overhead for switching task contexts. As a result, creating more than one thread in backend tasks may actually worsen the performance, not improve it.

Therefore, at present, support for clean in-core concurrency has been of relatively low priority[4].

3.7.1 Example: parallel colMeans, rowMeans using Scala parallel collections

Example 3.7 demonstrates that it is safe to create parallel iterators both column-wise and row-wise on a `DenseMatrix`. Here, we rely on Scala parallel iterators (`par` method in infix use), which by default use thread pools of size equal to number of cores. Similarly, it should be safe to iterate in parallel over rows of row-major sparse matrix JVM-native implementations, or over columns of column-major sparse matrix JVM-native implementations.

3.7.2 Example: parallel matrix multiplication

Another simple example is parallel matrix multiplication.

Suppose we want to compute a matrix-matrix product **AB**.

---

[4]While the search for ideas of bare-metal algebra accelerations in Mahout is still underway, MAHOUT-1791 suggests to enable full-bandwidth multicore in-memory algebraic operations for the front end applications automatically, while perhaps doing some reasonable over-subscription of CPU cores in backend operations. This should be a low-cost performance improvement effort meanwhile.

■ Example 3.9 Multicore in-memory multiplication using Scala futures and promises API.

```
1   /** Parallelize over vertical blocks of A operand */
2   def mmulParA(mxA: Matrix, mxB: Matrix): Matrix = {
3
4     val result = if (mxA.getFlavor.isDense)
5       mxA.like(mxA.nrow, mxB.ncol)
6     else if (mxB.getFlavor.isDense)
7       mxB.like(mxA.nrow, mxB.ncol)
8     else mxA.like(mxA.nrow, mxB.ncol)
9
10    val nsplits =
11      Runtime.getRuntime.availableProcessors() min mxA.nrow
12
13    val ranges = createSplits(mxA.nrow, nsplits)
14
15    val blocks = ranges.map { r ⇒
16      Future {
17        r → (mxA(r, ::) %*% mxB)
18      }
19    }
20
21    Await.result(Future.fold(blocks)(result) {
22      case (result, (r, block)) ⇒
23
24      result(r, ::) := block
25      result
26    }, Duration.Inf)
27  }
```

■ Example 3.10 Unit test for the parallel multiplication routine.

```
test("mthread-mmul") {

    val m = 5000
    val n = 300
    val s = 350

    val mxA = Matrices.symmetricUniformView(m, s, 1234).cloned
    val mxB = Matrices.symmetricUniformView(s, n, 1323).cloned

    // Just to warm up
    mxA %*% mxB
    MMul.mmulParA(mxA, mxB)

    val ntimes = 30

    val controlMsStart = System.currentTimeMillis()
    val mxControlC = mxA %*% mxB
    for (i ← 1 until ntimes) mxA %*% mxB
    val controlMs = System.currentTimeMillis() - controlMsStart

    val cMsStart = System.currentTimeMillis()
    val mxC = MMul.mmulParA(mxA, mxB)
    for (i ← 1 until ntimes) MMul.mmulParA(mxA, mxB)
    val cMs = System.currentTimeMillis() - cMsStart

    debug(f"control: ${controlMs/ntimes.toDouble}%.2f ms.")
    debug(f"mthread: ${cMs/ntimes.toDouble}%.2f ms.")
    trace(s"mxControlC:$mxControlC")
    trace(s"mxC:$mxC")

    (mxControlC - mxC).norm should be < 1e-5
}
```

We can split the operand **A** into vertical blocks, evenly:

$$\mathbf{A} = \begin{pmatrix} \mathbf{A}_1 \\ \mathbf{A}_2 \\ \vdots \\ \mathbf{A}_L \end{pmatrix}.$$

Then

$$\mathbf{AB} = \begin{pmatrix} \mathbf{A}_1\mathbf{B} \\ \mathbf{A}_2\mathbf{B} \\ \vdots \\ \mathbf{A}_L\mathbf{B} \end{pmatrix}. \tag{3.1}$$

The idea is to compute vertical blocks in (3.1) in parallel assigned to different CPU cores and then copy them into blocks of the final product.

The first step is to split operand **A** into L vertical blocks. This is done in example 3.8. Given the total number of rows and the desired number of vertical blocks (splits) of **A**, it produces Scala ranges corresponding to such vertical blocks. These ranges then could be used directly to create *block views* of matrix **A**.

Suppose m is the number of rows. We take split step as $s = \lfloor m/L \rfloor$ in line 4. It is easy to see that the "most even" splitting will be produced if we create $(m \bmod L)$ splits of size $(s+1)$ and the rest of the splits with the size s. We call the quantity $(m \bmod L)$ a "slack" (line 5). The formation of the range starting values using the aforementioned splitting rule is performed in lines 9 ($[s+1]$-wide ranges) and 12 (s-wide ranges). The formation of actual ranges out of a sequence of starting values if finalized in line 13.

After we are done with finding vertical split ranges, we can take on the actual multithreaded multiplication routine. This is shown in example 3.9. This time we use the Scala multithreading *futures and promises* API.

First, we prepare the result as a dense or sparse matrix of desired geometry. As a simple rule (which is often not true, but good enough for this example) we assume that if both of operands are sparse, then the result will also be better served by a sparse matrix structure. Otherwise, the result is assumed to be a dense structure just like one of the operands (lines 4-8).

Second, we decide on the number of vertical blocks (lines 10-11). For this example we take it as the number of available CPUs in the computer, but not to exceed m. Once we have decided on the number of splits L, we obtain the actual split ranges using the previously discussed function `createSplits` from example 3.8 (line 13).

Third, we create the Scala *futures* that perform formation of one single block view and multiply it by **B**, in lines 15-19. We return the block range (`r`) along with the multiplication result from each of the futures. This code will be done in parallel.

Finally, we use `Future.fold()` API to copy future results in a thread-safe manner to their corresponding vertical blocks of the final product as the futures complete, and wait for the fold to complete using `Await.result()` (lines 21-26).

Example 3.10 shows a unit test for our multithreaded procedure. In the test, we both measure average performances of standard multiplication and of our multithreaded version, and also assert the correctness of the result.

For simplicity, we use dense matrices of shape as set in lines 3-5 of the test. Matrices are copied into materialized clones out of random matrix views (lines 7,8). Lines 11, 12 just run both standard and multithreaded procedures just to ensure all classes are loaded and the JVM is warmed up for performance comparison.

We perform the standard, single-threaded multiplication procedure (we call it the "control" procedure) in lines 16-19. In order to be able to better account for the uncertainties of the measurements, we repeat the procedure 30 times while clocking the execution. We do the same thing in lines 21-24 for the multithreaded procedure. We print out average processing time in lines 26 and 27 for both cases. We also assert equivalence of the results (down to a rounding error) in line 31.

Running this unit test on an older Intel dual-core machine produces the following output:

```
Testing started at 2:06 PM ...
0 [ScalaTest-run-running-MThreadSuite] DEBUG myMahoutApp.mthread.
    MThreadSuite  - control: 905.07 ms.
1 [ScalaTest-run-running-MThreadSuite] DEBUG myMahoutApp.mthread.
    MThreadSuite  - mthread: 319.40 ms.
```

As shown, we get roughly 2 times speed up as expected[5].

3.8 Pitfalls

There are a few things that may lead to undesired effects. "Pitfalls" is probably too strong a word to describe these. For most part, they are not Mahout-specific problems but rather general mistakes people might make in other programs as well (such as by-reference argument side effects). However, these problems did occur in our testing of Mahout programs, and it would be prudent to assume they may occur to other Mahout users as well, so we would like to shed a bit of extra light to these corners.

3.8.1 Implicit side effects of shared reference

This is one pitfall people who are accustomed to writing R linear algebra will probably find quite easy to run across.

R has a nice property called "copy-on-write" which causes all variables to appear to act as by-value or scalar-like variables. All assignments and parameter passing appear to be as if by value. Since Scala always assigns by reference (except for AnyVal types which are assigned by value), it is easy to fall prey to involuntary side effect modifications like in example 3.11.

---

[5]In fact, as of release 0.10.2+, multiplication on dense matrix views is running a little faster than on the matrix itself, due to peculiarities of a perfomance patch applied in that release.

■ Example 3.11 Side effect on a shared reference.

```
val m1 = m
m1 += 5.0 // modifies m as well
```

■ Example 3.12 Cloned reference.

```
val m1 = m cloned
m1 += 5.0 // now m is intact
```

■ Example 3.13 Pitfalls of the '^' operator.

```
// Shortcut to compute distance between a and b
val dist = sqrt((a - b) ^= 2 sum)
// element-wise xor
val x = 2 ^ 2 // 0, not 4!
```

The fix is not to share the original reference but rather produce and share a deeply-cloned snapshot of the original reference (example 3.12). Unfortunately, it is not as convenient as an automatic copy-on-write feature.

3.8.2 The caret operator ('^')

Special case operators are 'matrix ^ double' and 'vector ^ double' (element-wise power). The right hand side of the operation is constrained to double (numeric) value type only. A bit of a semantic problem here is that unlike in R, the '^' operator in Scala also has the meaning of "exclusive or" (see example 3.13).

However, the convenience of the element-wise power operator is hard to ignore. Indeed, it is incredibly convenient when trying to avoid multiple lines while taking a square. For example, without the '^' operator, the distance computation requires more lines (example 3.14) — which is still pretty tidy but will be annoying when inlined repeatedly in a program.

In any case, overriding the '^' operator is consistent with the intent of creating an R-like DSL in Mahout "Samsara". Any other power operator notation would have created a precedence of divergence from R-likeness in the operator space. Eventually, combined, these arguments tipped the scales on the side of using the caret as the power element-wise operator over matrices and vectors.

■ **Example 3.14 Distance without the ^ operator.**
```
val diff = a - b
val dist = sqrt(diff * diff sum)
```

3.9 Example: Designing BFGS

The math is taken off-the-shelf from [Nocedal and Wright, 2006], which will be our main bibliography reference in this section.

3.9.1 Overview

The method we are going to consider is named after its authors, Broyden, Fletcher, Goldfarb and Shanno. It belongs to a class of numerical optimization algorithms, namely, algorithms that, given some starting point x_k, try to find a local minimum of some known function $f(\mathbf{x})$. This is also known as a convex optimization problem.

BFGS, in particular, is a numerical optimizer that assumes that the values of $f(\mathbf{x}_k)$ and $\nabla f(\mathbf{x}_k)$ are observable (or can be analytically computed) at any given point $\mathbf{x}_k$ in the domain of multivariate function f, even if such observations come at a high cost.

3.9.2 Quick background on BFGS

The general approach of a big class of optimization algorithms is to rely on (multivariate) Taylor series approximations in order to make a guess about the direction toward a local minimum.

Let's start with a case of a univariate function $f(x)$. Suppose we fix the variable x_k and we know how to compute or observe quantities $f(x_k), f'(x_k), f''(x_k) \ldots$. The univariate form of the Taylor series expansion approximates the value of $f(x_k + \Delta x)$ where Δx is small, variable step away from fixed location x_k

$$f(x_k + \Delta x) = f(x_k) + f'(x_k)\Delta x + \frac{1}{2}f''(x_k)\Delta^2 x + \frac{1}{6}f'''(x_k)\Delta^3 x + \ldots + \frac{1}{n!}f^{(n)}(x_k)\Delta^n x + \ldots .$$

Notice that the farther to the right we go, the less significant the contribution of the series members becomes. Because of that we can throw away the rightmost part altogether and use only a few first members for approximation. For example, the following is called "second degree approximation":

$$f(x_k + \Delta x) \approx f(x_k) + f'(x_k)\Delta x + \frac{1}{2}f''(x_k)\Delta^2 x.$$

In multivariate form, this approximation works out as

$$f(\mathbf{x}_k + \Delta\mathbf{x}) \approx \underbrace{f(\mathbf{x}_k) + \nabla f(\mathbf{x}_k)^\top \Delta\mathbf{x} + \frac{1}{2}\Delta\mathbf{x}^\top \mathbf{H}(\mathbf{x}_k)\Delta\mathbf{x}}_{\hat{f}(\mathbf{x}_k, \Delta\mathbf{x})}, \tag{3.2}$$

where ∇f is the *gradient* of function f (roughly, a multivariate generalization of the first derivative) and matrix $\mathbf{H}$ is a Hessian matrix (a multivariate generalization of the second derivative).

We will denote the second degree approximation as $\hat{f}(\mathbf{x}_k, \Delta\mathbf{x})$, i.e., the right-hand side of (3.2).

Newton's method uses (3.2) for its iterative step[6]. It takes

$$\mathbf{x}_{k+1} = \mathbf{x}_k + \underset{\Delta\mathbf{x}}{\operatorname{argmin}} \hat{f}(\mathbf{x}_k, \Delta\mathbf{x})$$

until convergence. Note that at every k-th iteration $\mathbf{x}_k$ becomes our best guess about the exact location of a minimum.

Let us denote $\mathbf{p}_k \triangleq \underset{\Delta\mathbf{x}}{\operatorname{argmin}} \hat{f}(\mathbf{x}_k, \Delta\mathbf{x})$.

Thus, our guess about function extremum location is $\mathbf{x}_{k+1} = \mathbf{x}_k + \mathbf{p}_k$, i.e., $\mathbf{p}_k$ is the step of Newton's method iteration.

By differentiating (3.2) over $\Delta\mathbf{x}$, Newton's method step estimate is obtained:

$$\mathbf{p}_k = -\mathbf{H}_k^{-1}\nabla f_k. \tag{3.3}$$

Here, ∇f_k and $\mathbf{H}_k$ are the gradient and Hessian matrix of $f(\mathbf{x})$ obtained during k-th step.

For brevity we denote $f_k \triangleq f(\mathbf{x}_k)$, $\nabla f_k \triangleq \nabla f(\mathbf{x}_k)$.

In practice, however, many methods choose to approach true minimum in step increments smaller than those in the classic Newton's method:

$$\mathbf{x}_{k+1} = \mathbf{x}_k + \alpha_k \mathbf{p}_k, \tag{3.4}$$

where α_k is chosen within the range $0 < \alpha_k \leq 1$. In that case the convergence, in practice, is often faster as staying in the neighborhood of $\mathbf{x}_k$ implies smaller Taylor expansion errors.

We can visualize the process easily as soon as we start thinking of the quantity $\mathbf{p}_k$ as the *step direction*, and of α_k as the *step length*. In this form it resembles gradient descent methods which take the negative gradient as their descent direction. Hessian matrix correction is what makes Newton's method converge faster than the gradient descent method since it captures information from the second degree partial derivatives.

Methods that do not compute a Hessian matrix and second degree partial derivatives exactly, instead using Hessian matrix approximation, are called *quasi-Newton* methods.

---

[6]Technically, Newton's method searches for *roots* of a function, i.e., the solution of $f(x) = 0$. But it also can be considered as a method of finding extrema of the antiderivative of f.

Equation (3.3) for quasi-Newton methods is rewritten using the Hessian approximation $\mathbf{B}$ as

$$\mathbf{p}_k = -\mathbf{B}_k^{-1}\nabla f_k. \tag{3.5}$$

Quasi-Newton methods mostly differ in the ways they approximate the Hessian matrix inverse. BFGS method uses the recursive formula:

$$\boxed{\mathbf{B}_{k+1}^{-1} = \left(\mathbf{I} - \rho_k \mathbf{s}_k \mathbf{y}_k^\top\right)\mathbf{B}_k^{-1}\left(\mathbf{I} - \rho_k \mathbf{y}_k \mathbf{s}_k^\top\right) + \rho_k \mathbf{s}_k \mathbf{s}_k^\top.} \tag{3.6}$$

Here, $\mathbf{y}_k$ is the gradient increment, $\mathbf{s}_k$ is the the quasi-Newton step between iterations, and ρ is the inverse dot-product of the gradient and argument steps:

$$\begin{cases} \mathbf{y}_k = \nabla f_{k+1} - \nabla f_k, \\ \mathbf{s}_k = \mathbf{x}_{k+1} - \mathbf{x}_k = \alpha_k \mathbf{p}_k, \\ \rho_k = \left(\mathbf{y}_k^\top \mathbf{s}_k\right)^{-1}. \end{cases} \tag{3.7}$$

This approximation is computationally useful because firstly we now do not need to know how to compute the second partial derivatives, and secondly we do not have to compute any matrix inversions.

Expressions (3.6) and (3.7) now start looking beyond what is immediately intuitive for most people. Delving deeper into understanding the reasons for and the inferences behind (3.6) and (3.7) is a problem unto itself. Instead of our doing so, as usual in this book, we suggest just to take this result off the shelf, and for the sake of a pragmatic hands-on approach realize that any formula is just an encoded computational algorithm. As we will see, the BFGS formula and algorithms are not that complicated – actually, most computer science algorithms are much more complex than this.

And now we are almost done with the math. But before we can outline the BFGS algorithm, we still need two things.

The first issue, and this is a very important one, is how to choose the step length α_k. Classic Newton's method suggests to always take $\alpha_k = 1$. The problem with this choice is that unless we are already very close to the solution, at this step length we are likely to have left the neighborhood of $\mathbf{x}_k$, and the Taylor approximation of f_k — and, therefore, the $\mathbf{x}_{k+1}$ estimate of extremum too — will be wildly inaccurate. Even though Newton's method, with assumptions, eventually converges, in practice we can reach convergence much better by choosing steps $\mathbf{s}_k$ wisely.

A special class of algorithms called "line search" deals with this problem. We will not consider details of these algorithms here. For the purposes of this tutorial we are going to assume that a proper line search procedure has been performed having given us a step length α_k. We refer readers who are interested in details of line search to [Nocedal and Wright, 2006] where these solutions are discussed at length.

The second issue is choice of $\mathbf{B}_0$. For simplicity, in the first step we will take $\mathbf{B}_0 = \mathbf{I}$ (identity), although there are other ways to bootstrap BFGS iterations. Therefore, in our version of the algorithm it simply does the first step in the direction of steepest descent

---

■ **Algorithm 3.1 Base BFGS iteration.**

Given starting point $\mathbf{x}_0$, convergence tolerance $\varepsilon > 0$, inverse Hessian inverse approximation $\mathbf{B}_0^{-1}$, as well as functions f, ∇f, this algorithm finds a local minimum of function f.

$k \leftarrow 0$

while iteration limit not reached **do**

    search direction $\mathbf{p}_k \leftarrow$ per (3.5)

    $\alpha_k \leftarrow$ **line search** $(f, \nabla f, \mathbf{x}_k, \mathbf{p}_k)$

    $\mathbf{s}_k \leftarrow \alpha_k \mathbf{p}_k$ per (3.7)

    $\mathbf{x}_{k+1} \leftarrow \mathbf{x}_k + \mathbf{s}_k$

    if $\|\nabla f_{k+1}\| \leq \varepsilon$

        return $\mathbf{x}_{k+1}$

    end-if

    $(\mathbf{y}_k, \rho_k) \leftarrow$ per (3.7)

    $\mathbf{B}_{k+1}^{-1} \leftarrow$ per (3.6)

end-while

error – convergence not reached in maximum time allowed

■ **Example 3.15 Functional type declarations used in BFGS.**

```
type MVFunc = Vector ⇒ Double
type MVFuncGrad = Vector ⇒ Vector
type LineSearchFunc =
  (MVFunc, MVFuncGrad, Vector, Vector) ⇒ Double
```

(the negative gradient). The second degree approximation thus kicks in with the second iteration.

Our variation of the BFGS iteration is given in Alg. 3.1. We start off the outer iteration by computing descent direction $\mathbf{p}_k$ and its length α_k. We subsequently compute the BFGS step $\mathbf{s}_k$ and arrive at the next location $\mathbf{x}_{k+1}$. At this point we are ready to test for convergence, which is determined by checking whether the gradient norm is below the threshold ε. If convergence checks out, we return $\mathbf{x}_{k+1}$ as our numerical estimate of the function's local minimum. Otherwise, we compute the next approximation of the inverse Hessian $\mathbf{B}_{k+1}^{-1}$ and continue to the next iteration. We keep iterating until we either return the result or exhaust the maximum allowed number of iterations. We treat the latter condition as an error, since it is a failure to reach convergence given the specified time (iteration) limit.

3.9.3 Implementation of BFGS iteration

The BFGS iteration implementation is shown in examples 3.15 and 3.16.

To simplify computation, we introduce an inner loop substitution here, $\mathbf{T} \triangleq \mathbf{I} -$

■ **Example 3.16 BFGS. cf. Alg. 3.1.**

```
def bfgs(f: MVFunc,
         grad: MVFuncGrad,
         x0: Vector,
         maxIterations: Int = 0,
         lineSearch: LineSearchFunc,
         epsilon: Double = 1e-7): Vector = {
  val d = x0.length
  var mxBInv = eye(d):Matrix
  var stop = false
  var k = 0
  // xₖ
  var x = x0
  // ∇fₖ
  var gradk = grad(x)
  while (k < maxIterations && ! stop)  {
    // Step direction pₖ (3.5).
    val p = (mxBInv %*% gradk) := (-_)
    // Step length.
    val alpha = lineSearch(f, grad, x, p)
    // Step sₖ (3.7).
    val s = alpha * p
    // xₖ₊₁.
    val x1 = x + s
    // Compute and cache ∇fₖ₊₁.
    val gradk1 = grad(x1)
    // Check convergence.
    stop = gradk1.norm(2) < epsilon
    if (! stop ) {
      // Update BInv.
      // yₖ,ρₖ per (3.7).
      val y = gradk1 - gradk
      val rho = 1.0 / (y dot s)
      // T ← I − ρₖsₖyₖᵀ
      val mxT = - rho * s cross y
      mxT.diagv += 1.0
      // Bₖ₊₁⁻¹ ← TBₖ⁻¹Tᵀ + ρₖsₖsₖᵀ which is (3.6)
      mxBInv = mxT %*% mxBInv %*% mxT.t + (rho * s cross s)
    }
    // Next iteration:
    x = x1
    gradk = gradk1
    k += 1
  }
  require(stop,
    s"Convergence not reached in $k iterations.")
    trace(s"BFGS convergence reached after $k iterations.")
  x
}
```

■ **Example 3.17 BFGS unit test.**

```
test("bfgs") {
  setLogLevel(Level.TRACE)
  getLog(BFGS.getClass).setLevel(Level.TRACE)

  // Simple parabaloid with minimum at x0=(3,5)
  val xminControl = dvec(3, 5)
```

$$// \ \mathbf{Q} \triangleq \begin{pmatrix} 2 & 0 \\ 0 & 0.5 \end{pmatrix}$$

```
  val mxQ = diagv((2, .5))
```

$$// \ f(\mathbf{x}) = (\mathbf{x} - \mathbf{x}_0)^\top \mathbf{Q} (\mathbf{x} - \mathbf{x}_0) + c$$

```
  val f: MVFunc = x => {
    val xp = x - xminControl
    xp dot (mxQ %*% xp) - 3.5
  }
```

$$// \ \nabla_x f = 2\mathbf{Q}(\mathbf{x} - \mathbf{x}_0)$$

```
  val gradF: MVFuncGrad = x => {
    2 *=: (mxQ.diagv *=: (x - xminControl))
  }

  // Where to start the search.
  val x0 = dvec(45, -32)
  val xargmin = BFGS.bfgs(f, gradF, x0, 40, BFGS.newtonStep)

  trace(s"xMin found:$xargmin")

  (xargmin - xminControl).norm(1) should be < 1e-7
}
```

$\rho_k \mathbf{s}_k \mathbf{y}_k^\top$, after which update (3.6) really becomes just $\mathbf{T} \mathbf{B}_k^{-1} \mathbf{T}^\top + \rho_k \mathbf{s}_k \mathbf{s}_k^\top$. Our substitution $\mathbf{T}$ thus becomes a *common computational path*.

To test this algorithm, we will use a line search strategy that is a simple Newton step which just returns a constant step of maximum length:

```
def newtonStep(f: MVFunc, fgrad: MVFuncGrad,
    x: Vector, p: Vector) = 1.0
```

As we have mentioned, in practice more sophisticated line search methods are used. For example, the line search with strong Wolfe conditions from [Nocedal and Wright, 2006] is recommended[7].

In the test itself, we need the function $f(\mathbf{x})$ and its gradient $\nabla_x f$. To conduct a very simple test, we will use a paraboloid with a single minimum at $\mathbf{x}_0$:

$$f(\mathbf{x}) = (\mathbf{x} - \mathbf{x}_0)^\top \mathbf{Q} (\mathbf{x} - \mathbf{x}_0) + c.$$

The gradient of this function is:

$$\nabla_x f = \left(\mathbf{Q} + \mathbf{Q}^\top \right) (\mathbf{x} - \mathbf{x}_0);$$

or, as long as we use diagonal $\mathbf{Q}$, this could simply be:

$$\nabla_x f = 2\mathbf{Q} (\mathbf{x} - \mathbf{x}_0).$$

The unit test is given in example 3.17. First, we set up $f(\mathbf{x})$ and $\nabla_x f$, to produce a paraboloid with its minimum at $\begin{pmatrix} 3 & 5 \end{pmatrix}^\top$ and start the search off from an arbitrarily chosen point $\begin{pmatrix} 45 & 32 \end{pmatrix}^\top$. The test output is:

```
TRACE BFGS$: BFGS convergence reached after 5 iterations.
TRACE MyAppSuite: xMin found:
    {0:3.0000000003401897,1:5.000000000002691}
```

As we see, the test succeeds and it takes the optimizer 5 iterations to converge on the minimum within the requested ε.

This seems like a good result. However, in practice the surface will not be an ideal paraboloid, and its laws are not going to be as easy to predict. Which is why a high quality line search procedure is important when searching over complex surfaces.

What did this example teach us?

This example shows that even relatively complicated methods from a mathematical point of view can receive very hands-on, simple treatment in code.

Certain details draw our attention to tips given in this chapter. For example, direction could be computed using much more explicit notation:

---

[7]The algorithm referenced here in practice may not be as useful for thin distributed optimizers, as it assumes that while computation of $\nabla_x f$ is expensive, computation of $f(\mathbf{x})$ is not as expensive. In practice, both distributed loss and its gradient computations are of course just as expensive under distributed settings.

```
val p = - mxBInv %*% gradk
```

But this would have done an extra matrix clone via application of the unary '-' operator. We chose to do a slightly less intuitive functional assignment to apply the sign change instead because for one thing it does not involve matrix cloning (§ 3.5), and for another it is optimized for order of traversal based on the underlying matrix structure (§ 3.4.4):

```
val p = (mxBInv %*% gradk) := (-_)
```

Similarly, in the test we prefer the in-place variant

```
2 *=: (<vector-expr>)
```

to cloning variant

```
2 * (<vector-expr>)
```

It also shows us the power of formula substitutions that enable clarity of mathematical formulation and readability and maintainability of the code. We seek the simplest expressions as building blocks of algorithms. We also seek decomposition into quantities that are intuitively clear ("step," "step direction," "step length," etc.)

Why is fast convergence so important?

Remember we said that observing or computing $f(\mathbf{x}_k)$ and $\nabla f(\mathbf{x}_k)$ could be expensive. In fact, if these are distributed computations, such as exact loss function estimates, then they will be orders of magnitude more expensive than even the original algorithm assumed. We ideally would like to converge in just a handful of steps.

Under these circumstances BFGS becomes a "thin" distributed iterative procedure meaning input sets have large cardinality but reasonable or low dimensionality. Reducing the number of iterations and algorithm convergence speed in absolute terms all of a sudden becomes very important.

4

Distributed Algebra

In this chapter we will talk about distributed algebraic operations in Mahout 0.10+.

Optimization and deferred execution of distributed algebra expressions is the key to the flexibility of creating and maintaining distributed R-like algorithms. The framework looks at expressions as a whole and subsequently creates a distributed execution plan before any actual execution can occur.

A deferred execution (or *lazy evaluation* in terms of Spark) allows for relaxation of the execution requirements in a sense that only the inputs and the final execution result must be formed in their entirety at some point in time. There is no guarantee that a logical operator in the middle of an expression will be formed at all, or formed in its entirety at any given moment of time. This relaxation of the execution requirements is a fundamental assumption that provides a basis for distributed pipeline optimizations.

We will look closer at building distributed matrices and the algebraic expressions that manipulate them. We may omit explanation of some details related to DSL operators. For details, please refer to the appendix C.

All examples in this chapter assume that the imports are performed per § C.1.

Whenever backend-specific issues are concerned, we will be talking specifically about the Mahout on Spark deployment, as this happens to be a common way of Mahout use for the authors of this book.

Coding conventions are per § A.1. In-core matrix variables (of `org.apache.mahout.math.Matrix` type) start with the prefix 'mx', e.g.: mxA. Variables for distributed row matrices (`DrmLike[K]`) use the prefix 'drm', e.g.: drmA.

4.1 Synergy of the in-core and distributed operations

In the previous chapter we looked at different R-like operations over the in-core algebra types: vectors (`o.a.m.math.Vector` trait) and in-core matrices (`o.a.m.math.Matrix` trait). A lot of logical operations applicable to the in-core matrix types are also applicable to the distributed types.

One of the principles of the Mahout DSL design is to be consistent regardless of operand types.

For example,

```
a + b
```

will logically mean element-wise addition regardless whether a and b are vector, in-core matrix, or distributed matrix arguments. Similarly, a matrix multiplication

```
A %*% B
A %*% x
```

implies the same logical outcome for any combination of in-core and out-of-core operands. Same goes for many R-like operations such as `nrow`, `rowSums`, `rowMeans` etc.

The idea here is that even though we may go after quite different implementations of the operation, the visual form of the operation will *look* the same for the same logical operation regardless of the operand types.

That said, the set of distributed matrix operations is not without some important distinctions.

First and foremost, distributed matrix data is not naively iterable. Rather, it is block-wise, shared-nothing iterable. We will have to resort to some functional programming to achieve effects similar to the effects of iterations over in-core matrix data.

Second, distributed data is logically immutable. This means there are no assignment counterparts such as '+=' for distributed matrices.

Now we will look at our single most important distributed matrix type at finer detail.

4.2 Distributed Row Matrix

The main distributed type used in Mahout distributed algebra is the distributed row matrix, or the DRM. The persistence format of the DRM is inherited from Mahout's MapReduce days. Therefore, all map-reduce Mahout methods that output DRMs are format-compatible with the Samsara DRMs on the persistence level. We will use this quality later in the Naive Bayes tutorial (chapter 8).

Mahout consciously makes the decision to have just one distributed matrix type that can "do it all." That way, the user does not have to adapt inputs and outputs of algorithms while scripting out pipelines.

Within Mahout, a distributed row matrix is an unordered set of (presumably) uniquely keyed row vectors. Thus, every row must have its key; moreover, the optimizer needs to

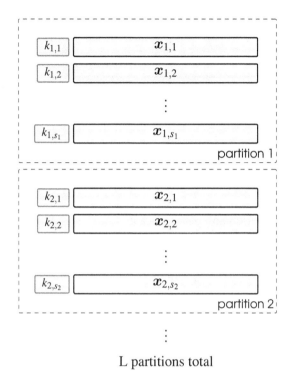

L partitions total

Figure 4.1: The DRM row-wise in-memory representation. $s_1, s_2, \ldots s_L$ represent partiton sizes in terms of number of rows held.

keep track of the key type via a `ClassTag` *context view* (in Scala terms). In Samsara, the Scala DRM trait is defined as:

```
trait DrmLike[K: ClassTag] ...
```

The key uniqueness is *implied*, mostly, to ensure correctness of some algebraic operations. Uniqueness is not always *required* (for example, see the operation of aggregating transpositon in § 4.10). It is certainly never *validated* or *enforced*.

There is only one *native persistence* format for a DRM (as opposed to other formats a DRM could be *exported* to or *imported* from). A DRM in HDFS is a sequence file with the row key being a sequence file key, and the vector being packed into a sequence file record value via the `VectorWritable` decorator. The `VectorWritable` is found in the *mahout-hdfs* module, which contains the very few parts of Mahout Samsara that happen to require direct Hadoop dependencies.

4.2.1 Row key contracts

Matrix row keys generally can be anything, as long as the backend provides proper serialization and persistence for them. Since row keys in a matrix imply uniqueness of a row, they must adhere to the *equals/hashcode* contract.

The concerns of "serialization" and "persistence" for the keys however are different.

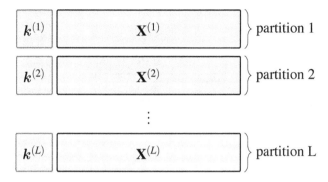

Figure 4.2: The block-wise DRM in-memory representation.

We will consider serialization and persistence contracts for the row keys in the following paragraph.

4.2.2 DRM persistence and serialization

In this section, *serialization* means the ability of the backend to serialize objects for the purposes of shuffles and other exchanges between machine nodes, at will. With the Spark backend, this implies a pretty generous scope of types supported out of the box. Mahout in-memory tensors, however, are not such types; so Mahout defines Kryo serialization for its tensor types (in the Spark backend case). Hence, the Spark Kryo serializer must be enforced in Mahout applications, and Mahout's Kryo registrator must be chain-linked with a backend platform (which is done automatically if the Mahout context factory methods are used).

On the other hand, *persistence* implies loading matrices from and saving to native DRM format on HDFS. DRM persistence format is a Hadoop sequence file as discussed above. Reading/writing this format relates, mostly, to the methods 'drmDfsRead()' and 'drmA.dfsWrite()'. This requires type support in terms of the Hadoop Writeable API, and also communicating such Writeable support to the particular backend being used. With Spark, as of the time of this writing, the DRM row key types supported for DRM persistence are `Int`, `Long`, `Double`, `Float`, `Boolean`, `String`, and `Array[Byte]`.

This set of types is also the common denominator for both persistence and serialization and across all the supported back-ends.

4.2.3 In-memory DRM representation

There are two in-memory representations of a DRM: the row-wise representation and the block-wise representation.

The row-wise in-memory representation.

The row-wise representation (Fig. 4.1) is the default representation after a matrix is restored from a DFS medium. This format is similar to the persistence format of a DRM. Just like a DRM sequence file, it is also organized into a set of tuples (*i*-th key, *i*-th row). We will formally denote this tuple as a sequence (k_i, x_i). The entire DRM dataset is therefore $\mathcal{D}^{\mathrm{DRM}} \triangleq \{(k_i, x_i) : i = 1, 2, \ldots m\}$. This dataset is further partitioned into L

Spark partitions, as shown. In the figure, for illustration we assign double-subscripts to show partition membership of the elements, and the order of an element inside the partition. However, in reality, outside of performance considerations, it is logically irrelevant which partition a data tuple belongs to. The number of data points in each partition may vary, and is denoted as s_j, $j = 1, 2, \ldots L$.

The dataset payload sequence (k_i, x_i) is defined by the following type:

```
type DrmTuple[K] = (K, Vector)
```

The block-wise in-memory representation.

Some physical operators may indicate to the optimizer that they can only consume the block-wise matrix representation as their input. When this happens for the first time in a physical plan, the optimizer lazily performs a conversion of the matrix data into the block-wise format (Fig. 4.2). After that, any row-wise physical operators (if any are encountered) continue working on the row-wise vector *views* of the blocks. That is, the reverse data transformation from block-wise format into row-wise format is never actually performed.

Block-wise in-memory representation is normally preferred. All operators that require block-wise input also produce block-wise output, so conversions do not take place often. In reality perhaps the only operators that produce row-wise output are the operation of reading DRM from HDFS, and the Spark-specific operation of wrapping an external row-wise RDD drmWrap.

Note that we can represent the entire dataset $\mathcal{D}^{\mathrm{DRM}}$ as a tuple of a key vector $k \triangleq \begin{pmatrix} k_1 & k_2 & \cdots & k_m \end{pmatrix}^\top$, and a matrix $\mathbf{X}$ induced row-wise: $\mathbf{X}_{i*} \triangleq x_i$. The "blockified" format vertically blocks both the key vector k and the payload matrix $\mathbf{X}$:

$$k = \begin{pmatrix} k^{(1)} \\ k^{(2)} \\ \vdots \\ k^{(L)} \end{pmatrix};$$

$$\mathbf{X} = \begin{pmatrix} \mathbf{X}^{(1)} \\ \mathbf{X}^{(2)} \\ \vdots \\ \mathbf{X}^{(L)} \end{pmatrix}.$$

The vertical blocks are created by combining row sets in every individual partition into zero or more (but usually just one) tuple of the form $\left(k^{(j)}, \mathbf{X}^{(j)} \right)$. As the result, every partition maps into exactly one pair of a key block and a corresponding matrix block. Also, all the keys in each key block come in the same order as their corresponding rows come inside the $\mathbf{X}$-block. The entire dataset therefore can now be represented as $\mathcal{D}^{\mathrm{DRM}} = \left\{ \left(k^{(j)}, \mathbf{X}^{(j)} \right) : j = 1, 2, \ldots L \right\}$. In particular, the blockified dataset is exactly the dataset that the operators mapBlock and allreduceBlock (§ 4.6) iterate over. There, the closure arguments (keys, block) correspond to the $\left(k^{(j)}, \mathbf{X}^{(j)} \right)$ sequence.

The block-wise dataset payload tuple $\left(k^{(j)}, \mathbf{X}^{(j)} \right)$ is defined as follows:

```
/** Drm block-wise tuple:

  Array of row keys and the matrix block. */


type BlockifiedDrmTuple[K] = (Array[K], _ <: Matrix)
```

That is, the block $k^{(j)}$ is represented by an array type, and the block $\mathbf{X}^{(j)}$ is represented by an in-core matrix type.

4.2.4 Integral type row keys

Row keys of `Int` type have a special meaning: they enable certain algebraic expressions to be formed, which will not be available to operands with non-`Int` key types. For example, it is possible to form an $\mathbf{A}^{\top}\mathbf{A}$ execution plan with any row key type in $\mathbf{A}$; but to compute $\mathbf{A}^{\top}$, the row keys must have Int type in order for the transposition to be defined. Restrictions and optimizations related to the transposition operation with `Int` keys vs. non-`Int` keys are described in more detail in § 4.10.

Row keys of the `Int` type also have a special effect on the matrix geometry. The matrix height, m, is computed per $m = \max_i (k_i) + 1$, i.e., it adheres to 0-based ordinal row labeling rules. If there are gaps in row keys between 0 and $m - 1$, the DRM contract just considers these missing rows to be *sparse*, i.e., filled with all zeros.

On the other hand, for DRMs with non-`Int` keys, m is computed by just taking the count of the rows in the DRM dataset.

As it was mentioned above, `Int` keys may lead to a situation where the distributed matrix has missing rows. However, some physical operators require all rows to be present. For example, element-wise application of an unary function may be changing zero elements to non-zero elements. In such a situation the physical operator communicates to the optimizer that it requires *all* rows.

The distributed optimizer keeps track of whether a physical node in a plan may have missing rows and makes sure that additional operations are inserted to ensure all rows are present when required. Such operations of finding and inserting empty rows with missing keys are an extra expense, so they are performed conservatively. Most physical operators in reality will always produce matrices with *all* rows present. An `Int`-keyed matrix loaded off HDFS by default does not assume it can have missing rows. Perhaps the only situation that assumes that there may be missing rows in a sparse distributed matrix is when the matrix is created out of a custom RDD with the help of `drmWrap(...,` `canHaveMissingRows = true)`.

4.3 Initializing Mahout distributed context running on Spark

 Spark-specific section. Examples require Spark-specific imports per § C.1.

Many (if not all) operations will require a specific Mahout object called a "distributed context."

> ■ **Example 4.1 Initialization of Spark-backed Mahout context.**
>
> ```
> implicit val mahoutCtx = mahoutSparkContext(
>   masterUrl = "local",
>   appName = "MahoutLocalContext"
>   // ...
> )
> ```

A distributed context is essentially bound to a physical engine session: Spark, H2O or Flink. Without a context, a Mahout session cannot be identified. Fortunately, in Scala we do not have to pass it explicitly to every method or operator. It is enough to throw it into an implicit parameter or variable, and all the methods that need it will pick it up implicitly. Alternatively, a distributed session context may be passed in while encapsulated inside a distributed argument of the method (similarly to how a Spark RDD encapsulates its Spark context).

To initialize a Mahout session, just create an implicit value of a specifically prepared Spark context (example 4.1).

There, the parameter `masterUrl` defines a Spark cluster URL. Note that Mahout expects either the MAHOUT_HOME environment or -Dmahout.home= ... Java system variable to point to the Mahout home directory in order to collect relevant jar files for Spark sessions.

From there on, as long as the Mahout distributed context is exposed through a Scala implicit value, attribute or parameter, there is no need to specify it explicitly for any of the successive operations.

Creating a Mahout distributed context of course depends on the backend we want to use. If we want to work with an H2O or a Flink session, we need to use the factory methods for these concrete engines.

4.4 The distributed optimizer architecture

The distributed algebra application architecture stack of Mahout is shown in the figure 4.3.

On top of the stack there is an algebraic application. Most of the code examples in this book are Mahout applications. Mahout applications speak the Mahout Scala DSL.

The in-core Scala DSL executes in-core algebraic operations. This evaluation is immediate.

The distributed Scala DSL builds a DAG (directed acyclic graph) made of distributed *logical* operators. Distributed algebra is subject to lazy planning and evaluation provisions as will be further discussed in § 4.5. At the moment of an optimizer planning action,

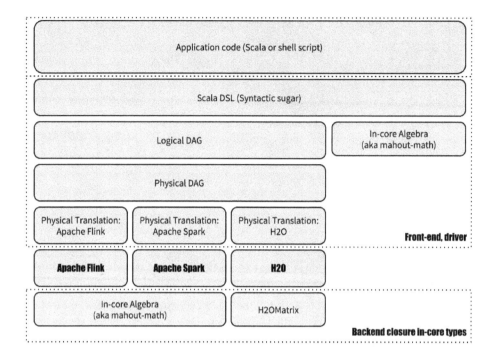

Figure 4.3: Algebraic optimizer architecture stack.

logical plans are rewritten into physical plans. This process of rewriting into a set of physical operators is largely shared between all engines, although specific engines have a chance to implement custom rewrite rules and add engine-specific physical operators.

The execution engine-specific translations also attach engine-specific evaluation strategies to the physical plan operators. Once a lazy evaluation is triggered, the plans are to be executed.

In the backend closures, algorithms once again deal with blocks of tensor data which adheres to the in-core tensor types of o.a.m.math.Vector and o.a.m.math.Matrix. In the case of a Spark backend, these are *mahout-math* implementations; and in the case of an H2O backend, the Mahout in-core API is bridged to the H2O-specific matrix representations. Thus in-core algebra appears both in the front end and in the backend closures.

The Mahout algebraic optimizer does a few quite useful things. For example, it has nine or so physical operators to choose from for the distributed matrix multiplication on Spark – and we can plug more in as we find more efficient ways of doing things. It simplifies expressions, e.g., it can fuse element-wise and other obvious map-only operations into one task. It tracks dataset partition identities in order to automatically rule in favor of "zip" vs. "join" Spark merges in case of identically partitioned datasets. It detects common computational paths (except for the cases requiring explicit checkpoints as discussed at the conclusion of § 4.5.1). It makes decisions on split sizes of operation products. It tracks data deficiency in matrix data sets and automatically applies fixes before carrying out operations sensitive to such deficiency, and so on.

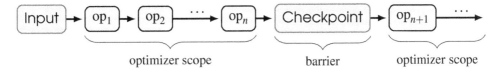

(a) checkpoint barrier and optimizer scopes

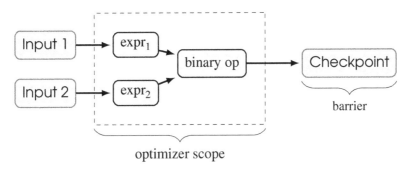

(b) binary operator inside an optmizer scope

Figure 4.4: The optimizer actions and barriers.

4.5 Logical Expressions and Checkpoints

Mahout defines a logical set of operators that are familiar to users of R. Those include element-wise +, -, *, / as well as matrix multiplication %*% and transposition t(). The general rule for designing distributed algebra operators is that we implement a subset of the same things found in the in-core algebraic DSL. The most significant difference is that since all the distributed matrices are logically immutable, there are no assignment operations (for example, drmA += drmB is nonsensical). The immutability of distributed matrices arises, for the most part, from the backend architecture specifics imposed on distributed datasets.

Logical operators are composed into expressions. We commonly refer to this composition as a "logical" plan. Elements of a logical plan are all the operators that are available to the user, such as an element-wise sum or a matrix multiplication.

The physical plan is also a graph consisting of abstract elementary physical operators. Examples of a physical operator are applying a unary function to every element of a matrix, or computing a "self-squared" matrix product $\mathbf{A}^\top\mathbf{A}$. An algebraic expression physical plan however is not materialized until the expression is "checkpointed" – directly or indirectly. In terms of Spark this is called a "delayed action," or a "lazy evaluation."

Unlike Spark, Mahout discerns between two types of "actions": *an optimizer action* and *a computational action*.

4.5.1 Optimizer actions and checkpoints

An *optimizer action* triggers materialization of a physical plan, backed by a Checkpointedrm. The optimizer action does not trigger an actual computation of the result dataset. The boundaries of such optimizer work are determined by a *checkpoint*.

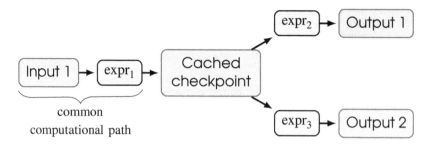

Figure 4.5: Using a cached checkpoint to combine common computational paths.

A checkpoint creates an optimizer *barrier*. Conceptually, this is not unlike the concept of memory barriers for compiler optimizations [Wikipedia.org, 2015b]. This simply means that the optimizer is prohibited from rewriting expressions spanning over checkpoints. Thus, every optimizer action is subject to its *scope*. An example of a chain of unary algebraic operations along with checkpoints, scopes, and barriers is illustrated in Fig. 4.4 (a).

A checkpoint can be created either explicitly, by inserting the `checkpoint(...)` method into an algebraic expression, or implicitly. For now, we will focus on explicit checkpoints; implicit checkpoints are considered further in this section.

For example, in the case of the expression '$(\mathbf{A}^\top \mathbf{A})$.checkpoint()', the optimizer is allowed to rewrite the whole computation as a single physical step 'self-squared(A)'. At the same time in the expression '$(\mathbf{A}^\top)$.checkpoint()$\cdot \mathbf{A}$', the optimizer is explicitly prohibited from doing a similar rewrite and would have to consider $\mathbf{A}^\top$ and $\mathbf{A}$ as two separate expressions, which makes the use of the "self-squared" physical operator impossible. The execution actually has to form $\mathbf{A}^\top$ in its entirety first, and only then can it proceed to form the final result $\mathbf{A}^\top \mathbf{A}$.

Just like with memory barriers, the important notion about checkpoints is that only the input and the checkpoint datasets connected by a single, continuous, optimizer scope are guaranteed to be formed in their proper entirety and orientation. Any logical operator *inside* the optimizer scope is not guaranteed to be either formed at all, or formed entirely at any given moment in time. This very notion is very important, and is what enables any optimization at all.

Since linear algebra operators also include binary operators (operators accepting two operands), a single optimizer action associated with a single checkpoint may relate to more than one input. An example of one such situation is shown in Fig. 4.4 (b). In the most general case, a logical execution plan may become a DAG (directed acyclic graph).

A checkpoint may also be an input to multiple optimization scopes, as shown in Fig. 4.5. In this case, the checkpoint may serve to mark common computational paths while producing multiple outcomes. This situation is further clarified in the example that follows.

Let us consider the following:

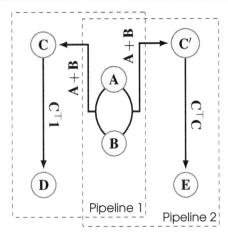

Figure 4.6: Two independent pipelines for **D** and **E**.

```
1   val drmA = drmParallelize(...)
2   val drmB = drmParallelize(...)
3   val drmC = drmA + drmB
4   val drmD = drmC.colSums
5   val drmE = drmC.t %*% drmC
6
7   ...
8
9   drmD.dfsWrite(<path>)
10  drmE.dfsWrite(<path>)
```

This example defines two input matrices: **A** and **B**.

It produces and saves two outputs according to the formulas:

(1) $\mathbf{D} = (\mathbf{A}+\mathbf{B})^{\top}\mathbf{1}$: column-wise sums of $\mathbf{A}+\mathbf{B}$; and

(2) $\mathbf{E} = (\mathbf{A}+\mathbf{B})^{\top}(\mathbf{A}+\mathbf{B})$.

While processing this example, the optimizer looks at and rewrites expressions (1) and (2) completely independently using the matrices **A** and **B** as the root (input) nodes for both computation plans. This corresponds to two pipelines shown in Fig. 4.6.

But it does not take a lot of effort to notice that these two pipelines have a *common computational path*: $\mathbf{C} = \mathbf{A}+\mathbf{B}$. To hint the optimizer at the common computational path, we need to modify line 3 of the original example and equip the intermediate result **C** with a checkpoint:

```
val drmC = (drmA + drmB).checkpoint()
```

The new code after the modification still computes the same results **D** and **E**. But now, the intermediate result **C** is fully formed and pinned into the machine cluster memory cache, and the subsequent plan to compute **E** takes **C** directly instead of computing it again. This may (or may not) result in a better wall time for the entire computation. The

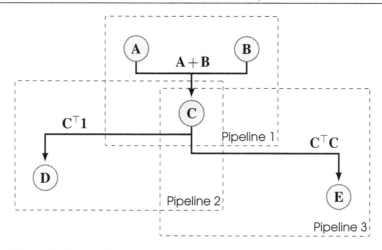

Figure 4.7: Three pipelines with a common computational path. $\mathbf{C}$ acts as a checkpoint and an optimizer barrier.

optimizer internally now produces three plans: (1) $\mathbf{C} = \mathbf{A} + \mathbf{B}$, (2) $\mathbf{D} = \mathbf{C}^\top \mathbf{1}$ (row sums of $\mathbf{C}$), and (3) $\mathbf{E} = \mathbf{C}^\top \mathbf{C}$. This is shown in Fig. 4.7.

Why would we need this kind of flexibility?

Well, unfortunately with Mahout's current code an optimizer action cannot be triggered for $\mathbf{D}$ and $\mathbf{E}$ at the same time, so the optimizer does not support multiple sinks in the computation DAG. This is something to be potentially improved on. Therefore, an optimization of a computational graph with multiple sinks and common computational paths unfortunately still relies on explicit checkpointing as a form of an optimization hint.

For the record though, even in the original example the optimizer will be able to optimize $\mathbf{E} = (\mathbf{A} + \mathbf{B})^\top (\mathbf{A} + \mathbf{B})$ as the 'square $(\text{sum}(\mathbf{A}, \mathbf{B}))$' pipeline, i.e., as only two sequential physical operators, and (at most) two Spark shuffles.

In either of the examples, no computations really happen in the backend until a computational action is triggered for either of $\mathbf{E}$ or $\mathbf{D}$ (lines 9 and 10 of the original example).

4.5.2 Checkpoint caching

Since a checkpoint is the only time the optimizer is asked to form the result in its complete form, orientation, and entirety, it is also an appropriate time to make arrangements for the result caching policy.

Every checkpoint can be pushed into the Spark memory block manager, if so desired. This is especially the case with the "common computational path" example earlier in this section. The default policy is MEMORY_ONLY, but the storage level can be specified explicitly as a parameter for the `checkpoint()` call. The actual push of data to the memory block manager happens no sooner than the partition computation actually occurs for the first time (i.e., at the first occurrence of a *computational action* of the pipeline involving the result in question).[1] Checkpointed DRMs may later be explicitly (asynchronously)

---

[1] See the Spark manual to understand interactions with the Block Manager and storage levels in detail.

■ **Example 4.2 Using framework's memory cache with checkpoints.**
```
val drmA = (/*..drm expression..*/).checkpoint(
  CacheHint.MEMORY_AND_DISK)

... some computational actions involving drmA
... drmA is not needed anymore

drmA.uncache()
```

■ **Example 4.3 An implicit checkpoint.**
```
val drmA:DrmLike[Int] = ...
...
// Implicit checkpoint(CACHE_NONE) and collect() here:
val mxA:Matrix = drmA
```

"unpinned" from the block manager if desired. This is shown in example 4.2.

If the argument is not cached by the time the uncache() call has occurred, nothing of substance happens.

 Spark-specific note: in release 1.1.x, Spark introduced memory-sensitive management of broadcasts and cached RDDs.

That means that cached RDDs are automatically freed once the JVM garbage collector suggests that there are no more strong references to the RDD in the driver application. This fact drastically discounts the need for explicit *uncache* calls in applications running on Spark.

4.5.3 Implicit checkpointing

There are several ways to create *implicit* checkpoints. An implicit checkpoint is formed without an explicit invocation of the checkpoint() method.

The mechanism of implicit checkpointing is by implicit Scala conversion. The situations that create checkpoints implicitly include, but are not limited to:

- Implicit conversion of a logical distributed algebraic expression to a Checkpoin-tedDrm type. This happens if code invokes any of the methods defined in the CheckpointedDrm: collect(), dfsWrite(), newRowCardinality() etc. All these operations imply either *computational action* (§4.5.5), or formation of the result in its entirety in order to carry out the requested action.
- Implicit conversion of a distributed matrix to an in-core matrix of the Matrix type (see example 4.3).
- The use of the Spark-specific operator rdd, which produces a Spark-specific RDD

representation of a distributed matrix.

Unlike with explicit checkpoints, the default policy for implicit checkpoints is CACHE_ NONE. This means that the results of implicit checkpoints are never committed to memory cache. Indeed, since implicit checkpoints never appear in the code, they can never be assigned to another variable, and, therefore, they can never be used for common computational paths. The result of implicit checkpoint will be used once and only once (such as saving it to a file system). Hence, the platform assumes that committing to cache in these situations is not required. Of course, we always can invoke the checkpoint() method explicitly to change the situation as needed.

4.5.4 Checkpoint masking

It does not matter how many times checkpointing is called for the same logical expression – checkpointing still happens only once. As a consequence, the checkpointing parameters (such as cache policy) are ignored for any checkpoint invocation except for the very first one:

```
val drmAcp1 = drmA.checkpoint(CacheHint.MEMORY_ONLY)
val drmAcp2 = drmA.checkpoint(CacheHint.MEMORY_AND_DISK)
```

In this case, assuming drmA had no previous checkpoints, drmAcp1 and drmAcp2 are logically the same checkpoint with the MEMORY_ONLY caching policy attached to it, and will create only one optimizer plan for drmA and its plan barrier.

The second checkpoint is thus completely masked by the first one. The second line has essentially no effect and is silently ignored. This is a bit of a problem. Indeed, we received no indication that our intent to back the checkpoint cache by hard drive memory had in fact no effect. However, during our experience of writing tens of thousands of lines of code using the Mahout Samsara environment we have been consistently getting the indication that the most common pattern is "lazy checkpointing," i.e., the most desired logic is "do a checkpoint only if has not been done already." That experience drove the Mahout project's decision not to produce an error on second-chance checkpoint attempts but rather ignore them silently.

 This is the opposite of what Apache Spark would do with attempts to set up an RDD cache policy if one has been already assigned. Spark would produce an error on such an attempt.

This approach may still be reviewed in the future.

In summary, it's recommended to create a checkpoint as soon as possible in order to lock the desired caching policy.

4.5.5 Computational actions

A *computational action* leads to the result's being computed and (optionally) placed into the distributed engine's cache. Such actions will also lazily and implicitly trigger linear algebra optimizer checkpointing. Currently, computational actions include dfsWrite(), collect() or any operation implicitly requiring a checkpoint, such as

■ **Example 4.4 The signature of the operator mapBlock().**

```
def mapBlock[R: ClassTag](ncol: Int = -1,
  identicallyParitioned: Boolean = true)
  (bmf: BlockMapFunc[K, R]): DrmLike[R]
```

computing row/column sums or means. Most notably, the operator `allreduceBlock()` (§ 4.6) also requires a checkpoint as it brings the reduced matrix to the driver application's memory.

For example, in the modified example above corresponding to Fig. 4.7, running

```
drmE.dfsWrite(path)
```

triggers the computational actions for **E** and, implicitly, for **C**.

4.6 Custom pipelines on matrix blocks

Pretty often there is a need to do something custom to a distributed matrix. The Mahout distributed DSL provides two main venues for performing custom computations over matrix data: the operator `mapBlock` (a custom functional iterator) and the operator `allreduceBlock` (a custom functional map-combine-reduce operator). These operators work with block-wise matrix data, as was described in § 4.2.3.

4.6.1 The mapBlock() operator

The idea behind the `mapBlock` operator is to provide an opportunity to perform a distributed matrix modification based on access to one vertical block at a time. The signature of that operator is given in example 4.4.

The `mapBlock` operator takes three parameters, which are divided into two sets for convenience: `ncol`, `identicallyPartitioned`, and a closure. The first two are optional, but we always need to specify the closure.

The closure signature takes block-wise in-memory representation of the distributed matrix as the argument, as has been discussed in § 4.2.3. The closure is to produce a modified block-wise representation of the matrix as well. To recap, the block-wise representation payload type is `BlockifiedDrmTuple[K]`. It means that the closure receives a vertical matrix block and its corresponding row keys of the generic type K. Note that the key type information is retained at the runtime. In case it is masked at compile time by a generic type variable, the closure code can still rely on Scala reflection mechanisms, as the class tag of K is passed implicitly all the way to the backend.

Example 4.5 demonstrates use of the `mapBlock` operator that produces $\mathbf{A} + 1.0$. For convenience of notation, we use Scala *partial function* in order to disassemble the closure argument into an array of row keys and a matrix block to be processed.

■ **Example 4.5 Unit test example for mapBlock().**

```
val mxA = dense((1, 2, 3), (2, 3, 4),

 (3, 4, 5), (4, 5, 6))

val drmA = drmParallelize(m = mxA, numPartitions = 2)
val drmB = drmA.mapBlock(/* Inherit width */) {
  case (keys, block) ⇒ keys → (block += 1.0)
}

val mxB = drmB.collect
val mxBControl = mxA + 1.0

// Assert they are the same
(mxB - mxBControl).norm should be < 1E-10
```

One constraint is that the *mapBlock* operator should not attempt to change the height of the block. If the operator were allowed to change block heights, that would invalidate internal assumptions of the algebraic plan optimizer about matrix geometry. A dynamic modification of a distributed matrix geometry is in general a pretty difficult challenge for the optimizer to tackle. It is significantly less of a problem if it is non-dynamic, i.e., if the optimizer knows the product geometry before any computation actually happens.

The mapBlock operator may change the *width* (column count) of the matrix; if it does so, it needs to supply it to the ncol parameter of the mapBlock() call. This is a hint to the optimizer to infer the product geometries at the time of the *optimizer action*. The default of this parameter assumes that the mapBlock product has inherited the width of the original matrix. At the time of building the execution plan the optimizer relies on that information in order to infer the product geometries in the plan and does not have a way of verifying its validity. However, this condition is also enforced during the actual execution, where the operator code checks that the closure indeed produces blocks of the expected width and height, in order to catch any unintended discrepancy. Assuming an algorithm is properly unit-tested, these problems will be detected before running in production.

The identicallyPartitioned parameter is also an optimizer hint. It indicates whether the output of the current operation may be presumed *identically partitioned* with respect to the input. It is usually the case when the key vector is not changed, i.e., rows in the matrix block retain their order and identity. Example 4.5 that produces $\mathbf{A} + 1$ is a typical instance of identically partitioned processing. Most map-only transformations produce identically partitioned results. In fact, we are yet to encounter a situation when we might want to override this parameter's default value.

There is another note about mapBlock. It is sometimes okay to return a reference to the modified input block passed in to a mapBlock() closure (as opposed to creating a new or cloned matrix block). But beware of the side effects while caching as discussed in

■ **Example 4.6 The signature of the operator allreduceBlock().**
```
def allreduceBlock(bmf: BlockMapFunc2[K],
  rf: BlockReduceFunc = _ += _): Matrix
```

■ **Example 4.7 allreduceBlock example.**
```
    val mxB = drmA.allreduceBlock(

    // Map
    { case (keys, block) ⇒

      // Return first row of the block
      block(0, ::).toColMatrix.t
    },

    // Optional reduce: stack results one on top another.
    _ rbind _
    )
  }
```

§ 4.14! These problems are potentially hard to catch and debug.

4.6.2 The allreduceBlock() operator

This operator could be thought of as map() and reduce() operations on vertical matrix blocks. As we will see in § 7.2, it is quite useful for computing data sketches and limited-size samples. The signature of this operator is shown in example 4.6.

The `allreduceBlock` operator takes two functions: map and reduce. The map function takes a (keys, block) pair, just like in the case of the `mapBlock`'s functional argument, and is expected to return an in-core matrix. The reduce function takes two matrices produced by executions of the map function, and reduces (combines) them into one in-core matrix. There are no constraints on the returned matrix geometries beyond those that may be imposed by the reduce function itself.

The reduce function is optional and by default it tries to sum the arguments up into a single new one. This implies identical geometry of all matrices output by the map closures; otherwise, the default reduce function would fail.

The result of `allreduceBlock` is one reduced in-core matrix collected to the driver process.

Naturally, unlike `mapBlock`, the `allreduceBlock` operator triggers immediate optimizer and computational actions.

Of course, the same result – and much more – can be achieved by switching to the backend engine API. However, we felt that this reduce pattern is called for often enough that we might abstract it from any particular backend engine API and thus keep significantly more algorithms backend-agnostic.

On the other hand, we did not want to make it too flexible. For example, we could have extended type support to more than just matrix types. However, that means that we would have to relay arbitrary type support requirements to the back-ends, and make things potentially incompatible across them. So the Mahout project felt we should maintain the balance between introducing new useful abstractions and keeping back-end requirements as conservative and simple as possible, while retaining the compatibility guarantee.

4.6.3 Effect of block operators on missing rows

As it has been discussed in § 4.2.4, there are some fairly rare situations when distributed matrices with row keys of type `Int` may have missing rows. Neither the `mapBlock` operator nor the `allReduceBlock` operator require all rows to be present. Although such situations may be rare, they may not always be suited for things that require changing zero elements.

For example, if we want to perform an element-wise exponent, then implementing `block.cloned := { x ⇒ exp(x) }` inside the `mapBlock()` operator will not produce correct result on matrices with missing rows. Use the function `dexp(drmA)` instead, which guarantees that the operation is applied to all rows, even the missing ones. The optimizer knows whether locating missing rows may be necessary. In most cases it is not, so the additional expense for locating missing row keys is rarely incurred.

4.7 Attaching non-algebraic pipelines

Entry/exit points for Apache Spark.

 This is a Spark-specific section. The examples require Spark-specific imports per § C.1.

If the flexibility of the DRM API is not enough, it is always possible to exit out of the optimizer-based algebra pipeline into the native Spark environment. Such a transition is possible at optimizer checkpoints, which are presented by the `CheckpointedDrm-Base[K]` trait. This trait has an `rdd:DrmRdd[K]` getter method, which returns a row-wise RDD with `DrmTuple[K]` payload type.

The row-wise RDDs and their payload types are defined as follows:

```
/** Drm row-wise tuple */
type DrmTuple[K] = (K, Vector)
/** Row-wise organized DRM rdd type */
type DrmRdd[K] = RDD[DrmTuple[K]]
```

Here, the `Vector` type is `org.apache.mahout.math.Vector`.

If we want to convert a matrix to an RDD of the `DrmRdd` type, we can use the following statement:

```
val myRdd = (A %*% B).checkpoint().rdd
...
```

The import of the `sparkbindings` package adds an implicit Scala conversions to a checkpoint, and also enables Spark-specific operations on it. Thus, the example above could be simply written as:

```
val myRdd = (A %*% B).rdd
...
```

Keep in mind that an implicit conversion to a checkpoint creates a checkpoint with default checkpoint parameters (i.e., a checkpoint barrier without dataset caching). This should not be a worry, as this default is sensible. Indeed, since the created checkpoint is implicit, there is no chance to create a common computational path which would reuse it; therefore, it is extremely unlikely any caching is ever desired in this situation.

Similarly, an RDD conforming to the type of DrmRdd, can be re-wrapped into an optimizer's distributed matrix type as follows:

```
val rdd:DrmRdd[K] = ... // Rdd initialization
val A = drmWrap(rdd = rdd, nrow = 50000, ncol = 100)
... // use A in a DRM pipeline
```

The parameters "ncol" and "nrow" (geometry) are optional. If not supplied, they will be recomputed off a cached dataset. But if supplied, they *must* be accurate.

4.8 Broadcasting vectors and matrices to the backend closures

Generally, one can create and use one-way closure attributes and use them in the backend.

As an illustration, we can implement scalar matrix multiplication by a variable *factor* the following way:

```
val factor:Int = ...
val drm2 = drm1.mapBlock() {

  case (keys, block) ⇒ block *= factor
  keys → block

}
```

As we can see, even though the `factor` variable is initialized in the front end, it can be easily used in backend closures running on every matrix vertical block in parallel.

A slight wrinkle with this is that in order to serialize a Scala closure and send it to the backend workers, the closure attributes must also be Java-serializable. This is, as it stands, not currently the case with the in-core matrices and vectors. And even if they were, Java serialization would be less compact on the wire than a custom serialization that Mahout in-core matrices use. As an example the following fragment that implements a vector subtraction from every matrix row would fail with *NotSerializableException*:

```
val v:Vector = ...

val drm2 = drm1.mapBlock() { case (keys, block) ⇒

 for (row ← 0 until block.nrow) block(row,::) -= v
 keys → block

}
```

Spark and similar execution backends support a "broadcast" feature, which ensures that a broadcast variable is available to all code running in the backend. Mahout abstracts that away too. The fix to the previous fragment would be:

```
val v:Vector = ...
val bcastV = drmBroadcast(v)

val drm2 = drm1.mapBlock() { case (keys, block) ⇒

 for (row ← 0 until block.nrow) block(row,::) -= bcastV
 keys → block

}
```

A very small improvement to this code is possible. Notice that we use the `bcastV` value as if it were of a `o.a.m.math.Vector` type. In fact, the `drmBroadcast()` method returns a variable of `BCast[Vector]` type. Here is the signature of the `drmBroadcast` method, which is defined in the `o.a.m.math.drm` package:

```
/** Broadcast support API */
def drmBroadcast(v:Vector)(implicit ctx:DistributedContext)
  :BCast[Vector]
```

The reason why we can use the value of `BCast[Vector]` as just `Vector` is because the same `o.a.m.math.drm` package defines an implicit conversion from `BCast[T]` type to `T`:

```
/** Implicit broadcast → value conversion. */
implicit def bcast2val[T](bcast: BCast[T]): T = bcast.value
```

This implicit conversion is triggered by an unambiguous context. This is the Scala rule for applying implicits: of all the implicit conversions in the scope, one and only one must fit the expected type. In our case it works because there is exactly one implicit conversion in the scope that fits the expected type.

But it also means that, while fairly instantaneous, the implicit conversion unwinds into a `bcast2val(bcastV)` call, which in turn calls another getter method. This all happens inside a massively iterative code fragment. A small improvement is to pin the the actual vector to a value outside the iteration, thus avoiding the indirections of the implicit conversion. Here is our suggested final code pattern for the above example:

```
val v:Vector = ...
val bcastV = drmBroadcast(v)

val drm2 = drm1.mapBlock() { case (keys, block) ⇒

  // Pin the broadcast to a local value.
  // Calls the implicit conversion only once per closure.
  val v:Vector = bcastV

  for (row ← 0 until block.nrow) block(row,::) -= v
  keys → block

}
```

4.9 Parallelizing distributed algorithms

In the previous chapter we took a look at the application of simple parallelization techniques to the in-core tensor types. Actually, there was nothing really novel there: we just jumped on the back of Scala parallel collections and iterators. Mahout in-core tensors themselves however were not fundamentally developed with parallel access in mind.

In the case of distributed matrices though, parallelism is everything. Distributed matrices are designed to run in parallel.

One may wonder, aren't distributed matrix computations already parallelized? Yes, they are, of course. However, this process is not terribly smart by default. There is an automatic parallelism strategy, but it needs to be engaged explicitly, as is discussed a little later. And sometimes even using the automatic parallelism guess is not enough.

The issue of parallelism of distributed matrices boils down to one simple problem: how many partitions does our dataset need to be divided into to ensure more or less optimal efficiency of computations?

Let us recap the terminology of various frameworks. In parallel processing frameworks, datasets are divided into chunks. A "split" is an HDFS/Hadoop term implying an individual data chunk size, usually driven by a block size of a DFS medium where the chunk is currently persisted. A "partition" is a Spark term that means pretty much the same thing, except it is used almost exclusively with respect to in-memory data chunks rather than splits encompassed by a preset block size of a persistence medium. Finally, in Spark, one "task" means an algorithm (a closure) that operates on exactly one "partition."

In this section, we will use the terms "task," "partition," and "split" interchangeably. When we discuss a number of "tasks," we also mean the number of "partitions," When we discuss the size of a "task," we also mean the data size of a "partition" (but not necessarily the task execution time).

Parallelism of distributed computations is incredibly important.

Poor parallelism is the number one reason for poor performance. If there are too few tasks, then the job is potentially under-utilizing the machine cluster capacity. Or, perhaps, too much skew between task loads in absolute terms affects the wall time.

If there are too many tasks, or tasks are too small, then the job also runs slowly as task start-up costs start dominating the wall time. There are no systems that achieve ideal strong scalability. Therefore there is always a sweet spot here.

For distributed algebra the issues of parallelism and finding the sweet spots are even more important due to two specific reasons.

First, increasing the number of running tasks usually also means increased I/O due to highly interconnected nature of matrix-matrix operations. For example, it is very difficult to demonstrate good strong scaling for distributed matrix multiplication of two different and sufficiently big datasets.

Second, distributed pipelines behind more or less involved algebraic algorithms tend to produce a significant number of Spark stages. Therefore, even though the algebraic optimizer makes an attempt to maintain equivalent task sizes throughout the job, even a handful of shuffles may accumulate an error of such estimates significant enough to warrant redistribution of the data before continuing.

The logic of the algebraic optimizer probably deserves a separate discussion here.

The optimizer's rules of thumb for the task sizes.

There are approaches for balancing cluster load based on creating different task sizes in the same stage. Mahout Samsara, however, retains the much simpler approach found in Hadoop MapReduce and Spark. This approach assumes that the task loads have to be formed approximately uniformly among workers.

Obviously, the number of tasks (a.k.a. the "parallelism") is connected with the task average size: the more tasks we have, the less the average task size becomes, and vice versa. The number of tasks is also affected by the whole dataset size as well. If a dataset is currently an input to the physical plan, it is (potentially) cached, or we can load it from the medium and put into the cache with assumption that it is about to be used. Which means, the size of the initial dataset is available, at worst, at the cost of the operations to load and count the data size.

On the other hand, the size of the intermediate steps of the physical plan is not directly known. The optimizer at the planning stage has not formed the intermediate datasets yet, so it has to make a guess about them. This guess actually may not always be happily accurate, although in reality these errors seem to be of little consequence, unless the physical plan is long enough to accumulate errors of this type.

The errors in the estimates of the intermediate dataset sizes is not the only error that may accrue during a physical plan formation. Let us get back to the problem of a physical layer task translation. As a general rule, the optimizer tries to keep the tasks approximately the same size as in the previous physical stage of a pipeline. That means that the optimizer tries to maintain task sizes equivalent to the sizes of the initially formed tasks at the point of entry to the algebraic pipeline. In case of matrix-matrix operands, the optimizer takes operands with bigger splits as a guidance for product task size. This is at least true for the Spark optimizer backend and its physical operators. As the optimizer dumps more stages onto the physical plan, this estimate error also accrues.

Thus, normally the optimizer never takes default engine parallelism settings into account. It is quite oblivious of the actual number of tasks available in the machine cluster. The criterion of maintaining constant task size is the only driving logic. The only exception to this rule is the use of the operator `par(auto = true)` with automatic adjustment to the specified default parallelism. We will discuss this a little later in this section.

What this means is that the pipeline products may have a different number of tasks (a.k.a splits, partitions) compared to the stage inputs.

It also means that the initial input splitting is what drives the parallelism of the entire pipeline afterwards, by default.

Often in practice the DFS medium's input splits target relatively long running ETL tasks and therefore are too big for CPU-bound algebraic tasks, especially for tasks that need to provide "speed-of-thought" performance.

This means that we may want to repartition the data after loading it from HDFS. This first repartitioning will affect the performance of the rest of our pipeline, unless we choose to intervene somewhere in the middle again and repartition the dataset again.

Repartitioning of distributed matrices is driven by the operator `par()`. This operator exists in 3 mutually exclusive forms.

The first form has the goal of ascertaining the minimally acceptable parallelism:

```
drmA.par(min = minParallelism)
```

This ensures that the matrix is going to be split *at least* in `minParallelism` ways.

The second form ensures that the parallelism is equal to the parameter *exactly*:

```
drmA.par(exact = exactParallelism)
```

Finally, the third form is the `auto` guess mode. In this mode the operator consults engine-specific default parallelism settings, which it trusts to be the cluster capacity – or at least the capacity quota. Then it chooses between 95% cluster capacity and 190% cluster capacity – whichever mark the current number of partitions happens to be closer to. The "auto" mode will not change the number of tasks if they exceed 190% of the default parallelism setting; in this situation it is assumed that adjustments will not be effective.

```
drmA.par(auto = true)
```

Neither of these implementations is perfect. For example, the `auto` implementation does not take into account degenerate cases (the data is too small). It certainly does not do any attempt to predict the sweet spots mentioned earlier.

For that reason, setting exact parallelism is an indispensable tool once we are trying to run experiments with the purpose of finding a good balance. But automatic logic still provides a good enough guess in a sufficiently interesting number of situations.

In our experience, data loaded from HDFS must almost always be adjusted for parallelism to get closer to the optimal wall time.

4.10 The hidden powers of distributed transposition

Let us take a closer look at the operation of distributed matrix transposition.

The scope of the transpose definition.

Let us recall what the DRM in-memory representation is.

The DRM (distributed row matrix) format is, essentially, a partitioned set of row vectors and their keys. The Int-keyed matrices are distinguished as a special case. In this special case the keys are treated as ordinal row ids, and therefore the (logical) number of rows m equals to $m = \max_i (k_i) + 1$, and thus $k_i \in \{0, 1, \ldots m - 1\}$. Note that all keys are assumed to be 0-based (to be consistent with the in-memory Mahout tensor types which are also 0-based) for the purposes of matrix operations. Thus, the Int-keyed matrices are true matrices in their strict mathematical sense.

But row keys may also be of types different from integer, and then the natural order of the rows is not really defined.

The first peculiarity is that the operation of transposition does not apply to all matrices. This is not really surprising, given that distributed row matrices do not necessarily have to be identified by an ordinal number. However, the transposition may have a scope surprisingly larger than it may seem at the first glance.

Indeed, the transposition operation is always defined whenever the type of the matrix is DrmLike[Int]. On the other hand, a transposition of a matrix with a non-integer key type may or may not be defined. For example, if $\mathbf{A}$ is of DrmLike[String] type, then the expression

```
drmA.t.checkpoint()
```

will be rejected by the optimizer.

The checkpoint operation tells the optimizer that the result $\mathbf{A}^\top$ must be *formed in its entirety*. But with non-integer keys such formation is undefined, for there is no way to map non-integer row indexes of the input to the ordinal column indexes of the result $\mathbf{A}^\top$.

However, in many cases the logical transposition $\mathbf{A}^\top$ *as a part of an expression* is admissible even for matrices with non-integer row keys. A most simple example is the expression $\mathbf{A}^\top\mathbf{A}$. It can be demonstrated that the formation of the result is possible without having ordered row keys in the input $\mathbf{A}$. Similarly, the distributed stochastic SVD (dssvd()) and the stochastic PCA (dspca()) would accept matrices with non-integer keys: it turns out that the information about ordinal row positions is never actually needed in order to form the final results.

So, the coverage of the transposition operator for distributed matrix expressions, although not being totally complete, is still significant even for matrices that do not have

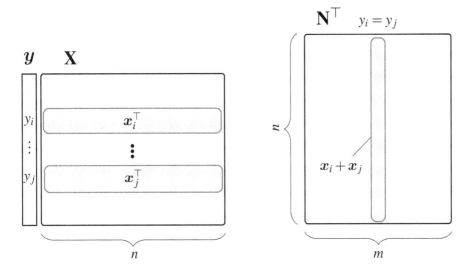

Figure 4.8: An illustration of the aggregating transposition: $\mathbf{N}^\top \leftarrow (\boldsymbol{y}|\mathbf{X})^\top$. Left: the DRM structure before the transposition. Two row vectors $\boldsymbol{x}_i$ and $\boldsymbol{x}_j$ are shown along with their respective row keys y_i and y_j. Right: the DRM result after the transposition. If $y_i = y_j$, then after the transposition the corresponding column of the result $\mathbf{N}^\top_{*,y_i} = \mathbf{N}^\top_{*,y_j} = \boldsymbol{x}_i + \boldsymbol{x}_j$. If $y_i \neq y_j$ for all the i and j, then the transposition is a regular, non-aggregating transposition: $\mathbf{N}^\top = \mathbf{X}^\top$.

their rows ordinally numbered.

Aggregating matrix rows using the transpose semantics.

Another unexpected property of simple transposition is the aggregation effect.

This is something that is specific to the integer-keyed distributed matrices. Remember that the number of rows for the integer-keyed matrices is assumed $m = \max_i (k_i) + 1$. However, it does not mean that such matrix necessarily contains exactly m rows. First, it could be of course less, due to missing rows. If rows are missing from such a matrix, this simply implies sparse data (such rows logically assume they consist of all zeros). Second, the DRM format technically admits existence of key duplicates. So it is also possible that the actual number of rows may be significantly larger than m. The situation when there are, for example, 20 rows labeled as row 3, scattered across the dataset, is possible, and sometimes is even intentionally created.

Multiclass classification training input may be one example when such situation exists. Let us assume we have an input matrix $\mathbf{X}$ induced by a dataset $\mathcal{D} = \{\boldsymbol{x}^{(i)} : i = 1, 2, \ldots m\}$ row-wise: $\mathbf{X}_{i*} \triangleq \boldsymbol{x}^{(i)}$. Suppose each datapoint also has a corresponding training target label expressed by an ordinal of the label inside ordered label set: $y_i \in \{1, 2, \ldots \ell\}$. The target vector therefore is $\boldsymbol{y} = \begin{pmatrix} y_1 & y_2 & \cdots & y_m \end{pmatrix}^\top$, and thus $\boldsymbol{y} \in \{1, 2, \ldots \ell\}^m$.

Very typically, we then want to encode both $\mathbf{X}$ and $\boldsymbol{y}$ inside one single DRM of type `DrmLike[Int]`. In order to achieve that, we can set the DRM keys to $\boldsymbol{y}$ and the vector payload part to $\mathbf{X}$. The input DRM will then represent the pair $(\boldsymbol{y}, \mathbf{X})$. However, note that points of the same class may appear more than one time, so it is possible that $y_i = y_j$

for some $i \neq j$.

Next, a thing that is also very typical is to aggregate rows of $\mathbf{X}$ by their classes into another matrix $\mathbf{N}$: $\mathbf{N}_{c*} \triangleq \sum_i^{y_i=c} \boldsymbol{x}_i \; \forall c \in \{1, 2, \dots \ell\}$. In an SQL-like form, this notation is equivalent to saying "select sum(x) group by y". This is, for example, a common first step over a labeled frequency matrix in a variety of Naive Bayes methods in [Rennie et al., 2003].

In Mahout semantics, that is exactly what the following transposition would do (producing $\mathbf{N}^\top$):

```
drmNt = drmX.t.checkpoint()
```

This happens due to the fact that Mahout transposition aggregates row conflicts by summing up the rows labeled by the same key before placing them into their destination column (Fig. 4.8). Since in our case rows are labeled by the ordinal class index, the transposition operation over the structure $(\boldsymbol{y}, \mathbf{X})$ creates the sum of all rows belonging to the same class, and places it into single column corresponding to the class ordinal. Note the *checkpoint* operation: it is required in this case. It ensures that the aggregated result is actually formed. Had we allowed the optimizer to continue without the checkpoint barrier, it might have rewritten the transposition operation into something else on physical level as a part of a larger expression.

This aggregation via transposition feels a bit like cheating with respect to the general contracts of algebra; and in fact, it certainly is. Indeed, we equip the matrix structure with "row doppelgangers," which is not a mathematically acceptable construct. But in practice this "cheating" turns out to be surprisingly useful, and, along with the `allreduceBlock` and `mapBlock` operators, allows avoiding direct uses of the backend APIs, thus keeping algorithms backend-agnostic.

4.11 Untangling $a\mathbf{1}^\top$, $\mathbf{A}\mathbf{1}$, and $\mathbf{A}\mathbf{1}\mathbf{1}^\top$

We often try to adjust formulas to correspond to what we are actually doing in the algorithms. Algorithm code often follows certain patterns, so the formulas follow patterns too. In this section we discuss some very common (for this book) formula patterns $a\mathbf{1}^\top$, $\mathbf{A}\mathbf{1}$, $\mathbf{A}\mathbf{1}\mathbf{1}^\top$, and their corresponding code patterns.

So, what is the "1" notation?

Some literature uses the notation of 1-vector (not to be confused with a unit vector):

$$\mathbf{1} \triangleq \begin{pmatrix} 1 \\ 1 \\ \vdots \\ 1 \end{pmatrix},$$

that is, the notation $\mathbf{1}$ (in bold) means a vector, all elements of which are equal to 1. The dimensionality of the vector is derived from the context. For example, in the expression $\mathbf{A}\mathbf{1}$, where $\mathbf{A} \in \mathbb{R}^{m \times n}$, the dimensionality of the vector $\mathbf{1}$ is implied to be $n \times 1$.

Similarly, say, **5**, implies a vector $\begin{pmatrix} 5 & 5 & \cdots & 5 \end{pmatrix}^\top$, although this is far more rare.

4.11.1 Untangling the $\mathbf{A1}$ and $\mathbf{A}^\top\mathbf{1}$

Very often our algorithms run column-wise or vector-wise aggregators such as column-wise means `colMeans()` or variance `colVars()`.

Remember that when we are computing a product $\mathbf{Ax}$, we are taking a linear combination of all the columns of $\mathbf{A}$, and then the result ends up in the column space of $\mathbf{A}$ (also called "the range" of $\mathbf{A}$). Notationally, a column space (or a range) of $\mathbf{A}$ is denoted as $C(\mathbf{A})$ or $R(\mathbf{A})$. So, when we compute $\mathbf{A1}$, this creates sum of all columns in $\mathbf{A}$, or, in other words, this produces the same thing as one of the simplest aggregate operators, the `rowSums()` operator would produce:

$$\mathbf{A1} = \sum_i^n \mathbf{A}_{*i}.$$

Thus, in Mahout the formula pattern $\mathbf{A1}$ corresponds to the code `A.rowSums()`. Similarly, $\mathbf{A}^\top\mathbf{1}$ is:

$$\mathbf{A}^\top\mathbf{1} = \sum_i^m \mathbf{A}_{i*},$$

and corresponds to the code `A.colSums()`. Here, we assume $\mathbf{A} \in \mathbb{R}^{m \times n}$.

4.11.2 Untangling $a\mathbf{1}^\top$

The notation $a b^\top$ means "the outer product of two vectors a and b." If $a \in \mathbb{R}^m$ and $b \in \mathbb{R}^n$, then $a b^\top \in \mathbb{R}^{m \times n}$. If we take an outer product $a\mathbf{1}^\top$, we simply clone the vector a as every column of the result matrix.

In Mahout algebra, there is no corresponding operator for the operation $a\mathbf{1}^\top$. It is always used in a context. The dimensionality of the vector $\mathbf{1}$ in this expression is also implied by the context. There are two patterns that notation pattern $a\mathbf{1}^\top$ usually implies:

(1) We compute a partial representation of a inside a `mapBlock` operator acting on some dataset that we apply $a\mathbf{1}^\top$ over (so a is never formed in its entirety); or

(2) We already have the vector a in the front-end code of the application and subsequently broadcast it to the `mapBlock` operator where closures perform the application of $a\mathbf{1}^\top$ over another dataset.

What do we mean by "application" of $a\mathbf{1}^\top$ on another dataset? Most of the time, it is an element-wise operation. Let us consider, for example:

$$\mathbf{C} \leftarrow \mathbf{A} - a\mathbf{1}^\top.$$

Here, the dimensionality of $\mathbf{1}$ is derived from context and is the same as the number of columns of $\mathbf{A}$. The whole operation simply implies subtracting a from every column of $\mathbf{A}$. In reality, an implementation would often follow the pattern (2) described above (example 4.8).

■ **Example 4.8 Computing** $C = A - a1^\top$.
```
// arguments: A, a.
val drmA: DrmLike[Int] = {...}
val a: Vector = {...}

// Broadcast the vector a
val aBcast = drmBroadcast(a)

// compute C ← A − a1⊤.
val drmC = drmA.mapBlock() { case (keys, block) ⇒

  val a:Vector = aBcast
  block ::= { (r, _, v) ⇒ v - a(keys(r)) }
  keys → block
}
```

■ **Example 4.9 Computing** $C = A - A11^\top$.
```
// argument: A.
val drmA: DrmLike[K] = { ... }

// compute C ← A − A11⊤
val drmC = drmA.mapBlock() { case (keys, block) ⇒

  val partialRS = block.rowSums()
  block ::= { (r, _, v) ⇒ v - partialRS(r) }
  keys → block
}
```

4.11.3 Untangling $A11^\top$

Let us start directly with an example. Suppose we consider

$$C \leftarrow A - A11^\top.$$

It is exactly the same as the previous example, $C \leftarrow A - a1^\top$, for as long as we substitute $a = A1^\top = \text{rowSums}(A)$. But rowSums$(A)$ can be computed partially inside the mapBlock closure, so in this case we are going to follow the algorithm pattern scenario (1) described above (example 4.9).

Note that now we do not need the input to be Int-keyed; previously a implied an integer ordinal adressing of the rows of A, but now we do not have such a constraint.

4.12 Example: distance and distance-based kernel matrices

4.12.1 Computing a distance matrix

We will start by giving a definition of a distance matrix.

> **Definition 4.12.1 Distance and Squared Distance matrices.**
>
> Let $\mathcal{D} = \{\mathbf{x}_i : i = 1, 2, ..m\}$. Let $\mathbf{X}$ be a matrix induced by $\mathcal{D}$ such that $\mathbf{X}_{i*} \triangleq \mathbf{x}_i$, in other words, the rows of $\mathbf{X}$ are our dataset points. (This convention will be used by default in this book).
>
> Distance matrix $\mathbf{D} \in \mathbb{R}^{m \times n}$ is a matrix such that $\mathbf{D}_{ij} \triangleq \left\| \mathbf{x}_i - \mathbf{x}_j \right\|_2$.
>
> Also, let the squared distance matrix, denoted as $\mathbf{D}^2$, be $\mathbf{D}^2 \triangleq \mathbf{D} \circ \mathbf{D}$.

Let us figure out how to compute distance or distance squared matrix.

> **Tip**
>
> Seek an algebraic presentation of the problem.

An element of the squared distance matrix:

$$\mathbf{D}_{ij}^2 = \left\| \mathbf{x}_i - \mathbf{x}_j \right\|_2^2 = \mathbf{x}_i^\top \mathbf{x}_i + \mathbf{x}_j^\top \mathbf{x}_j - 2\mathbf{x}_i^\top \mathbf{x}_j, \tag{4.1}$$

which yields

$$\mathbf{D}^2 = \mathbf{s}\mathbf{1}^\top + \mathbf{1}\mathbf{s}^\top - 2\mathbf{X}\mathbf{X}^\top, \tag{4.2}$$

where

$$\mathbf{s} = (\mathbf{X} \circ \mathbf{X})\mathbf{1}. \tag{4.3}$$

This may look a bit strange, but in reality it is very simple algebra.

Notation $\mathbf{A} \circ \mathbf{A}$ is the *Hadamard* (element-wise) self-product of $\mathbf{A}$, i.e., 'drmA * drmA' in Samsara's speak. Another possible syntax is 'drmA ^ 2'.

As it has been discussed in § 4.11.1, multiplying any matrix by $\mathbf{1}$ produces row-wise sums.

So the computation of (4.3) is simply:

```
val s = drmA * drmA rowSums
```

Now, the notation $\mathbf{s}\mathbf{1}^\top$ means "populate all *columns* of a matrix with the vector $\mathbf{s}$" (see § 4.11.2). Similarly, the expression $\mathbf{1}\mathbf{s}^\top$ means "populate all *rows* of a matrix with the vector $\mathbf{s}$." We do not have a single operator for these, as it stands, but these are still very simple operations. If we want to add $\mathbf{s}\mathbf{1}^\top$ or $\mathbf{1}\mathbf{s}^\top$ to a precomputed matrix $-2\mathbf{X}\mathbf{X}^\top$, this operation can be carried out with the help of operator `mapBlock` and by making $\mathbf{s}$ available to the the block code via a broadcast.

■ **Example 4.10 Distributed Squared Distance.**

```
private[math] def dsqDist(drmInput: DrmLike[Int]):
  DrmLike[Int] = {

  // We make several passes over X,
  // make sure it is pinned to cache.
  val drmX = drmInput.checkpoint()
  implicit val ctx = drmX.context

  val s = drmX * drmX rowSums // compute 4.3
  val sBcast = drmBroadcast(s) // Broadcast

  // Compute XᵀX first
  (drmX %*% drmX.t).mapBlock() { case (keys, block) ⇒
    // Pin s to a reference.
    val s:Vector = sBcast
    // Apply 4.2 to each distributed block
    val newBlock = block.cloned := { (r, c, x) ⇒
        s(keys(r)) + s(c) - 2 * x
    }
    keys → newBlock
  }
}
```

The observations (4.2) and (4.3) are presented in example 4.10. The code is self-explanatory per above.

As a more general case, for any two datasets $\mathbf{X} \hookleftarrow \mathcal{D}_1$ and $\mathbf{Y} \hookleftarrow \mathcal{D}_2$, a pairwise squared distance matrix of all combinations of data points in $\mathcal{D}_1$ and $\mathcal{D}_2$ will look like:

$$\mathbf{D}_{\mathbf{XY}}^2 = \mathbf{s}\mathbf{1}^\top + \mathbf{1}\mathbf{t}^\top - 2\mathbf{X}\mathbf{Y}^\top, \tag{4.4}$$

where

$$\begin{aligned}
\mathbf{s} &= (\mathbf{X} \circ \mathbf{X})\,\mathbf{1}, \\
\mathbf{t} &= (\mathbf{Y} \circ \mathbf{Y})\,\mathbf{1}.
\end{aligned}$$

A naive solution to the distance problem could include building a Cartesian product of all vectors and computing the distance formula directly.

Seeking an algebraic representation of a problem has multiple benefits in this case. First, we are able to sketch a solution quickly by reusing algebraic building blocks. Second, at the time of this writing, building a Cartesian product in Spark alone, for example, would cause a quadratic number of combined but tiny tasks, which in practice runs too slowly due to task startup costs, eclipsing the task load.

The procedures computing (4.2) and (4.4), both over in-core and distributed operands, are now part of Mahout and are mentioned in the appendix.

4.12.2 Computing a kernel matrix

We start with a definition of a kernel matrix.

> **Definition 4.12.2 Kernel matrix.**
> A kernel matrix $\mathbf{K}$ of input $\mathcal{D} = \{\mathbf{x}_i : i = 1, 2, \ldots m\}$ is a squared (and usually symmetric) matrix such that $\mathbf{K}_{ij} \triangleq \kappa(\mathbf{x}_i, \mathbf{x}_j)$, where function $\kappa(\cdot)$ is called a "kernel" function.

As usual, we assume a matrix $\mathbf{X}$ is induced by $\mathcal{D}$ row-wise: $\mathbf{X}_{i*} \triangleq \mathbf{x}_i$.

In practice, a lot of kernel functions act on the norm of the difference $d(\mathbf{x}_1, \mathbf{x}_2) \triangleq \|\mathbf{x}_1 - \mathbf{x}_2\|_2$ or on the squared norm of the difference between two data points $d^2(\mathbf{x}_1, \mathbf{x}_2) \triangleq \|\mathbf{x}_1 - \mathbf{x}_2\|_2^2$. For example, the standard exponential kernel is often defined as

$$\kappa_{SE}(\mathbf{x}_1, \mathbf{x}_2) = \exp\left(\frac{-d^2(\mathbf{x}_1, \mathbf{x}_2)}{h^2}\right),$$

where h is a so called "kernel bandwidth" parameter.

Therefore, it is easy to compute a kernel matrix induced by the standard exponential kernel on any input $\mathbf{X}$ (example 4.11).

■ **Example 4.11 Computing a standard exponential kernel matrix.**
```
val drmKSE = dexp(dsq(drmX) / (-h * h))
```

 Tip

Try to group scalar-only operands together when possible. E.g., `constA * constB * drmM` or `drmM * (constA * constB)`.

If they are not grouped together, it may, but not necessarily will, create additional composed function(s) applied element-wise.

In the context of a massive element-wise application, adding even one more function call may be a cost one may want to avoid.

In practice, however, we would probably rarely seek to form a full distance or kernel matrix unless we can impose an upper bound on m which is reasonably small. This is because quite often in practice input $\mathbf{X} \in \mathbb{R}^{m \times n}$ is a tall and thin matrix such that $m \gg n$, forming a kernel matrix would impose a significant memory requirement of $O\left(m^2\right)$ which is much more than the input size $O\left(mn\right)$. But partial kernel and distance matrices based on (4.4) are still quite useful in practice.

4.13 Example: scaling a dataset

Dataset scaling by standardization is a quite common feature transformation technique that forces all columns in the input to have mean of 0 and standard deviation of 1 (or 0 if there was no variance in data at all). A lot of algorithms such as algorithms fitting GLMs or clustering algorithms recommend or require this step as a part of input preprocessing.

If we have a set of values $\mathcal{D} \triangleq \{x_i : i = 1, 2, ...m\}$ then the scaling transformation is

$$y_i = \begin{cases} \frac{x_i - \mu}{\sigma}, & \sigma > 0; \\ 0, & \sigma = 0, \end{cases} \tag{4.5}$$

where μ is the mean and σ^2 is the variance of $\mathcal{D}$.

The problem of scaling is therefore a two-step problem:

(1) Compute column-wise μ, σ of $\mathcal{D}$;
(2) Apply scaling (4.5).

First, we will design a method computing both column-wise μ and σ (example 4.12)[2].

This is almost the same example mentioned in the preface of this book; we are using the fact that $\sigma^2 = \mathbb{E}\left(x^2\right) - \mathbb{E}\left(x\right)^2$.

---

[2] As of Mahout 0.10.2, these and some other functions given in examples are part of Mahout.

■ **Example 4.12 Computing column-wise** μ, σ **of X.**

```
def dcolMeanVars[K: ClassTag](drmA: DrmLike[K]):
(Vector, Vector) = {
  val drmAcp = drmA.checkpoint()
  val mu = drmAcp colMeans
  // Compute variance using mean(x^2) - mean(x)^2
  val variances = (drmAcp ^ 2 colMeans) -=: mu * mu
  mu → variances
}

def dcolMeanStdevs[K: ClassTag](drmA: DrmLike[K])
: (Vector, Vector) = {
  val (mu, vars) = dcolMeanVars(drmA)
  mu → (vars ::= math.sqrt _)
}
```

■ **Example 4.13 Dataset scaling.**

```
def dcolScale[K: ClassTag](drmX: DrmLike[K]): DrmLike[K] = {
  implicit val ctx = drmX.context
  // Multiple passes -- pin to cache if not yet pinned.
  val drmXcp = drmX.checkpoint()

  // Compute mean, deviation.
  val (mu, sigma) = dcolMeanStdevs(drmXcp)
  val (muBcast, sigmaBCast) =
 drmBroadcast(mu) → drmBroadcast(sigma)

  // Apply formula (4.5) to each block.
  drmXcp.mapBlock() { case (keys, block) ⇒
    val (mu, sigma) = (muBcast: Vector) → (sigmaBCast: Vector)
    val newBlock = block.cloned := { (_, c, v) ⇒
      (v - mu(c)) / sigma(c)
    }
    keys → newBlock
  }
}
```

Now we can trivially scale the input dataset per (4.5) (example 4.13). The unit test verifying scaling on simulated data is given in example 4.14.

■ **Example 4.14 Scaling unit test.**

```
test("dcolScale") {
  val m = 500
  val d = 25

  // Simulate noise, means and variances.
  val mxNoise = Matrices.symmetricUniformView(m, d, 12345)

  // Simulate random data means
  val mxDataMeans = Matrices
    .symmetricUniformView(d, 1, 134)(::, 0) * 100
  val mxDataSigmas = Matrices
    .symmetricUniformView(d, 1, 135)(::, 0) * 10

  // Test if column has no variance.
  mxDataSigmas(1) = 0.0

  // Unscaled simulated data.
  val mxA = mxNoise.cloned :=
    { (_, c, v) ⇒ v * mxDataSigmas(c) + mxDataMeans(c) }

  // Convert to a distributed matrix
  val drmA = drmParallelize(mxA, numPartitions = 2)

  // Standardize
  val drmScaled = dcolScale(drmA)

  // Compute means and variances of the scaled
  val (mxMeans, mxSigmas) = dcolMeanStdevs(drmScaled)

  // Assert that scaled data has standard mean (0) and dev (1 or 0)
  val mxMeansControl = new RandomAccessSparseVector(d)
  val mxSigmaControl = new DenseVector(d) := 1.0
  mxSigmaControl(1) = 0
  (mxMeans - mxMeansControl).norm(2) should be < 1e-7
  (mxSigmas - mxSigmaControl).norm(2) should be < 1e-7
}
```

4.14 Cache side effects of the mapBlock() operator

 Tip   Beware of the side effects on cached partition data.

Let us elaborate on this tip.

Notice that we clone the block during the `mapBlock` operation in example 4.13.

Since we pin X to cache, X is going to be reused. In case the Spark cache decides to keep object trees rather than write X to a serialized format, if we do not clone the block, we may cause side effects or non-idempotent computation effects by interfering with object trees in the Spark memory block manager.

The rule of thumb, therefore, is: `mapBlocks` running over a reused dataset that is pinned in cache should always clone the matrix blocks.

In general, if there is any doubt, it is prudent to clone partition content inside the `mapBlock`. There may be penalty for copying memory, but in reality it is still much faster than, for example, matrix multiplication computation, or for I/O expenses, and usually certainly not worth optimizing at the backdrop of much bigger task startup and I/O costs.

4.15 Example: testing regression slopes

We will conclude this chapter with yet another distributed algebra example.

In examples 2.3, 2.4, and 2.5 we have considered fitting a linear regression, and its regularized version, a ridge regression.

However, regression analysis does not stop upon model fitting. It also considers various metrics for goodness of fit. In particular, two tests are commonly run: Analysis of Variance (ANOVA) regression tests and individual slope tests.

Now we intend to continue working on the example of linear regression (ordinary least squares, OLS) from the point where it was left in § 2.4. In this section we consider regression slope tests. Various work, for example, [Montgomery et al., 2012], contains details of the formulas used further in this section.

To recap, the general linear regression model can be viewed as follows:

$$y_i = \hat{y}_i + \varepsilon,$$

where ε is a random variable distributed according to

$$\varepsilon \sim \mathcal{N}(0, \sigma),$$

and

$$\hat{y}_i = \boldsymbol{\beta}^\top \boldsymbol{x}_i.$$

The latter in the matrix form looks as

$$\hat{\boldsymbol{y}} = \mathbf{X}\boldsymbol{\beta}.$$

Here we assume that the bias component is already included into the input $\mathbf{X}$ so that $x_0 = 1$ for all rows of $\mathbf{X}$.

"Slope" is just another word for the elements of vector β. Indeed, β_j shows how much the estimator $\hat{y}$ changes per unit of change in the corresponding element of $\boldsymbol{x}$ if other predictor elements stay the same.

However, how can we be sure that the deduced value β_j has any likely contribution towards the target in the population, given our limited observed dataset? The classic statistical approach to address this question is to conduct a two-sided t-test of β_j against the null hypothesis H_0 which is, in this case, $\beta_j = 0$ for any β_j inside the β.

Since we are conducting a t-test, we require a computation of the t-statistics:

$$t = \frac{\hat{\beta}_j}{\operatorname{se}\left(\hat{\beta}_j\right)}, \tag{4.6}$$

where $\hat{\beta}_j$ is our obtained estimate for β_j, and $\operatorname{se}\left(\hat{\beta}_j\right)$ is the standard error of our slope estimate.

The construction of computation of the standard error $\operatorname{se}\left(\hat{\beta}_j\right)$ is as follows. First, we define a square matrix $\mathbf{C}$ as

$$\mathbf{C} \triangleq \left(\mathbf{X}^\top \mathbf{X}\right)^{-1}. \tag{4.7}$$

Then the standard error is:

$$\operatorname{se}\left(\hat{\beta}_j\right) = \sqrt{\sigma^2 \mathbf{C}_{jj}}, \tag{4.8}$$

where σ is the regression noise deviation parameter, and $\mathbf{C}_{jj}$ is the j-th element of the main diagonal of matrix $\mathbf{C}$.

In order to compute the standard error of a slope per above, we also need to estimate the regression variance σ^2. The regression variance estimator is computed according to the formula:

$$\hat{\sigma}^2 = \frac{\sum (y_i - \hat{y}_i)^2}{m - n}, \tag{4.9}$$

where m is the number of data points, and n is the number of predictor variables (including the "bias" predictor which is always 1). Note that by construction these are parameters of our input matrix $\mathbf{X}$: $\mathbf{X} \in \mathbb{R}^{m \times n}$. The expression $m - n$ represents the degrees of freedom when estimating the regression variance. Among other things, we must therefore require that $m > n$, implying an over-defined regression problem.

By sequentially applying formulas for regression variance (4.9), matrix $\mathbf{C}$ (4.7), slope standard error (4.8), and t-statistics (4.6) for every predictor coefficient in β, we compute everything that is needed for the two-sided t-test using the Student distribution with $m - n$ degrees of freedom and computation of the p-values.

These steps are shown in example 4.15. There, the inputs are: the input $\mathbf{X}$ without bias element, the observed values $\boldsymbol{y}$, and the fitted coefficients $\hat{\beta}$.

■ **Example 4.15 Distributed OLS slope t-test.**

```
def testBeta(drmX: DrmLike[Int], y: Vector, beta: Vector):
  (Vector, Vector, Vector) = {

  val m = drmX.nrow
  val n = drmX.ncol + 1

  require(beta.length == n, "beta.length must be X.ncol + 1.")
  require(y.length == m, "y.length must be X.nrow.")

  // We shy away from an underdefined problem
  require(m > n, "Underdefined problem")

  // Estimate regression variance.
  val drmBX = (1 cbind drmX).checkpoint()

  // Compute sum of square residuals.
  val ssr = ((drmBX %*% beta).collect(::, 0) - y) ^= 2 sum

  // Regression variance (sigma^2) estimator. DF = m - n
  val regVar = ssr / (m - n)

  // C := inv(X'X); compute main diagonal of C as c-vector
  val c = solve(drmBX.t %*% drmBX) diagv

  // Standard errors of all betas except intercept
  val seBeta = (c *= regVar) := sqrt _

  // t-statistics
  val tBeta = beta / seBeta

  // Standard t-distr for (n-p) degrees of freedom
  val tDistribution = new TDistribution(m - n)

  // p-values, 2-side test
  val pValBeta = tBeta.cloned := { t =>
    2 * (1 - tDistribution.cumulativeProbability(abs(t)))
  }

  (seBeta, tBeta, pValBeta)
}
```

■ Example 4.16 Unit test for distributed slope t-tests.

```
1   test("ols-coeff-tests") {
2     import LinearRegression._
3
4     // Simulated data
5     val betaSim = dvec(-4, 3, 25, 12)
6     val (mxX, y) = simData(betaSim, 250, noiseSigma = 10.0)
7
8     // Distributed X
9     val drmX = drmParallelize(mxX, numPartitions = 2)
10
11    val fittedBeta = dridge(drmX, y, 0)
12    trace(s"beta = $fittedBeta.")
13
14    // Coefficient t-tests
15    val (betaSE, betaT, betaPVal) = testBeta(drmX, y, fittedBeta)
16
17    println("Beta tests:\n  #          beta          SE       " +
18      "t-stat      p-value")
19    for (i ← 0 until fittedBeta.length) {
20      println(f"${i}%3d${fittedBeta(i)}%12.4f" +
21        f"${betaSE(i)}%12.4f${betaT(i)}%12.4f" +
22        f"${betaPVal(i)}%12.4f")
23    }
24  }
```

Since the input $\mathbf{X}$ does not include the bias element, this is corrected in lines 5 and 14. As the input with bias (drmBX) is used multiple times in the procedure, it is pinned to cache via checkpoint(). Alternatively, if the input without bias (drmX) is already pinned to cache and memory is a concern, then it may make sense to avoid caching.

The computation of (4.9) is performed in lines 17 and 20. First, the distributed evaluation of $\hat{y}$ is carried out in line 17, and the rest of the formula is finished in the front end.

The main diagonal of (4.7) is computed in line 23. The computation of $\mathbf{X}^\top\mathbf{X}$ is distributed, but the inversion is done in the driver application (as before in § 2.4, we assume the matrix $\mathbf{X}^\top\mathbf{X}$ to be small enough for that).

The rest of the formulas are computed in the front end (since the data at this point is small). Line 26 carries out (4.8), line 29 carries out (4.6), and lines 32, 35-37 compute the p-values of the two-sided t-tests. All of these computations happen for all regression coefficients at the same time.

The procedure returns three vectors containing the standard errors, the t-statistics, and the p-values for each of the coefficients β_j.

Now that the regression slope t-test procedure is defined, we can construct a unit test for it. This unit test code is shown in example 4.16. First we create a simulated regression data using the "ground truth" values of $\beta = \begin{pmatrix} -4 & 3 & 25 & 12 \end{pmatrix}$, and $\sigma = 10$ (lines 5, 6).

Line 9 creates the distributed input $\mathbf{X}$ (without the bias component). OLS is fitted via ridge regression in line 11 using the same procedure we have given previously in example 2.3. Line 15 executes test values computation. Lines 17-23 print the result.

The output of the test is shown below:

Test output

```
Beta tests:
 #         beta          SE       t-stat     p-value
 0      -3.5757      0.6549     -5.4598      0.0000
 1       5.9527      2.3299      2.5549      0.0112
 2      24.8379      2.2877     10.8573      0.0000
 3      10.0503      2.2892      4.3903      0.0000
```

Here, the first line corresponds to the intercept coefficient.

For good measure we dumped the dataset created in line 6 into a CSV file and fitted OLS using R's *glm* procedure. The output of the slope statistics done in R is shown below:

R output

```
glm(formula = y ~ X0 + X1 + X2, data = data)
Deviance Residuals:
    Min        1Q    Median        3Q       Max
-31.122    -7.275    -0.302     6.606    32.280
```

R output

```
Coefficients:
             Estimate Std. Error t value Pr(>|t|)
(Intercept)  -3.5757     0.6549   -5.460 1.16e-07 ***
X0            5.9527      2.3299    2.555  0.0112 *
X1           24.8379      2.2877   10.857  < 2e-16 ***
X2           10.0503      2.2892    4.390 1.68e-05 ***
---
Signif. codes:  0 '***' 0.001 '**' 0.01 '*' 0.05 '.' 0.1 ' ' 1
```

As observed, our values are identical to the values reported by R's *glm*.

The interpretation of the results is usually done based on p-values. At the 95% confidence level, the coefficients with p-values less than 5% (or 0.05) are considered significant. At higher p-values the null hypothesis (i.e., $\beta_j = 0$) cannot be rejected confidently. In this test, all coefficients seem to be very significant. The least significant estimate of $\hat{\beta}_1$ comes at 1.12% p-value which is still well below the 5% threshold. Choice of confidence level depends on the use case, but the 95% confidence level is commonly used.

As the formulas demonstrate, the results of the t-tests are driven by the variance of a predictor variable (higher variance driving lower p-values), the regression variance (higher value driving higher p-values), and the value of the β_j estimate itself (higher value driving higher t-statistics and lower p-value). As the simulated data procedure really used the same variance for all predictors (except for the bias), in this case the test results are mostly driven by the value of the slope estimate itself.

A word of caution is due about interpretation of the slope significance tests. There is sometimes a perception that the slope significance tests express a statistically asserted influence of a predictor variable on the target variable. For example, if we fit a regression that takes income and age of mortgage applicants as predictors of a company's approval/denial decision, then the slope tests supposedly would measure the likelihood that the company is making decisions based on income (legal to do) vs. applicant age (illegal to do). In general, however, this is not a correct interpretation of the regression slope tests.

Why?

A rejection of the slope test asserts high confidence that the differences in the regression residuals when using $\beta_j = 0$ and $\beta_j = \hat{\beta}_j$ are not due to chance, provided *the rest of the coefficients* $\beta_s : s \neq j$ *retain their estimated values*. In the multivariate case this means that this test is good for this particular model fit $\hat{\beta}$, and is not valid for any other model fit $\hat{\beta}' \neq \hat{\beta}$. Moreover, it does not even matter how well the model fits, the test only measures how well β_j works in this very model (even if the model does a poor job). So if the model exhibits poor goodness of fit, tests do not explain much as the model fails to align with the target in the first place. But even if the model fits well, it turns out that certain data situations may cause significant variance in optimal and near-optimal solutions that predict the target variable almost equally well. By a "significant variance of a solution" we imply a significant variance of estimated $\hat{\beta}$ and their respective p-values among models that fit the observed values equally well, or almost equally well. Model-fitting algorithms almost always exhibit non-deterministic "jitter" (for example, due to noise in the data and its non-deterministic splitting into train and test sets), and may spuriously arrive at one of the existing near-optimal solutions on the same training dataset. One near-optimal fit may tell us that the applicant's age was significant for the prediction of mortgage application approval, while the applicant's income was not; and another near-optimal model may tell us the opposite. This is the case with regressions when predictors are affected by a so-called *collinearity* condition. The regression slope tests themselves unfortunately do not account for such possibilities.

High variance of the near-optimal fit does not affect regressions only. For example, decision trees are even more prone to the variability of near-optimal fits. In fact, this is a fairly common problem for an attempt to interpret any model that contains latent (hidden) variables. It is important to realize that the statistical modelling exists primarily for predicting target variables but not necessarily for *explaining* them. It usually does not guarantee low variance of the near-optimal solution – or even provide such variance estimates.

Approximating Distributed Problems

In part III, we will mainly focus on the principles of building distributed math algorithms.

We will not focus on the detailed mathematical underpinnings of already published algorithms. With rare exceptions, these are already described in excellent detail in the references we give. Rather, we will only provide a minimal summary we would need to drive our distributed solution. We focus on what makes algorithms suitable for processing "Big Math" problems, as well as their final translation into distributed Mahout "Samsara" code. Similarly to how the Computer Science design principles of induction, dynamic programming, etc., can be taught by example, we believe we can improve the process of finding cues to a good algorithm by formulating a few principles and observing examples of the process of seeking a solution.

The design principles for distributed "Big Math" algorithms.

Let us consider a hypothetical example. What happens when we simply start increasing the amount of input for a traditional in-core algorithm such as PCA? Well, at some point we may see our data swollen so much that we cannot keep running the problem in a traditional way any longer without breaking some of the requirements or constraints.

As a next step, we might think to morph the solution into a distributed algorithm, and since it is scaling horizontally, by indiscriminately throwing hardware at it, we will be done. Right?

Actually, in a surprisingly large amount of cases *we will not* be. Anecdotally, quite a few companies made this argument while marketing their products, but alas, this was not always found to be a working truth. Adding resources at a linear cost does not solve mathematical problems that asymptotically exceede this linear cost.

So why may that strategy not work?

There is an old folklore story in which one rich and greedy merchant ("merchant A," say) made a deal with another merchant ("merchant B"). The terms were that merchant B would give merchant A one million coins every night, while merchant A would pay back merchant B just one coin on the first night. Every night after that, the payback would be doubled, and the deal could not be ended in less than 30 days.

The greedy merchant thought he was getting a good deal and some easy money, but actually he went broke before the month was over. Indeed, it is easily seen that he would get no more than 30 million over 30 days, but he would start paying more than he was getting back on the 21st night, and the 30th night alone would cost him more than half a billion coins.

This story reflects exactly what happens with naively scaled approaches. We call it "the greedy merchant problem." What people often neglect, willingly and unwillingly alike, is the fact that hardware cost scales only linearly whereas most naive traditional algorithms (even matrix multiplication) scale according to a power law. In the above story, merchant B's payments, which come at a constant rate, represent our ability for hardware growth. Merchant A's repayments are an analogy of the cost of algorithm growth. Time represents, well, the size of the problem. Sooner or later it simply would cost too much to add another data point to the algorithm input so that the product would have to abandon the entire approach. Usually this boundary is found as an unpleasantly abrupt, if not catastrophic, "hockey stick" drop in performance, and quite often it takes product management completely by surprise.

Often in this scenario, to cope with the unexpected stall in what otherwise seemed like a smoothly working mechanism, additional engineering resources are thrown at profiling the solution. The team tries to make improvements on the *cost of iteration* by engineering more effective code, trimming obvious and not so obvious waste, throwing hardware acceleration at it, and so on. After all, that is how the management has tackled engineering problems before.

This may buy the product some time; but inputs continue to grow and 2x, 5x or even 10x cost-of-iteration improvements are quickly overtaken by the power law of the increases in the algorithm. Eventually, the team would have no other options left but to *modify the math in the algorithm*. The team would finally tackle the problem mathematically, at which point most of the team members become convinced that perhaps they would have saved a lot of time by simply doing it that way outright, instead of spending all that effort on interim improvements, hardware investments, etc., which in the end did not fundamentally address the root of the problem.

As the authors have found over the years, in the case of mathematical problems, the costs of engineering aimed at profiling the cost of iteration and growing the hardware to solve issues associated with an input increase often end up being overwhelmingly more expensive than designing and applying a simple mathematical trick.

The design principles of large scale *numerical* problems.

In "Big Math", practical numerical methods of coping with the *"greedy merchant"* problem mostly revolve around these techniques:

(1) Obtaining a low-resolution problem sketch or approximation and applying a previously known high-cost naive algorithm to it. Since the low resolution problem size has an upper bound and is explicitly controlled, the asymptotic complexity of the naive solution can be ignored. The algorithm for finding a low resolution approximation itself must also be linear and embarrassingly parallel, in order to be worth the extra step. Simple uniform sampling is an example of such a technique.

(2) Replacing a high-cost naive algorithm with a less accurate but more favorably scaling approximate algorithm. Ditching the full-batch gradient descent in favor of stochastic gradient descent is an example of such a technique. Another example is using an ANN (approximate nearest neighbor) algorithm such as LSH (locality-sensitive hashing) to replace an exact nearest neighbor algorithm such as kd-tree or R-tree.

(3) Replacing a naive high-cost algorithm with an algorithm which has a parameter controlling trade-off between accuracy and speed. Thus, once the algorithm gets too expensive to run, we can still continue controlling its growth by relaxing accuracy expectations as input grows, perhaps for quite some time. This approach assumes we can run things faster at the expense of accuracy, of which we hopefully had some surplus initially, and which we can give up as the problem input grows in size.

Ideally, all these qualities are available in one solution.

We want to reduce a problem in order to keep running things we cannot feasibly re-design in a more favorable way any time soon.

We want to have the option of running an approximate numerical algorithm instead of, say, an exact analytic one upon reaching a certain resource pressure threshold.

Finally, we want to have control over the speed/accuracy trade-off.

It is important to learn what parts of the algorithm lead to problematic asymptotic behaviors with respect to the input size from the start. For example, a prototype in-core algorithm may involve the steps of computing a full distance matrix on a data set, or a full kernel matrix. This will immediately lead to, approximately, a dense $O\left(\frac{m^2}{n}\right)$ power law requirement for the memory; or just $O\left(m^2\right)$, under the "thin" assumption that $m \gg n$. Depending on the problem at hand, we may decide to accept the power law memory requirements of the algorithm, often to keep things simple. However, a good quality "Big Math" algorithm strives to avoid the power law memory or flops (floating-point operations) requirements all together. And indeed, the body of research on approximating kernel matrices is impressive.

In part III we will consider how some of these principles may be implemented, by using concrete examples.

5

Stochastic SVD

In this chapter, we will learn the design of the stochastic SVD algorithm and how it applies all three design principles described in the introduction to part III in practice.

5.1 The SSVD Problem

Problem 5.1 Given rather large matrix $\mathbf{A}$, compute reduced $k-$rank SVD such that

$$\mathbf{A} \approx \mathbf{U}\mathbf{\Sigma}\mathbf{V}^\top,$$

where $\mathbf{A} \in \mathbb{R}^{m \times n}$, $\mathbf{U} \in \mathbb{R}^{m \times k}$, $\mathbf{V} \in \mathbb{R}^{n \times k}$, and $\mathbf{\Sigma} \in \mathbb{R}^{k \times k}$.

The matrices $\mathbf{U}$ and $\mathbf{V}$ are column-orthonormal, meaning all column vectors are pairwise orthogonal to each other, and their norms are equal to 1. The columns of $\mathbf{U}$ are called "left singular vectors," and the columns of $\mathbf{V}$ are called "right singular vectors."

The matrix $\mathbf{\Sigma}$ is a diagonal matrix of the form

$$\mathbf{\Sigma} = \begin{pmatrix} \sigma_1 & 0 & \cdots & 0 \\ 0 & \sigma_2 & \cdots & 0 \\ \vdots & \vdots & \ddots & \vdots \\ 0 & 0 & \cdots & \sigma_k \end{pmatrix}$$

with the quantities σ_i also known as the singular values.

By convention, the decomposition sorts the singular values and their correspondent singular vectors in decreasing order of the singular values.

5.2 Quick background behind the Stochastic SVD

5.2.1 Johnson-Lindenstrauss lemma

Stochastic SVD exploits, in part, the Johnson-Lindenstrauss lemma. This lemma says that the length of a random vector projected into a sufficiently high dimensional space $\mathbb{R}^d$ from even a higher dimensional space space $\mathbb{R}^n$, $n \gg d$, will be tightly distributed around its mean. For more detailed information see, for example, [Dasgupta and Gupta, 2003, Wikipedia.org, 2015a].

What is important for us is that the projection length mean is non-zero, proportional to the mean length in the original space, and that the deviation of the distribution shrinks as the number of dimensions d grows. What is more, the same proportionality statement holds for the mean distances between the points, so the data structure is roughly preserved. Another way to interpret this is that for any random subspace, on average, we observe a very small probability of a random vector falling dangerously close to being entirely contained in the space orthogonal to the random projection basis.

the intuition goes as follows. Suppose $\mathbf{x} \in \mathbb{R}^n$ is a random unit Gaussian vector. We can construct this as follows: first, let $\mathbf{y} \triangleq \left(y_1 \sim \mathcal{N}(0,1) \quad \cdots \quad y_n \sim \mathcal{N}(0,1) \right)^\top$ and then let $\mathbf{x} \triangleq \frac{\mathbf{y}}{\|\mathbf{y}\|_2}$ in order to make it unitary.

Let us then consider a projection $\mathbf{z} \triangleq \left(x_1 \quad \cdots \quad x_d \right)^\top$ of $\mathbf{x}$ on the subspace of the first d coordinates. Since $\|\mathbf{y}\|_2^2 \sim \chi^2 (\mathrm{df} = n)$ by construction, it is easy to see that $\frac{n}{d} \|\mathbf{z}\|_2^2 \sim \chi^2 (\mathrm{df} = d)$, or

$$p\left(\|\mathbf{z}\|_2^2 \right) \propto \chi^2 (\mathrm{df} = \mathrm{d}).$$

This means that as d increases, the mean of the projection squared norm increases proportionally to d, but the standard deviation increases only proportionally to $\sqrt{d}$; i.e., projection lengths become grouped much tighter around its expectation.

Due to similar considerations, we can extend this notion to any random projection

$$\mathbf{z} = \mathbf{Q}^\top \mathbf{x}, \tag{5.1}$$

where $\mathbf{Q} \in \mathbb{R}^{n \times d}$ is an arbitrary orthonormal projection matrix.

5.2.2 Capturing the subspace with largest variances

The following retains the notation of [Halko et al., 2011], which is an excellent study regarding random projection based methods. We highly recommend it for further details on this family of methods.

We said previously that for a set of random vectors, only a very small portion of those is likely to fall dangerously close to the null space of $\mathbf{Q}^\top$. However, our data is not going to be random. Certain directions (principal singular vectors) will matter more than others. What we care about is capturing directions with the most data variance. For that reason, we need to enhance the construction of matrix $\mathbf{Q}$. If most of the action in our matrix $\mathbf{A}$ is happening in only k-dimensional subspace, we can model matrix $\mathbf{A}$ as

$$\mathbf{A} = \mathbf{B} + \mathbf{E}, \tag{5.2}$$

where $\mathbf{B} \in \mathbb{R}^{m \times n}$ is of exactly rank k, and $\mathbf{E}$ is a small perturbation. We are thus interested in finding column space $\mathbf{C}(\mathbf{B})$.

We also can think of $\mathbf{B}$ as a signal, and $\mathbf{E}$ as a noise. Assumption (5.2) is important, the subsequent logic relies on it.

Imagine we then start creating random linear combinations of columns of $\mathbf{B}$ via multiplying them by a random vector $\boldsymbol{\omega}^{(i)}$:

$$\boldsymbol{y}^{(i)} = \mathbf{B}\boldsymbol{\omega}^{(i)}.$$

We do this k times. The vectors $\boldsymbol{y}^{(1)}$, $\boldsymbol{y}^{(2)}$... $\boldsymbol{y}^{(k)}$ are highly likely to span the column space of $\mathbf{B}$.

But we do not know matrix $\mathbf{B}$, we only know $\mathbf{A}$. We continue building the procedure out by seeking $\boldsymbol{y}^{(i)} = \mathbf{A}\boldsymbol{\omega}^{(i)}$ instead. So our procedure actually becomes

$$\boldsymbol{y}^{(i)} = \mathbf{B}\boldsymbol{\omega}^{(i)} + \mathbf{E}\boldsymbol{\omega}^{(i)}.$$

It is possible that the noise component $\mathbf{E}\boldsymbol{\omega}^{(i)}$ will prevent the vectors $\left\{ \boldsymbol{y}^{(i)} : i = 1, 2, \ldots k \right\}$ from spanning the entire column space of our signal $\mathbf{B}$. It turns out that over-sampling linear combinations of columns by another p vectors and obtaining vectors $\left\{ \boldsymbol{y}^{(i)} : i = 1, 2, \ldots k \right\}$ will improve the accuracy of capturing the column-space $\mathbf{C}(\mathbf{B})$ inside the space spanned by $k + p$ vectors $\boldsymbol{y}^{(i)}$ quite dramatically.

By orthonormalizing the basis spanned by the vectors $\boldsymbol{y}^{(i)}$, we obtain our random projection matrix. That leads to the 2-step Alg. 5.1 for obtaining $\mathbf{Q}$ (5.1). This algorithm

---

■ **Algorithm 5.1** k-rank capturing random projection.
   (1) $\mathbf{Y} \leftarrow \mathbf{A}\mathbf{\Omega}, \mathbf{A} \in \mathbb{R}^{m \times n}, \mathbf{\Omega} \in \mathbb{R}^{n \times (k+p)}$. Here, $\mathbf{\Omega}$ is a matrix consisting of random unitary Gaussian vectors $\boldsymbol{\omega}^{(i)}$
   (2) Obtain $\mathbf{Q}$ by computing QR decomposition $\mathbf{Y} = \mathbf{QR}$
   (3) $\mathbf{B} \leftarrow \mathbf{Q}^\top \mathbf{A}$

---

is given in [Halko et al., 2011]. There, we replace the individual vectors we have just talked about, with the matrices:

$$\mathbf{Y} \triangleq \begin{pmatrix} \boldsymbol{y}^{(1)} & \boldsymbol{y}^{(2)} & \cdots & \boldsymbol{y}^{(k+p)} \end{pmatrix},$$

$$\mathbf{\Omega} \triangleq \begin{pmatrix} \boldsymbol{\omega}^{(1)} & \boldsymbol{\omega}^{(2)} & \cdots & \boldsymbol{\omega}^{(k+p)} \end{pmatrix}.$$

It further turns out that we are not constrained by the Gaussian sampling scheme for the vectors $\boldsymbol{\omega}^{(i)}$. Uniform sampling works just as well, and even fast sparse [Achlioptas, 2001] and very sparse [Li et al., 2006] sampling schemes work well.

5.2.3 The power iterations

Power iteration is a technique which has the purpose of improving the ratio of signal to noise in the data. In Alg. 5.2 it is represented by step 5.

A practical consideration: q=1 significantly improves the accuracy but potentially more than doubles the execution time. If you can afford the time, use q=1, otherwise use q=0. According to accuracy tests on Wikipedia data, using q = 2,3,... is not expected to be cost effective in terms of time investment; q =1 is already quite accurate.

5.2.4 The formulation of the Mahout SSVD algorithm

The publication [Halko et al., 2011] describes several methods based on random projections. The Mahout SSVD variation of this methodology family is given in Alg. 5.2. It adjusts the ideas given in the publication a little in order to achieve somewhat better compactness of communications in a shared-nothing distributed system, especially with respect to communication between a driver node and worker nodes.

5.2.5 Coding the in-core SSVD version

Using the formulations given in Alg. 5.2, we can now undertake the in-core implementation of SSVD using Mahout "Samsara" as shown in example 5.1.

There, we inline the Cholesky QR formulas instead of actually running a QR procedure[1].

---

[1] In practice, since in SSVD the QR decomposition is performed over a thin matrix $\mathbf{Y}$, $\mathbf{Y}^\top \mathbf{Y}$ is easier to

> ■ **Algorithm 5.2 Modified SSVD Algorithm.**
> Given an $m \times n$ matrix $\mathbf{A}$, a target rank k, and an oversampling parameter p, this procedure computes a k-rank SVD $\mathbf{A} \approx \mathbf{U}\mathbf{\Sigma}\mathbf{V}^\top$:
> (1) Create seed for random $n \times (k+p)$ matrix $\mathbf{\Omega}$.
> (2) $\mathbf{Y}_0 = \mathbf{A}\mathbf{\Omega}$, $\mathbf{Y} \in \mathbb{R}^{m \times (k+p)}$.
> (3) Column-orthonormalize $\mathbf{Y}_0 \to \mathbf{Q}$ by computing thin decomposition $\mathbf{Y}_0 = \mathbf{Q}\mathbf{R}$. Also, $\mathbf{Q} \in \mathbb{R}^{m \times (k+p)}$, $\mathbf{R} \in \mathbb{R}^{(k+p) \times (k+p)}$.
> (4) $\mathbf{B}_0 = \mathbf{Q}^\top \mathbf{A}$: $\mathbf{B} \in \mathbb{R}^{(k+p) \times n}$.
> (5) For i in $1..q$ repeat (power iterations):
>   (a) $\mathbf{Y}_i \leftarrow \mathbf{A}\mathbf{B}_{i-1}^\top$;
>   (b) Column-orthonormalize $\mathbf{Y}_i \to \mathbf{Q}$ by computing thin decomposition $\mathbf{Y}_i = \mathbf{Q}\mathbf{R}$;
>   (c) $\mathbf{B}_i \leftarrow \mathbf{Q}^\top \mathbf{A}$.
> (6) Compute the Eigen-solution of a small symmetric $\mathbf{B}_q\mathbf{B}_q^\top = \hat{\mathbf{U}}\mathbf{\Lambda}\hat{\mathbf{U}}^\top$: $\mathbf{B}_q\mathbf{B}_q^\top \in \mathbb{R}^{(k+p) \times (k+p)}$.
> (7) Singular values $\mathbf{\Sigma} = \mathbf{\Lambda}^{\circ 1/2}$, or, in other words, $\sigma_i = \sqrt{\lambda_i}$.
> (8) If needed, compute $\mathbf{U} = \mathbf{Q}\hat{\mathbf{U}}$.
> (9) If needed, compute $\mathbf{V} = \mathbf{B}^\top \hat{\mathbf{U}} \mathbf{\Sigma}^{-1}$. Another way is $\mathbf{V} = \mathbf{A}^\top \mathbf{U} \mathbf{\Sigma}^{-1}$.

> ■ **Example 5.1 SSVD.**
>
> ```
> /**
>  * In-core SSVD algorithm.
>  *
>  * @param a input matrix A
>  * @param k request SSVD rank
>  * @param p oversampling parameter
>  * @param q number of power iterations
>  * @return (U,V,s)
>  */
> def ssvd(a: Matrix, k: Int, p: Int = 15, q: Int = 0) = {
>   val m = a.nrow
>   val n = a.ncol
>   if (k > min(m, n))
> ```

compute under distributed settings (a one step all-reduce operation). Also, step 4 in algorithm 5.2 becomes

$$\mathbf{B} = \mathbf{Q}^\top \mathbf{A}$$
$$= \left(\mathbf{Y}\left(\mathbf{L}^\top\right)^{-1} \right)^\top \mathbf{A}$$
$$= \mathbf{L}^{-1}\mathbf{Y}^\top \mathbf{A}.$$

```
    throw new IllegalArgumentException(
      "k cannot be greater than smaller of m,n")
  val pfxed = min(p, min(m, n) - k)
  // Actual decomposition rank
  val r = k + pfxed
  val rnd = RandomUtils.getRandom
  // We approximate Ω as matrix of symmetric uniform values
  val omega = Matrices.symmetricUniformView(n, r, rnd.nextInt)
```

// $\mathbf{Y} \leftarrow \mathbf{A}\mathbf{\Omega}$

```
  var y = a %*% omega
```

// compute $\mathbf{Y}^\top \mathbf{Y}$

```
  var yty = y.t %*% y
  val at = a.t
```

// Cholesky of $\mathbf{Y}^\top \mathbf{Y}$

```
  var ch = chol(yty)
  assert(ch.isPositiveDefinite, "Rank deficiency detected")
```

// $\mathbf{B}_0^\top \leftarrow \mathbf{A}^\top \mathbf{Y} \left(\mathbf{L}^\top\right)^{-1}$:
// inlining Cholesky QR per § 5.3

```
  var bt = ch.solveRight(at %*% y)
  // Power iterations
  for (i <- 0 until q) {
```

// $\mathbf{Y} \leftarrow \mathbf{A}\mathbf{B}_i^\top$

```
    y = a %*% bt
    yty = y.t %*% y
```

// $\mathbf{Y}^\top \mathbf{Y} = \mathbf{L}\mathbf{L}^\top$

```
    ch = chol(yty)
```

// $\mathbf{B}_i \leftarrow \mathbf{A}^\top \mathbf{Y} \left(\mathbf{L}^\top\right)^{-1}$: inlining Cholesky QR again.

```
    bt = ch.solveRight(at %*% y)
  }
  // compute $\mathbf{B}_q \mathbf{B}_q^\top$
  val bbt = bt.t %*% bt
  // eigen decomposition $\mathbf{B}_q \mathbf{B}_q^\top = \hat{\mathbf{U}}\mathbf{\Lambda}\hat{\mathbf{U}}$
  // d represents $\mathbf{\Lambda}$'s diagonal (eigenvalues)
  val (uhat, d) = eigen(bbt)
  // Singular values $\mathbf{\Sigma} \leftarrow \mathbf{\Lambda}^{\circ 0.5}$
  val s = d.sqrt
```

```
// U ← Q̂U
// We already have last Cholesky solution around, use it.
val u = ch.solveRight(y) %*% uhat
// V ← BᵀÛΣ⁻¹
val v = bt %*% (uhat %*% diagv(1 / s))
// Report only first k singular vectors and values.
(u(::, 0 until k), v(::, 0 until k), s(0 until k))
}
```

What assumption (5.2) means.

The rank assumption (5.2) may be interpreted in terms of singular values $\{\sigma_i\}$. Remember that the singular values are ordered from largest to smallest, by convention. The entire ordered sequence of decaying singular values is referred to as a "spectrum." We essentially assumed that the singular values of the signal (the first k values) are going to be significantly larger, on average, than the values indexed by $k+1$ and on. In other words, we assume that the spectrum will exhibit a significant decay between the first k values and the rest of them. If the spectrum is "flat" for more than $k + p$ singular values (as, for example, in a randomly generated dataset), then our procedure falls apart.

In particular, a failure of the rank assumption (5.2) in a dataset is the reason why SSVD does not work for a randomly generated matrix input. Such input would have a perfectly ideal flat spectrum (the same data variance in every orthogonal direction of $\mathbb{R}^n$).

But then, who would want to analyze random noise? In practice, if there is any useful information to be had in the data, the spectrum will decay, and will decay soon enough for us to be able to extract some useful information.

So, in practice, how important is the rate of the spectrum decay? The work [Halko et al., 2011] gives the following pessimistic upper bound estimate for the expectation of the truncated stochastic SVD error:

$$\mathbb{E}\left\| \mathbf{A} - \mathbf{U\Sigma V}^\top \right\|_2 \leq \sigma_{k+1} + \underbrace{\left[1 + 4\sqrt{\frac{2\min\{m, n\}}{k-1}}\right]^{1/(2q+1)}}_{\text{geometry-dependent factor}} \sigma_{k+1}.$$

This means that effectively the error is controlled by the $[k+1]$-st singular value σ_{k+1}, and the input geometry-dependent factor. The latter can be significantly reduced by the power iterations (i.e., $q > 0$); it also shows that the power iterations drive the geometry-induced factor down quite aggressively.

If the accuracy is important, as a matter of practical advice it is suggested to use the power iterations for matrices with a large geometry (large m and n) where the spectrum decay σ_1/σ_{k+1} does not exceed two orders of magnitude.

■ **Algorithm 5.3 Cholesky QR.**

Given an input matrix $\mathbf{A}$, this algorithm computes a QR decomposition $\mathbf{A} = \mathbf{QR}$.

   (1) Compute $\mathbf{S} = \mathbf{A}^\top \mathbf{A}$.
   (2) Compute the Cholesky decomposition $\mathbf{S} = \mathbf{LL}^\top$.
   (3) Return $(\mathbf{Q} \leftarrow \mathbf{A}\left(\mathbf{L}^\top\right)^{-1}, \mathbf{R} \leftarrow \mathbf{L}^\top)$.

5.3 Cholesky QR and its application for *thinQR*

5.3.1 The formulation of the Cholesky QR decomposition

It is possible to take another route in order to orthonormalize $\mathbf{Y}$ using so called Cholesky QR. To show how, let us do some substitutions:

$$
\begin{aligned}
\mathbf{A}^\top \mathbf{A} &= (\mathbf{QR})^\top (\mathbf{QR}) \\
&= \mathbf{L}(\mathbf{Q}^\top \mathbf{Q})\mathbf{L}^\top \\
&= \mathbf{LL}^\top.
\end{aligned}
$$

Since $\mathbf{Q}$ is orthonormal, $\mathbf{Q}^\top \mathbf{Q} = \mathbf{I}$. It tells us that the $\mathbf{R}$ matrix of the QR decomposition can be obtained by running the Cholesky decomposition on $\mathbf{A}^\top \mathbf{A}$ and flipping (transposing) the result matrix $\mathbf{L}$.

From there, $\mathbf{Q} = \mathbf{AR}^{-1} = \mathbf{A}\left(\mathbf{L}^\top\right)^{-1}$. This is summarized in Alg. 5.3. For the sake of further references, this algorithm is mentioned, for example, in [Demmel et al., 2012].

5.3.2 A distributed thin QR decomposition

We can now map Alg. 5.3 into Samsara distributed algebra as a "thin" procedure.

In this case the term "thin" means that we can assume that we can fit a square matrix of the smaller of the input dimensions into memory of one machine for implementation purposes. In particular, in terms of the thin QR decomposition (in the sense that is defined in [Golub and Van Loan, 2012]):

$$
\mathbf{A} = \mathbf{QR},
$$

where $\mathbf{A} \in \mathbb{R}^{m \times n}$, $m \gg n$, we assume that a dense matrix of the $n \times n$ geometry fits into one machine memory (comfortably). I.e., n is perhaps upper-bound by a number in the area of $\sim$1000...5000. Example 5.2 shows the outline of the thin QR algorithm. The full source of *thinQR* is implemented in the Mahout procedure `org.apache.mahout.math.decompositions.thinQR()`.

We rely on the thin Cholesky QR procedure heavily for the *dssvd* and the *dspca* routines. In the context of these methods, the n of the thin Cholesky decomposition implies the quantity $k + p$ of SSVD. Therefore, in these methods n would normally not exceed $\sim$300.

The contracts of the in-core Cholesky decomposition are explained in the § B.16.1.

Some comments for example 5.2:

■ **Example 5.2 The distributed thin Cholesky QR procedure.**

```scala
def dqrThin[K: ClassTag](drmA: DrmLike[K], <...>)
  : (DrmLike[K], Matrix) = {
  if (drmA.ncol > 5000)
    warn("A is too fat. A'A must fit in memory.")

  implicit val ctx = drmA.context
  val mxAtA:Matrix = drmA.t %*% drmA
  val bcastAtA = drmBroadcast(inCoreAtA)
  val ch = chol(mxAtA)
  val mxR = (ch.getL cloned) t
  // Compute Q = A (Lᵀ)⁻¹ -- we can do it blockwise.
  val Q = drmA.mapBlock() {
    case (keys, block) ⇒ keys → chol(bcastAtA)
      .solveRight(block)
  }
  Q → mxR
}
```

- Line 6: we need to declare an implicit distributed Mahout context since broadcast routines require it.
- Line 7: `drmA.t %*% drmA` is a distributed computation, which is implicitly executed and collected to the in-core matrix `mxAtA` since this latter value is declared as an in-core matrix type. Mahout provides an implicit conversion from the distributed matrix type (`DrmLike`) to the in-core matrix type (`Matrix`). This conversion implicitly calls `collect()`.
- Lines 12-15: $\mathbf{Q}$ is computed block-wise via a map-only procedure and a broadcast of the "small" matrix $\mathbf{A}^\top \mathbf{A}$.

Indeed, if $\left(\mathbf{A}^{(i)} : i = 1, 2 \ldots \ell\right)$ are vertical blocks of $\mathbf{A}$, then the result $\mathbf{Q}$ may be formed as

$$
\mathbf{Q} = \begin{pmatrix} \mathbf{A}^{(1)} \left(\mathbf{L}^\top\right)^{-1} \\ \mathbf{A}^{(2)} \left(\mathbf{L}^\top\right)^{-1} \\ \vdots \\ \mathbf{A}^{(\ell)} \left(\mathbf{L}^\top\right)^{-1} \end{pmatrix}.
$$

This fact, and the fact that $\mathbf{A}^\top \mathbf{A}$ is a small matrix that is easy to broadcast, helps us to devise an embarrassingly parallel formation of the result $\mathbf{Q}$ with the help of the *mapBlock()* operator.

5.4 Distributed SSVD

The code for the distributed version of SSVD, dssvd(), is given in example 5.3. The parameters have the same meaning as in the in-core version, ssvd().

DSSVD input parameters summary.

drmA the input, a distributed matrix.

k requested decomposition rank (one probably should keep $k \leq \sim 200$).

p oversampling parameter. Note that k, p must satisfy requirement $k + p \leq \mathrm{rank}\,(\mathbf{A})$. Since the upper bound for rank is $\min\,(m, n)$, the method reduces p automatically as needed. However, if the actual rank happens to be still less than $k + p$ then the method will report it as a problem. The remedy in this case is perhaps to retry to recompute with smaller $k + p$. *This is not common.* $p = 15$ (default) is usually a good value in most cases.

q the number of power iterations to run ($q \geq 0$). Use $q = 0$ for a faster result (especially if spectrum decay is good). If running time can tolerate the extra expense, use $q = 1$. In practical applications $q = 2$ and above will not make much difference in accuracy.

DSSVD output summary.

drmU matrix $\mathbf{U}$ of the decomposition. One special note: matrix $\mathbf{U}$ will contain the same row keys as input matrix $\mathbf{A}$, even if they are not integers (e.g., Strings). This allows for the tying of rows of $\mathbf{U}$ directly to rows of input $\mathbf{A}$.

drmV matrix $\mathbf{V}$ of the decomposition. Since row indices of $\mathbf{V}$ correspond to column indices of the input $\mathbf{A}$, the rows of this matrix are always Int-keyed.

s vector of length k containing first k singular values (diagonal of the matrix Σ) *in decreasing order.* Sorting right/left singular vectors and singular values in order of decreasing singular values is contractually guaranteed here.

Usage example:

```
val (drmU, drmV, s) = dssvd(drmA, k = 90)
```

Due to a lazy evaluation, the returned matrices $\mathbf{U}$ and $\mathbf{V}$ are not actually formed once the routine exits. Nothing but a logical plan exists for these products upon such an exit. Therefore, if any of these outputs are not actually used in a subsequent program, no wasted computational cost will incur.

We can even ignore the parameters we do not need with no cost consequences. For example, if we need only the $\mathbf{U}$ output of the decomposition, we can ignore the rest of the output as follows:

```
val (drmU, _, _) = dssvd(drmA, k=90)
```

5.5 Folding in new values and incremental SVD

Let us consider a scenario of an incremental SVD application.

■ **Example 5.3 Distributed Stochastic SVD.**

```
 1  def dssvd[K: ClassTag](drmA: DrmLike[K], k: Int, p: Int = 15,
 2  q: Int = 0): (DrmLike[K], DrmLike[Int], Vector) = {
 3    val drmAcp = drmA.checkpoint()
 4    val m = drmAcp.nrow
 5    val n = drmAcp.ncol
 6    assert(k <= (m min n), "k cannot be greater than smaller of m, n.")
 7    val pfxed = safeToNonNegInt((m min n) - k min p)
 8    // Actual decomposition rank
 9    val r = k + pfxed
10    // We represent Omega by its seed.
11    val omegaSeed = RandomUtils.getRandom().nextInt()
12    // Compute Y = A*Omega. Instead of redistributing view,
13    // we redistribute the Omega seed only.
14    var drmY = drmAcp.mapBlock(ncol = r) {
15      case (keys, blockA) =>
16        val blockY = blockA %*% Matrices.
17          symmetricUniformView(n, r, omegaSeed)
18        keys -> blockY
19    }.checkpoint()
20    var drmQ = dqrThin(drmY)._1
21    // Checkpoint Q if last iteration
22    if (q == 0) drmQ = drmQ.checkpoint()
23    trace(s"dssvd:drmQ=${drmQ.collect}.")
24    var drmBt = drmAcp.t %*% drmQ
25    // Checkpoint B' if last iteration
26    if (q == 0) drmBt = drmBt.checkpoint()
27    trace(s"dssvd:drmB'=${drmBt.collect}.")
28    for (i <- 0  until q) {
29      drmY = drmAcp %*% drmBt
30      drmQ = dqrThin(drmY.checkpoint())._1
31      // Checkpoint Q if last iteration
32      if (i == q - 1) drmQ = drmQ.checkpoint()
33      drmBt = drmAcp.t %*% drmQ
34      // Checkpoint B' if last iteration
35      if (i == q - 1) drmBt = drmBt.checkpoint()
36    }
37    val mxBBt:Matrix = drmBt.t %*% drmBt
38    trace(s"dssvd: BB'=$mxBBt.")
39    val (inCoreUHat, d) = eigen(mxBBt)
40    val s = d.sqrt
41    val drmU = drmQ %*% inCoreUHat
42    val drmV = drmBt %*% (inCoreUHat %*% diagv(1 /: s))
43    (drmU(::, 0 until k), drmV(::, 0 until k), s(0 until k))
44  }
```

Suppose we have previously "*trained*" an SVD on a matrix **A** and have obtained products of the decomposition. Let us assume that at some point in time (rather soon) new observations become available as additional *rows* of the input matrix **A**. We denote them as $\tilde{\mathbf{A}}$. Our task is to obtain *new* rows of the matrix **U**, denoted as $\hat{\mathbf{U}}$, that correspond to the rows[2] of the matrix $\tilde{\mathbf{A}}$.

One way to solve that is to run a new decomposition on the vertically concatenated input $\begin{pmatrix} \mathbf{A} \\ \tilde{\mathbf{A}} \end{pmatrix}$. This will work and this is also a most accurate approach. However, it is also a most expensive approach. In particular, if the number of the new rows is much less than the number of the previously decomposed rows, a full SVD re-run may not necessarily be warranted on the grounds of the merit vs. cost trade-off. We can run a much quicker cycle by *folding in* the new observations into the row space of **U**. A simple formula for that is

$$\tilde{\mathbf{U}} \approx \tilde{\mathbf{A}} \mathbf{V} \mathbf{\Sigma}^{-1}.$$

Since the size of the new observation is small, the cost of this computation is much smaller than that of a full SVD re-run on the $\begin{pmatrix} \mathbf{A} \\ \tilde{\mathbf{A}} \end{pmatrix}$ input. The overall incremental run formula would therefore be

$$\mathbf{U}^{(k+1)} \leftarrow \begin{pmatrix} \mathbf{U}^{(k)} \\ \tilde{\mathbf{A}} \mathbf{V} \mathbf{\Sigma}^{-1} \end{pmatrix}. \tag{5.3}$$

An implementation for the incremental SVD cycle (5.3) using Mahout is very simple:

```
val drmUnext = drmU rbind drmAnew %*% drmV %*% diagv(1 / s)
```

This assumes that the values `drmU`, `drmV` and `s` are $\mathbf{U}^{(k)}$, **V** and diagonal of $\mathbf{\Sigma}$, respectively; the computed value `drmUnext` is the sought value of $\mathbf{U}^{(k+1)}$.

 See the documentation for the MapReduce version of DSSVD for more details:
http://mahout.apache.org/users/dim-reduction/ssvd.page/SSVD-CLI.pdf
http://mahout.apache.org/users/dim-reduction/ssvd.html

The catch is that (5.3) only rotates the new observations into the already known row space of **U**, but does not modify its basis based on the new data available. One can think of a "full" SVD run as a "training," the matrices **U**, **V** and $\mathbf{\Sigma}$ as a model, and the procedure (5.3) as a "scoring" of the new data. This analogy fully holds – especially in the sense that no new model training information is extracted during the incremental "scoring" run.

This means that we cannot keep running the incremental procedure indefinitely without eventually significantly losing on "training". At some point we would certainly want to run a full SVD again. At that point, we may want to siphon some older, "obsolete" data points off in order to keep the problem size in check.

---

[2]As we will see a little later, the problem of new observations as *columns* is completely symmetrical.

In case new observations are *columns* rather than rows, all discussion is very similar — we swap $\mathbf{U}$ and $\mathbf{V}$. The incremental procedure (5.3) in this case becomes:

$$\mathbf{V}^{(k+1)} \leftarrow \begin{pmatrix} \mathbf{V}^{(k)} \\ \tilde{\mathbf{A}}^{\top}\mathbf{U}\mathbf{\Sigma}^{-1} \end{pmatrix}. \tag{5.4}$$

The situation where we would want to have both new row and new column observations incrementally usually does not exist in practice. If it does, we can only speculate that alternating between (5.3) and (5.4) may work, barring hard-to-see engineering difficulties. In particular, the processes that acquire new observations would need to have a way of adapting to accruals in the attribute sets.

5.6 LSA and its term/document spaces

One more topic closely relates to the previously discussed problem of folding in new observations.

Suppose we want to compute Latent Semantic Analysis (LSA).

We will not go into depth on the background of LSA here. For details the reader may consult [Deerwester et al., 1990]. Our input matrix is computed based on the *TF-IDF* values of the correspondent document/term entries. Let us assume document entries correspond to the rows of the input, and the term entries correspond to the columns.

In this situation typically a document-document similarity implies computing the cosine similarity between rows of $\mathbf{U}\mathbf{\Sigma}$ (the document space), and a term-term similarity implies computing the cosine similarity between rows of $\mathbf{V}\mathbf{\Sigma}$ (the term space).

A similarity between a term and a document is not as easy to compute because the term and the document vectors are not in the same low dimensional space. However, they can be converted into same document/vector space. For documents the conversion is $\mathbf{U}\mathbf{\Sigma}^{\circ 0.5}$, and for terms the conversion is $\mathbf{V}\mathbf{\Sigma}^{\circ 0.5}$. Here, the notation $\mathbf{\Sigma}^{\circ 0.5}$ means a diagonal matrix with its diagonal entries equal to the square roots of the singular values of the decomposition[3]:

$$\mathbf{\Sigma}^{\circ 0.5} = \begin{pmatrix} \sqrt{\sigma_1} & 0 & \cdots & 0 \\ 0 & \sqrt{\sigma_2} & \cdots & 0 \\ \vdots & \vdots & \ddots & \vdots \\ 0 & 0 & \cdots & \sqrt{\sigma_k} \end{pmatrix}.$$

Using Mahout, and assuming an SVD is already computed on the input *TF-IDF* matrix, the code for such projections will look like:

```
val drmDocuments = drmU %*% diagv(s.sqrt)
val drmTerms = drmV %*% diagv(s.sqrt)
```

Now we can compute similarities between a term and a document, too.

---

[3] See "Hadamard root" in the notations appendix of the book.

5.7 Why all the trouble

Nathan Halko's dissertation [Halko, 2012] gives a detailed investigation of accuracy vs. speed trade-offs. The reader is welcome to examine the accuracy of SSVD as compared to the now deprecated Apache Mahout distributed Lanczos method.

This dissertation, in the end, shows that the SSVD method provides superior asymptotic complexity and speed control while retaining quite comparable accuracy with respect to other methods. The SSVD algorithm discussed is a MapReduce version of the same SSVD engine neutral algorithm implemented in the Samsara environment.

The SSVD algorithm is quite successful in applying all three principles of "Big Math": (1) it takes on the issue of the problem approximation immediately at the very first step, and it does so sub-exponentially. The dimensionality problem is controlled by the $k + p$ parameters, which for the purposes of algorithm asymptotical complexity over an input size we can consider constant; (2) it re-designs traditional in-core algorithms to avoid the "greedy merchant" problem of exponential growth by controlling the width of the intermediate products; (3) finally, it provides parametric levers for controlling the accuracy/cost (i.e., speed) trade-off.

Due to these properties the algorithm is known to run in "speed-of-thought" applications where solutions are sought in a matter of seconds for relatively decently sized problems.

5.8 Where to next

SVD has been a major component of many practical algorithms we have encountered, and at the same time it has a fairly limited use on its own. One very famous application of SSVD almost "on its own" is latent semantic analysis (LSA). A complete tutorial on LSA using Mahout is beyond the scope of this book edition.

6

Stochastic PCA

In this chapter we will look more closely at the design of the Stochastic Principal Component Analysis implementation in Mahout.

Just like in the case of SSVD, Mahout provides both in-core and distributed versions of PCA: `spca` and `dspca`. The stochastic design of PCA to the best of our knowledge was, at the time of its inception in Mahout, unique to Mahout and was created specifically for Mahout[1].

---

[1] For working notes on the MapReduce version, see MAHOUT-817.

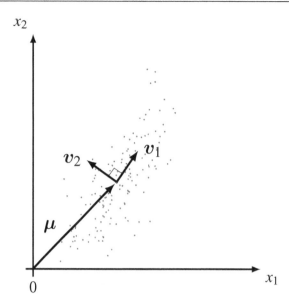

Figure 6.1: 2D PCA transformation example.

6.1 The PCA problem

Standard PCA is a popular technique and is described in a quite wide range of literature, ranging from Wikipedia [Wikipedia.org, 2015c] to more established texts on Machine Learning such as [Bishop, 2006]. It is suggested that the reader familiarizes herself or himself with the standard problem setting using one of these sources.

In this chapter we will briefly introduce the PCA problem by means of construction and intuition.

Suppose we have some dataset $\mathcal{D} \triangleq \{x_i : i = 1, 2, ...m\}$, where $x_i \in \mathbb{R}^n$, such as perhaps in Fig. 6.1. For as long as the dataset is interestingly different from a random noise, some directions will exhibit more data variance than the others. Perhaps some directions will have *significantly* more variance than the others (and in practice they indeed do).

The problem of PCA is to find such directions. PCA has an additional restriction: the directions found have to form an orthonormal basis. "Orthonormal" means every vector of the basis is a unit vector which is orthogonal to every other vector. The term "unit vector" denotes vectors that have their second norm equal to 1.

Additionally, the directions (axes) of the basis must be ordinally indexed in the order of decreasing data variance along every such direction.

An example of the result of such a search in a two dimensional situation is shown in Fig. 6.1: the offset μ and the orthonormal basis $\{v_1, v_2\}$. Every point could be therefore expressed in terms of coordinates projected on this new basis. The space spanned by this basis is called the "principal components space". The first coordinate of the basis is called "the first principal component", as the variance is greatest along that coordinate axis; the second coordinate is called "the second principal component", and so on.

A transformation from the original space into the PCA space therefore includes two steps: an offset and a rotation. Mathematically, this transformation is described as follows.

Suppose we have a matrix

$$\mathbf{V} \triangleq \begin{pmatrix} \boldsymbol{v}_1 & \boldsymbol{v}_2 & \cdots & \boldsymbol{v}_k \end{pmatrix},$$

$\mathbf{V} \in \mathbb{R}^{n \times k}$, such that vectors $\boldsymbol{v}_1$, $\boldsymbol{v}_2$ ... $\boldsymbol{v}_k$ form an orthonormal PCA basis. Then a transformation of any point $\boldsymbol{a}$ in the original space into the PCA space will look like

$$\boldsymbol{a}_{pca} = \mathbf{V}^\top (\boldsymbol{a} - \boldsymbol{\mu}). \tag{6.1}$$

The operation of subtraction represents the offset, and the matrix multiplication represents the rotation. Pretty simple, isn't it?

Similarly, to convert any point in the PCA space back into the original coordinates, we will use

$$\begin{aligned} \boldsymbol{a} &= \left(\mathbf{V}^\top\right)^{-1} \boldsymbol{a}_{pca} + \boldsymbol{\mu} \tag{6.2} \\ &= \mathbf{V} \boldsymbol{a}_{pca} + \boldsymbol{\mu}. \tag{6.3} \end{aligned}$$

Here, since $\mathbf{V}$ is orthonormal, the left inverse of $\mathbf{V}^\top$ is simply $\mathbf{V}$.

Now we can define the PCA problem a little more formally in terms of these quantities.

Problem 6.1 For a given dataset $\mathcal{D} : \mathcal{D} \triangleq \{\boldsymbol{a}_i : i = 1, 2, ...m\}$ and a matrix $\mathbf{A}$ induced by this dataset $\mathbf{A}_{i*} \triangleq \boldsymbol{a}_i$, find the PCA transformation quantities $\boldsymbol{\mu}$, $\mathbf{V}$ and a full translation of the original dataset into the PCA space, denoted as $\mathbf{A}^{(pca)}$.

6.2 The "standard" solution

Actually, there is more than one "standard" approach to a PCA solution. We will consider one of them.

First off, we start with finding $\boldsymbol{\mu}$, which is easy: $\boldsymbol{\mu}$ is taken as the mean of the dataset $\mathcal{D}$:

$$\begin{aligned} \boldsymbol{\mu} &= \frac{1}{m} \sum_i \boldsymbol{a}_i \tag{6.4} \\ &= \frac{\mathbf{A}^\top \mathbf{1}}{m}. \tag{6.5} \end{aligned}$$

For implementation purposes both of those expressions are simply A.colMeans(); also, recollect that A.colSums can also be formally written as $\mathbf{A}^\top \mathbf{1}$ (§ 4.11.1). So the equation (6.5) translates verbatim to A.colSums/A.nrow.

Next, we need to come up with an orthogonal basis $\mathbf{V}$.

Let us build a little bit of intuition about constructing this basis. Note that the principal direction $\boldsymbol{v}_1$ in Fig. 6.1 suspiciously resembles a "least squares" fit. Indeed, in the formulation of a standard PCA solution, one approach is to minimize the sum of squared *distances* from every point to the direction v_1 (after the mean subtraction)[2]. Once the direction v_1 is found, it is added to the matrix $\mathbf{V}$: $\mathbf{V} \leftarrow (v_1)$. By construction, all the original data points $a_i \in \mathbb{R}^n$. All the data points are then projected into the null row space of $\mathbf{V}$, denoted as $N\left(\mathbf{V}^\top\right)$.[3] Next, we minimize the square distances in $N\left(\mathbf{V}^\top\right)$ to find the new most significant variance direction, and rotate the result back to the original data point space $\mathbb{R}^n$, thus obtaining v_2. Since $v_2 \in N\left(\mathbf{V}^\top\right)$ and $v_1 \in C(\mathbf{V})$ (column-spanned subspace of $\mathbf{V}$), $v_1 \perp v_2$. Next, append the new vector to $\mathbf{V}$: $\mathbf{V} \leftarrow (\mathbf{V} \quad v_2)$ so now $\mathbf{V}$ becomes $(v_1 \quad v_2)$. Then the process repeats again starting from the projection step into $N\left(\mathbf{V}^\top\right)$. At any point $C(\mathbf{V}) \cup N\left(\mathbf{V}^\top\right) = \mathbb{R}^n$. Thus, we start off with $C(\mathbf{V}) = \emptyset$ and $N\left(\mathbf{V}^\top\right) = \mathbb{R}^n$ and then grow $C(\mathbf{V})$ by "biting off" dimensions from $N\left(\mathbf{V}^\top\right)$, one basis dimension at a time per every iteration. We repeat the process until $\mathbf{V}$ reaches some number of column vectors k, $k \leq n$, that we deem satisfactory based on some criterion.

We do not go beyond this intuitive construction in this book. We refer readers curious about the details to [Bishop, 2006] where this process is described with the necessary mathematical rigor. We will jump right to one of the standard solutions.

The next step in the standard approach is to compute a Singular Value Decomposition or a reduced-rank Singular Value Decomposition if only few principal components are sought:

$$\mathbf{A} - \mathbf{1}\mu^\top \approx \mathbf{U}_k \mathbf{\Sigma}_k \mathbf{V}_k^\top. \tag{6.6}$$

Here, $\mathbf{A} \in \mathbb{R}^{m \times n}$, $\mu \in \mathbb{R}^n$, $\mathbf{U}_k \in \mathbb{R}^{m \times k}$, $\mathbf{\Sigma}$ is a diagonal matrix, $\mathbf{\Sigma} \in \mathbb{R}^{k \times k}$, and $V_k \in \mathbb{R}^{n \times k}$. The parameter k is the rank of decomposition and is chosen so that $1 \leq k \leq \text{rank}\left(\mathbf{A} - \mathbf{1}\mu^\top\right)$. In practical PCA use cases, one of which is the dimensionality reduction use case, k is chosen to be $k \ll \text{rank}\left(\mathbf{A} - \mathbf{1}\mu^\top\right)$, and the input rank is upper-bound by $\min(m, n)$, which can be used as a crude approximation of the rank. The expression $\mathbf{A} - \mathbf{1}\mu^\top$ is simply the input $\mathbf{A}$ with the mean subtracted from every row, i.e., from every data point a_i.

It turns out that the right singular vectors (i.e., the columns of the matrix $\mathbf{V}_k$) are the very orthonormal basis $v_1, v_2, \ldots v_k$ we seek.

Now, what about the final question — how do we get $\mathcal{D}$ projected to the PCA space? One way is to use a matrix version of formula (6.1):

$$\mathbf{A}^{(pca)} = \left(\mathbf{A} - \mathbf{1}\mu^\top\right)\mathbf{V} \tag{6.7}$$

$$\approx \left(\mathbf{A} - \mathbf{1}\mu^\top\right)\mathbf{V}_k. \tag{6.8}$$

In practice, however, it is often more convenient to use the results of the decomposition itself. Based on equation (6.6), we infer that $\left(\mathbf{A} - \mathbf{1}\mu^\top\right)\mathbf{V}_k \approx \mathbf{U}_k\mathbf{\Sigma}_k$. In other words,

---

[2]This analogy is not absolute: the *"best fit"* solution minimizes the sum of squared *residuals*.

[3]$C(\mathbf{X})$ denotes the column space of $\mathbf{X}$. Alternatively, it sometimes is also called the "range" of a matrix $\mathbf{X}$ and is then denoted as $R(\mathbf{X})$. $N\left(\mathbf{V}^\top\right)$ denotes the null row space of $\mathbf{X}$.

This discussion relies on some familiarity with the "Fundamental theorem of Linear Algebra" and the Four Fundamental subpaces to visualize the process. See [Strang and Press, 1993, Strang, 1993].

■ **Algorithm 6.1 Stochastic PCA Algorithm.**

Given an $m \times n$ matrix $\mathbf{A}$, a target rank k, and an oversampling parameter p, this procedure computes a k-rank PCA by finding the unknowns in $\mathbf{A} - \mathbf{1}\mu^\top \approx \mathbf{U}\Sigma\mathbf{V}^\top$:

(1) Create seed for random $n \times (k+p)$ matrix Ω.

(2) $s_\Omega \leftarrow \Omega^\top \mu$. $\leftarrow$--

(3) $\mathbf{Y}_0 \leftarrow \mathbf{A}\Omega - \mathbf{1}s_\Omega^\top, \mathbf{Y} \in \mathbb{R}^{m \times (k+p)}$. $\leftarrow$--

(4) Column-orthonormalize $\mathbf{Y}_0 \rightarrow \mathbf{Q}$ by computing thin decomposition $\mathbf{Y}_0 = \mathbf{QR}$. Also, $\mathbf{Q} \in \mathbb{R}^{m \times (k+p)}$, $\mathbf{R} \in \mathbb{R}^{(k+p) \times (k+p)}$.

(5) $s_Q \leftarrow \mathbf{Q}^\top \mathbf{1}$. $\leftarrow$--

(6) $\mathbf{B}_0 \leftarrow \mathbf{Q}^\top \mathbf{A} : \mathbf{B} \in \mathbb{R}^{(k+p) \times n}$.

(7) $s_B \leftarrow \mathbf{B}_0^\top \mu$ $\leftarrow$--

(8) For i in $1..q$ repeat (power iterations):

    (a) For j in $1..n$ apply $(\mathbf{B}_{i-1})_{*j} \leftarrow (\mathbf{B}_{i-1})_{*j} - \mu_j s_Q$. $\leftarrow$--

    (b) $\mathbf{Y}_i \leftarrow \mathbf{A}\mathbf{B}_{i-1}^\top - \mathbf{1}\left(s_B - \mu^\top \mu s_Q\right)^\top$. $\leftarrow$--

    (c) Column-orthonormalize $\mathbf{Y}_i \rightarrow \mathbf{Q}$ by computing thin decomposition $\mathbf{Y}_i = \mathbf{QR}$.

    (d) $s_Q \leftarrow \mathbf{Q}^\top \mathbf{1}$. $\leftarrow$--

    (e) $\mathbf{B}_i \leftarrow \mathbf{Q}^\top \mathbf{A}$.

    (f) $s_B \leftarrow \mathbf{B}_i^\top \mu$ $\leftarrow$--

(9) Let $\mathbf{C} \triangleq s_Q s_B^\top$.
$\mathbf{M} \leftarrow \mathbf{B}_q \mathbf{B}_q^\top - \mathbf{C} - \mathbf{C}^\top + \mu^\top \mu s_Q s_Q^\top$. $\leftarrow$--

(10) Compute an eigensolution of the small symmetric $\mathbf{M} = \hat{\mathbf{U}}\Lambda\hat{\mathbf{U}}^\top$:
$\mathbf{M} \in \mathbb{R}^{(k+p) \times (k+p)}$.

(11) The singular values $\Sigma = \Lambda^{\circ 0.5}$, or, in other words, $\sigma_i = \sqrt{\lambda_i}$.

(12) If needed, compute $\mathbf{U} = \mathbf{Q}\hat{\mathbf{U}}$.

(13) If needed, compute $\mathbf{V} = \mathbf{B}^\top \hat{\mathbf{U}}\Sigma^{-1}$. Another way is $\mathbf{V} = \mathbf{A}^\top \mathbf{U}\Sigma^{-1}$.

(14) If needed, items converted to the PCA space can be computed as $\mathbf{U}\Sigma$. $\leftarrow$--

the projection to the PCA space can be alternatively computed as

$$\mathbf{A}^{(pca)} \approx \mathbf{U}_k \Sigma_k. \tag{6.9}$$

This formula is actually what we suggest to use with the distributed results as one that is much more practical than (6.8). Indeed, hopefully $\mathbf{U}_k$ is much thinner than $\mathbf{A}$, and Σ_k is a diagonal matrix – we are just scaling up each column of the $\mathbf{U}_k$ according to the singular values of the decomposition.

6.3 Stochastic PCA

6.3.1 The problem of "big data" PCA

As we have shown in the last section, PCA is mostly about running an SVD on a re-centered input $\mathbf{A} - \mathbf{1}\mu^\top$. It would seem that the task is pretty straightforward now: we just subtract the mean from every row and then run an SVD.

In reality, however, often times PCA inputs $\mathbf{A}$ are sparse – some are very sparse. Some very typical cases may have 0.1% or fewer non-zero elements. The distributed stochastic SVD algorithm handles such cases fairly well; at least, it was designed to handle sparse cases as well as dense, and so it does, within its limits.

The problem, however, is that the mean (6.5) is not sparse even if the input is sparse. If the mean is not sparse, then $\mathbf{A} - \mathbf{1}\mu^\top$ is not sparse either – not even for the rows of $\mathbf{A}$ that *are* 100% sparse. If we try to actually form $\mathbf{A} - \mathbf{1}\mu^\top$, then for our hypothetical case of a 0.1%-sparse input we would need a thousand times more memory than for the input (which perhaps is already quite big).

In other words, the "standard" approach may only work for very dense inputs.

Hopefully, we can modify the SSVD($\mathbf{A}$) algorithm and turn it into a PCA($\mathbf{A}$) algorithm with almost the same cost as the SSVD($\mathbf{A}$), for sparse and dense inputs alike.

6.3.2 The Stochastic PCA algorithm

The main idea of the SPCA algorithm is to re-trace the steps of the SSVD algorithm 5.2 while keeping intermediate product memory requirements under control. We are going to "pretend" we are still computing an SSVD of the sparse input $\mathbf{A}$ while pushing the effects of subtracting the $\mathbf{1}\mu^\top$ component down the computation pipeline for as long as needed.

Some algebraic inferences are to follow. But they are fairly simple. So take a breath, or perhaps just skip to the end result given in Alg. 6.1. There, the SSVD parts that have been adapted for the purpose of the SPCA, are annotated with '$\leftarrow$--'.

To reiterate, throughout the following discussion we keep referring to the steps of the SSVD Alg. 5.2, while mending them for the purpose of the SPCA.

First, we consider the computation of $\mathbf{Y}_0$ there:

$$
\begin{aligned}
\mathbf{Y}_0 &= \left(\mathbf{A} - \mathbf{1}\mu^\top\right)\Omega \\
&= \mathbf{A}\Omega - \mathbf{1}\left(\mu^\top\Omega\right) \\
&= \mathbf{A}\Omega - \mathbf{1}s_\Omega^\top,
\end{aligned}
$$

where we have defined a new vector s_Ω as

$$
s_\Omega \triangleq \Omega^\top\mu.
$$

This is nice: we need to form a dense but thin $\mathbf{A}\Omega$ as in SSVD, so the cost of that is the same. On top of it we just need to compute one tiny k-long vector s_Ω and subtract it from every row of $\mathbf{A}\Omega$. An additional computational cost notwithstanding, this is actually minimal in terms of memory requirements, and the explosive formation $\mathbf{A} - \mathbf{1}\mu^\top$ is completely avoided! As noted, the correction $-\mathbf{1}s_\Omega^\top$ simply means subtracting the tiny vector s_Ω from every row of $\mathbf{A}\Omega$, which is very easy and fairly inexpensive. These are the steps (2) and (3) of the algorithm.

So far so good.

The next step that involves the input $\mathbf{A} - \mathbf{1}\boldsymbol{\mu}^\top$ again is forming $\mathbf{B}_0$. Similarly,

$$
\begin{aligned}
\mathbf{B}_0 &= \mathbf{Q}^\top \left(\mathbf{A} - \mathbf{1}\boldsymbol{\mu}^\top \right) \\
&= \mathbf{Q}^\top \mathbf{A} - \mathbf{Q}^\top \mathbf{1}\boldsymbol{\mu}^\top \\
&= \mathbf{Q}^\top \mathbf{A} - \boldsymbol{s}_Q \boldsymbol{\mu}^\top,
\end{aligned}
$$

where $\boldsymbol{s}_Q \triangleq \mathbf{Q}^\top \mathbf{1}$ (column sums of $\mathbf{Q}$).

The cost of computing $\mathbf{Q}^\top \mathbf{A}$ is no different from that in SSVD. Length of the vector $\boldsymbol{s}_Q$ is k and computing it is just `colSums` on $\mathbf{Q}$. This is acceptable in terms of additional costs.

As for the outer product $\boldsymbol{s}_Q \boldsymbol{\mu}^\top$, it matches $\mathbf{B}_0$ itself in size. But we do not have to form it: we can update $\mathbf{B}_0$ inside a `mapBlock` operator column by column, knowing that $\left[\boldsymbol{s}_Q \boldsymbol{\mu}^\top \right]_{*j} = \mu_j \boldsymbol{s}_Q$. So we can just "fix" $\mathbf{B}_0$ column by column while broadcasting relatively modestly sized quantities of $\boldsymbol{\mu}$ and $\boldsymbol{s}_Q$: $(\mathbf{B}_0)_{*j} \leftarrow (\mathbf{B}_0)_{*j} - \mu_j \boldsymbol{s}_Q$ for all $j = 1, 2 \ldots n$. In the actual implementation this is quite trivial because the SSVD code (example 5.3) computes a transposed orientation of $\mathbf{B}_i$, i.e., $\mathbf{B}_i^\top$, so a column-wise iteration over $\mathbf{B}_i$ becomes a row-wise iteration over $\mathbf{B}_i^\top$. Note that the formation of matrices $\mathbf{B}_i$ is identical inside and outside of the power iterations, so this "fix" step can be the same for all of them. This is the step (8)(a) of the algorithm.

The next situation that involves the re-centered input $\mathbf{A} - \mathbf{1}\boldsymbol{\mu}^\top$ again is computing $\mathbf{Y}_i$ within the power iteration loop:

$$
\begin{aligned}
\mathbf{Y}_i &= \left(\mathbf{A} - \mathbf{1}\boldsymbol{\mu}^\top \right) \mathbf{B}_{i-1}^\top \\
&= \mathbf{A}\mathbf{B}_{i-1}^\top - \mathbf{1}\boldsymbol{\mu}^\top \mathbf{B}_{i-1}^\top \\
&= \mathbf{A}\mathbf{B}_{i-1}^\top - \mathbf{1}\boldsymbol{\mu}^\top \left(\mathbf{Q}^\top \mathbf{A} - \boldsymbol{s}_Q \boldsymbol{\mu}^\top \right)^\top \\
&= \mathbf{A}\mathbf{B}_{i-1}^\top - \mathbf{1}\left(\boldsymbol{s}_B - \mathbf{t}_B \right)^\top,
\end{aligned}
$$

where $\boldsymbol{s}_B \triangleq \mathbf{Q}^\top \mathbf{A}\boldsymbol{\mu}$, $\mathbf{t}_B \triangleq \boldsymbol{\mu}^\top \boldsymbol{\mu} \boldsymbol{s}_Q$.

The computations of the vector $\boldsymbol{s}_B$ correspond to the steps (7) and (8)(f). The $\mathbf{t}_B$ vector can be easily computed in-core on the driver program's side.

Note the similarities to "fixing" $\mathbf{Y}_0$. The cost of computing $\boldsymbol{s}_B$ is somewhat greater than the cost of computing $\boldsymbol{s}_\Omega$, since the matrix $\boldsymbol{\Omega}$ is merely a random view and has virtually zero memory requirements. But at least this matrix-vector multiplication is carried out in parallel, so in practice this is also quite acceptable in terms of additional costs as well.

The cost of $\mathbf{A}\mathbf{B}_{i-1}$ is high – but it is no costlier than that in SSVD. $\mathbf{A}$ is (possibly) sparse, $\mathbf{B}_{i-1}$ is skinny-dense, so the mileage may vary.

As in the case of $\mathbf{Y}_0$, the expression $-\mathbf{1}\left(\boldsymbol{s}_B - \mathbf{t}_B \right)^\top$ simply means subtracting a tiny vector $\boldsymbol{s}_B - \mathbf{t}_B$ from every row of the $\mathbf{A}\mathbf{B}_{i-1}$. The adjustment of $\mathbf{Y}_i$ is carried out in the step (8)(b) of the algorithm.

Now for the final observation. SSVD computes a product $\mathbf{M} = \mathbf{B}_q \mathbf{B}_q^\top$ which is a tiny $k + p \times k + p$ squared symmetric matrix, and then performs an eigendecomposition of it.

We can optimize the procedure a little more by pushing the step of "fixing" $\mathbf{B}_q$ further down into the computation of the $\mathbf{M}$ product. Let us assume that the final matrix $\mathbf{B}_q$ (and only $\mathbf{B}_q$) stays without the correction $-s_Q \mu^\top$: let $\mathbf{B}_q \triangleq \mathbf{Q}_q^\top \mathbf{A}$. Then

$$
\begin{aligned}
\mathbf{M} &= \left[\mathbf{Q}^\top \left(\mathbf{A} - \mathbf{1}\mu^\top \right) \right] \left[\mathbf{Q}^\top \left(\mathbf{A} - \mathbf{1}\mu^\top \right) \right]^\top \\
&= \left(\mathbf{Q}^\top \mathbf{A} - s_Q \mu^\top \right) \left(\mathbf{Q}^\top \mathbf{A} - s_Q \mu^\top \right)^\top \\
&= \mathbf{B}_q \mathbf{B}_q^\top - \mathbf{Q}^\top \mathbf{A}\mu s_Q^\top - s_Q \mu^\top \mathbf{A}^\top \mathbf{Q} + \mu^\top \mu s_Q s_Q^\top \\
&= \mathbf{B}_q \mathbf{B}_q^\top - s_B s_Q^\top - s_Q s_B^\top + \mu^\top \mu s_Q s_Q^\top \\
&= \mathbf{B}_q \mathbf{B}_q^\top - \mathbf{C} - \mathbf{C}^\top + \mu^\top \mu s_Q s_Q^\top.
\end{aligned}
$$

Here, for the sake of a cleaner formula we denote $\mathbf{C} \triangleq s_Q s_B^\top$.

That way we can save on the distributed $\mathbf{B}_q$ correction step and perform corrections on the tiny $(k+p) \times (k+p)$ in-core components of the computation of $\mathbf{M}$-computation. In reality, a lot of pragmatic tasks would run with $q = 0$, and some would run with $q = 1$, which means that half of the time we will need to "fix" only $\mathbf{B}_0$ but not $\mathbf{B}_1$, and another half of the time we will not be needing any $\mathbf{B}_i$ "fixes" at all.

Note that all elements needed for the adjustment are already available: s_Q, s_B and self dot-product $\mu^\top \mu$.

The implementation of the Distributed Stochastic PCA algorithm is given in example 6.1.

■ **Example 6.1 Distributed Stochastic PCA (cf. Alg. 6.1).**

```
1   def dspca[K: ClassTag](drmA: DrmLike[K], k: Int, p: Int = 15, q: Int = 0):
2   (DrmLike[K], DrmLike[Int], Vector) = {
3
4       val drmAcp = drmA.checkpoint()
5       implicit val ctx = drmAcp.context
6       val m = drmAcp.nrow
7       val n = drmAcp.ncol
8       assert(k <= (m min n), "k cannot be greater than smaller of m, n.")
9       val pfxed = safeToNonNegInt((m min n) - k min p)
10
11      // Actual decomposition rank
12      val r = k + pfxed
13
14      // Dataset mean
15      val mu = drmAcp.colMeans
16      val mtm = mu dot mu
17
18      // We represent Omega by its seed.
19      val omegaSeed = RandomUtils.getRandom().nextInt()
20      val omega = Matrices.symmetricUniformView(n, r, omegaSeed)
```

```
21    val s_o = omega.t %*% mu
22    val bcastS_o = drmBroadcast(s_o)
23    val bcastMu = drmBroadcast(mu)

24
25    var drmY = drmAcp.mapBlock(ncol = r) {
26      case (keys, blockA) ⇒
27        val s_o:Vector = bcastS_o
28        val blockY = blockA %*% Matrices.symmetricUniformView(n, r, omegaSeed)
29        for (row ← 0 until blockY.nrow) blockY(row, ::) -= s_o
30        keys → blockY
31    }
32        // Checkpoint Y
33        .checkpoint()

34
35    var drmQ = dqrThin(drmY, checkRankDeficiency = false)._1.checkpoint()
36    var s_q = drmQ.colSums()
37    var bcastVarS_q = drmBroadcast(s_q)

38
39    var drmBt = (drmAcp.t %*% drmQ).checkpoint()
40    var s_b = (drmBt.t %*% mu).collect(::, 0)
41    var bcastVarS_b = drmBroadcast(s_b)

42
43    for (i ← 0 until q) {
44      val bcastS_q = bcastVarS_q
45      val bcastMuInner = bcastMu

46
47      // Fix Bt as B' -= xi cross s_q
48      drmBt = drmBt.mapBlock() {
49        case (keys, block) ⇒
50          val s_q: Vector = bcastS_q
51          val mu: Vector = bcastMuInner
52          keys.zipWithIndex.foreach {
53            case (key, idx) ⇒ block(idx, ::) -= s_q * mu(key)
54          }
55          keys → block
56      }

57
58      drmY.uncache()
59      drmQ.uncache()

60
61      val bCastSt_b = drmBroadcast(s_b -=: mtm * s_q)

62
63      drmY = (drmAcp %*% drmBt)
64          // Fix Y by subtracting st_b from each row of the AB'
65          .mapBlock() {
66        case (keys, block) ⇒
67          val st_b: Vector = bCastSt_b
68          block := { (_, c, v) ⇒ v - st_b(c) }
69          keys → block
70      }
```

```
71          // Checkpoint Y
72          .checkpoint()
73
74        drmQ = dqrThin(drmY, checkRankDeficiency = false)._1.checkpoint()
75        s_q = drmQ.colSums()
76        bcastVarS_q = drmBroadcast(s_q)
77
78        drmBt = (drmAcp.t %*% drmQ).checkpoint()
79        s_b = (drmBt.t %*% mu).collect(::, 0)
80        bcastVarS_b = drmBroadcast(s_b)
81      }
82
83      val c = s_q cross s_b
84
85      val inCoreBBt = (drmBt.t %*% drmBt).checkpoint(CacheHint.NONE).collect -=:
86          c -=: c.t +=: mtm *=: (s_q cross s_q)
87
88      val (inCoreUHat, d) = eigen(inCoreBBt)
89      val s = d.sqrt
90
91      val drmU = drmQ %*% inCoreUHat
92      val drmV = drmBt %*% (inCoreUHat %*% diagv(1 / s))
93
94      (drmU(::, 0 until k), drmV(::, 0 until k), s(0 until k))
95    }
```

DSPCA input parameter summary.

drmA the input, a distributed matrix to compute the PCA for. The matrix is assumed to be induced by the input dataset *row-wise*, that is $\mathbf{A}_{i*} \triangleq \boldsymbol{x}_i$.

k the requested PCA rank (one probably should keep $k \leq\sim 200$ or so.

p the oversampling parameter of SSVD. See the SSVD parameter notes in § 5.4.

q the number of power iterations. See SSVD parameter notes. Recommended values are 0 or 1.

DSPCA output summary.

drmU the **U** matrix of the SVD step. $\mathbf{U} \in \mathbb{R}^{m \times k}$. This matrix retains row keys from the original input drmA.

drmV the **V** matrix of the SVD step. $\mathbf{V} \in \mathbb{R}^{n \times k}$. This matrix contains integer row keys.

s vector of length k containing singular values from the SVD step.

The output singular vectors and the singular values will be sorted in the decreasing order of the corresponding singular values.

As it stands, this PCA implementation outputs all products of the final SVD step. It does not perform the last step (14) of Alg. 6.1 on its own, so if the PCA space conversion $\mathbf{A}^{(pca)}$ is needed, it can be trivially obtained using (6.9). One reason why the SPCA does not scale the result into the PCA space is because the scaled $(\mathbf{U}_k \boldsymbol{\Sigma})$ and the unscaled $(\mathbf{U}_k)$ conversions could be equally useful.

Usage example:

```
val (drmU, _, s) = dspca(drmA, k = 90)
// Input rows converted to PCA space per (6.9):
val drmPCA = drmU %*% diag(s)
```

7

Data Sketching with Bahmani sketch

In the introduction to part III we considered a few principles important for "Big Math" algorithms, one of which being how to obtain a low resolution representation of a problem. We have previously seen how it was addressed in the stochastic SVD algorithm. In this chapter we will give an example of computing a probabilistic low resolution representation of a dataset $\mathcal{D}$ we call "Bahmani sketch."

Sketches are important techniques as they are often used to seed non-deterministic algorithms for better stability or obtain a low-resolution representation of a particular problem.

■ **Algorithm 7.1 "Bahmani sketch."**

Given dataset $\mathcal{D} = \{x_i \in \mathbb{R}^n : i = 1, \ldots m\}$ and oversampling parameter ℓ, this algorithm computes an approximate data sketch of size k, $k \ll m$:

(1) $\mathcal{C} \leftarrow$ sample a point uniformly at random from $\mathcal{D}$
(2) $\psi \leftarrow \phi_X(\mathcal{C})$
(3) for $O(\log \psi)$ times do
    (a) $\mathcal{C}' \leftarrow$ sample each point $x \in \mathcal{D}$ independently with probability $p_x = \frac{\ell \cdot d^2(x, \mathcal{C})}{\phi_{\mathcal{D}}(\mathcal{C})}$
    (b) $\mathcal{C} \leftarrow \mathcal{C} \cup \mathcal{C}'$
(4) end-for
(5) For $c_i \in \mathcal{C}$ set w_i to be the number of points in $\mathcal{D}$ closer to c_i than any other point in $\mathcal{C}$
(6) Recluster the weighted points in $\mathcal{C}$ into k clusters $\mathcal{C}''$
(7) Return $\mathcal{C}''$

7.1 The sketch problem

Problem 7.1 **Density sketch problem.**

Given m data points in n-dimensional space, obtain k data points, $k \ll N$ retaining an approximation of required dataset statistics as best as possible, at CPU and memory cost no worse than $O(m)$.

7.2 The Bahmani sketch formulation

The algorithm we are exploring here is actually algorithm 2 from [Bahmani et al., 2012] called "k-means∥(k,l) initialization". This is a bit of a mouthful, so in this book we refer to it as the "Bahmani sketch" after the name of the paper's first author.

In line with the stated approach of this book, we are leaving it to the reader to study the details of this paper, but we will now take the math and show how to parse and translate it into distributed Mahout Samsara code. For our purposes it is enough to say that this algorithm approximates the k-means problem using sampling techniques. Another intuitive way to think about it is of a problem of finding means of k distributions, the mixture of which may, however crudely, approximate our input dataset density.

Using sampling techniques is usually good news for a distributed algorithm, as it both is embarrassingly parallel and removes any interconnectedness (that is, a significant shuffle I/O) from the procedure.

Let us consider our input dataset, $\mathcal{D} = \{x_i \in \mathbb{R}^n : i = 1, 2, \ldots m\}$.

We are going to need the quantity $\phi_{\mathcal{D}}$ given in the paper. This quantity is computed for our dataset $\mathcal{D}$ against some other dataset $\mathcal{C} = \{c_i \in \mathbb{R}^n : i = 1, \ldots k\}$:

$$\phi_{\mathcal{D}}(\mathcal{C}) = \sum_{x \in \mathcal{D}} \min_{c \in \mathcal{C}} \|x - c\|_2^2.$$

Let us parse this into common language: "$\phi_D(C)$ is the sum of of squared distances between every point in a set D to the closest point in another set C to that point". To make things easier, the authors of the paper define a function of the distance from any point y to the closest point in C:

$$\mathrm{d}(y, C) = \min_{c \in C} \|y - c\|_2, \tag{7.1}$$

so that the $\phi_D(C)$ formula becomes even simpler notationally –

$$\phi_D(C) = \sum_{x \in D} \mathrm{d}^2(x, C). \tag{7.2}$$

The "Bahmani sketch" algorithm is given in Alg. (7.1).

For the purposes of this algorithm, we assume that the sets C and C', which mutate with time, are *ordered*. A union of two ordered sets C and C' implies ordered concatenation, i.e., the first element of C' becomes the $(|C|+1)$-th element of $(C \cup C')$, and so on. So thus the union product is also ordered.

If ordered datasets C and C' are represented by matrices with the rows being the data points then such a union operation corresponds to the vertical concatenation of the matrices. In Mahout Samsara this operation is `rbind`.

From here on we will denote points of an ordered set C as $\{c^{(i)} : i = 1, 2, \ldots\}$ and points of the ordered set C' as $\{c'^{(i)} : i = 1, 2, \ldots\}$.

7.3 Coding the Bahmani Sketch with Samsara

Now we will give a translation of Alg. 7.1 into Mahout Samsara code.

For the purpose of this example, we will focus on how to sample the initial set of points, i.e., on steps (1) to (5).

The weighted reclustering step (6) is left as an exercise. There, weighted in-memory k-means or k-means++ are among the fastest approaches to be used, although a bottom-up in-memory weighted agglomerative clustering would perhaps provide a more appropriate result for this step (since n is single order factor multiple of k).

Parallelizing the sampling algorithm.

Let a matrix $\mathbf{X}$ be induced by D such that $\mathbf{X}_{i*} \triangleq x_i$, i.e., the dataset D points are forming the rows of the matrix $\mathbf{X}$.

First, let us determine what the biggest thing is here.

The cardinality $|D| = m$. Obviously, it is the biggest dataset here in the general case, so the decision to keep it in a distributed row matrix is pretty obvious.

Next, let us look at the number of sampled points $|C|$ after the last algorithm iteration is complete.

Since $\sum_{x \in D} \frac{\mathrm{d}^2(x, C)}{\phi_D(C)} = 1$, it is easy to see that expectation of the number of newly sampled points in step (3)(a) is $\mathbb{E}(|C'|) = \ell$. The parameter ℓ is usually chosen to be

---

■ **Algorithm 7.2 Simplified distributed Bahmani sampling.**

Given a number of iterations I, an input $\mathbf{X}$ induced by a dataset $\mathcal{D}$, and a final sketch size k, perform the Bahmani sampling, thus obtaining $\mathcal{C}$ after step (4) of Alg. 7.1:

set $\ell \leftarrow 2I/k$
initialize $\mathbf{Y} \leftarrow \text{cbind}\,(0, +Inf, \mathbf{X})$
sample $\mathcal{C}$ uniformly with approximately ℓ points
updateY$(\emptyset, \mathcal{C})$
for $I-1$ times **do**
  $\phi_{\mathcal{D}}(\mathcal{C}) \leftarrow \langle \mathbf{Y}_{*2}, \mathbf{1} \rangle$: sum of closest squared distances saved in $\mathbf{Y}_{*2}$
  for each $y^{(i)} \triangleq \mathbf{Y}_{i*}$: $i = 1, 2 \ldots m$
    $x^{(i)} \equiv y^{(i)}\,(3 : n+2)$: by construction of $\mathbf{Y}$
    $d_i^2 \leftarrow y_2^{(i)}$: closest squared distance
    $p_i \leftarrow \dfrac{\ell d_i^2}{\phi_{\mathcal{D}}(\mathcal{C})}$: probability of sampling
    sample, add $x^{(i)}$ with probability p_i to $\mathcal{C}'$
  end-for
  updateY$(\mathcal{C}, \mathcal{C}')$
  $\mathcal{C} \leftarrow \mathcal{C} \cup \mathcal{C}'$: uses rbind concatenation
end-for
return $\mathcal{C}, \mathbf{Y}$

$\sim 0.5k\ldots2k$, so the expectation of the number of final points sampled after all iterations is a multiple of k by a small factor, and therefore $\mathbb{E}\,(|\mathcal{C}|) \ll m$.

Furthermore, we see that we will need to compute squared distances $\mathrm{d}^2\,(x_i, \mathcal{C})$ in every iteration, so we would need to access all the points in $\mathcal{C}$.

Therefore, we assume that the sampled dataset $\mathcal{C}$ (a) is of a limited size, and (b) is modified (augmented) in every iteration. All of this means that $\mathcal{C}$ can, and must, be collected into the driver program memory and then re-broadcast for every iteration.

Finally, we also notice that the quantity $\phi_{\mathcal{D}}\,(\mathcal{C})$ does not change within each iteration regardless of which point x_i the quantity p_x is evaluated for.

This leads us to the conclusion that we need to complete at least 2 passes over $\mathcal{D}$ for each of the outer sampling iterations – one is to compute $\phi_{\mathcal{D}}\,(\mathcal{C})$ as per (7.2), and the other one is to run the sampling part.

We also notice that both passes share the quantities $\mathrm{d}^2\,(x_i, \mathcal{C})$, which means that perhaps it is easier to compute squared closest distances in the first pass and share it with the second. With this purpose in mind, we construct the following blocking algorithm.

■ **Algorithm 7.3 UpdateY($\mathcal{C}$, $\mathcal{C}'$).**

Given a new set of sample points $\mathcal{C}'$ and an existing matrix $\mathbf{Y}$ per (7.3), this algorithm updates the first two columns of the matrix $\mathbf{Y}$ with the ordinal index of, and the squared distance to, the closest point in $(\mathcal{C} \cup \mathcal{C}')$:

compute the squared distance matrix $\mathbf{D}$: $\mathbf{D}_{ij} = \left\| \mathbf{c}'^{(i)} - \mathbf{c}'^{(j)} \right\|_2^2$, $\mathbf{c}'^{(i)} \in \mathcal{C}'$, $\mathbf{c}'^{(j)} \in \mathcal{C}'$

for each $\mathbf{y}^{(i)} \triangleq \mathbf{Y}_{i*} : i = 1, 2, \ldots m$:

$\quad \mathbf{x}^{(i)} = \mathbf{y}^{(i)}(3 : n+2)$**:** by construction of $\mathbf{Y}$

$\quad d_i^2 \leftarrow y_2^{(i)}$**:** closest squared distance

$\quad j \leftarrow 1$

$\quad d_{\min}^2 \leftarrow \left\| \mathbf{c}'_j - \mathbf{x}^{(i)} \right\|_2^2$

$\quad$**for** each $\mathbf{c}'_s$ in $\mathcal{C}' \backslash \mathbf{c}'_1$ **do**

$\quad\quad$**if** $\mathbf{D}_{js} < 4d_{\min}^2$

$\quad\quad\quad d_s^2 \leftarrow \left\| \mathbf{c}'_s - \mathbf{x}^{(i)} \right\|_2^2$

$\quad\quad\quad$**if** $d_s^2 < d_{\min}^2$

$\quad\quad\quad\quad j \leftarrow s, d_{\min}^2 \leftarrow d_s^2$

$\quad\quad\quad$**end-if**

$\quad\quad$**end-if**

$\quad$**end-for**

$\quad$**if** $\mathcal{C} = \emptyset$ or $d_{\min}^2 < d_i^2$**:** found closer point in $\mathcal{C}'$

$\quad\quad$**Update** first and second columns of $\mathbf{Y}$ with sample index ς_i and minimal squared distance $d^2(\mathbf{x}_i, \mathcal{C} \cup \mathcal{C}')$:

$\quad\quad y_1^{(i)} \leftarrow \varsigma_i = j + |\mathcal{C}|$

$\quad\quad y_2^{(i)} \leftarrow d^2(\mathbf{x}_i, \mathcal{C} \cup \mathcal{C}') = d_{\min}^2$

$\quad$**end-if**

end-for

■ **Example 7.1 Y construction per (7.3).**
```
private def drmAtoY[K: ClassTag](drmA: DrmLike[K])
: DrmLike[K] =
  drmA.mapBlock(drmA.ncol + 2) { case (keys, block) ⇒
    val yBlock = new DenseMatrix(block.nrow, 2) cbind block
    keys → yBlock
  }
}
```

Distributed blocking algorithm for the Bahmani sketch sampling.

Let ς_i (sigma) be the ordinal index of a data point $c_{\varsigma_i} : c_{\varsigma_i} \in \mathcal{C}$ inside an ordered set $\mathcal{C}$ such that

$$\varsigma_i = \underset{j}{\operatorname{argmin}} \left[\operatorname{d} \left(\boldsymbol{x}_i, \boldsymbol{c}_j \right) \right].$$

In other words, ς_i is the ordinal index of the closest point in $\mathcal{C}$ to $\boldsymbol{x}_i$. Also, $\operatorname{d} \left(\boldsymbol{x}_i, \mathcal{C} \right) = \operatorname{d} \left(\boldsymbol{x}_i, \boldsymbol{c}_{\varsigma_i} \right)$.

If we collect all ς_i together, we get the vector $\varsigma = \begin{pmatrix} \varsigma_1 & \varsigma_2 & \cdots & \varsigma_m \end{pmatrix}^{\top}$

We now start building a composite matrix $\mathbf{Y}$: $\mathbf{Y} \in \mathbb{R}^{m \times (n+2)}$ as follows.

We allocate the first column in the $\mathbf{Y}$ for the vector ς. We allocate another, second, column for the values $\left\{ \operatorname{d}^2 \left(\boldsymbol{x}_i, \mathcal{C} \right) : i = 1, 2, \ldots m \right\}$. The rest of the columns to the right are occupied by the input $\mathbf{X}$. The total construction of the matrix $\mathbf{Y}$ is shown below:

$$\mathbf{Y} \triangleq \left(\begin{array}{c|c|c} \varsigma_1 & \operatorname{d}^2 \left(\boldsymbol{x}_1, \mathcal{C} \right) = \operatorname{d}^2 \left(\boldsymbol{x}_1, \boldsymbol{c}_{\varsigma_1} \right) & \boldsymbol{x}_1^{\top} \\ \varsigma_2 & \operatorname{d}^2 \left(\boldsymbol{x}_2, \mathcal{C} \right) & \boldsymbol{x}_2^{\top} \\ \vdots & \vdots & \vdots \\ \varsigma_m & \operatorname{d}^2 \left(\boldsymbol{x}_m, \mathcal{C} \right) & \boldsymbol{x}_m^{\top} \end{array} \right). \tag{7.3}$$

  Tip Note that encoding more complex structures into a single matrix as blocks is a useful practical trick.

Encoding different statistics of the algorithm this way may create a small additional overhead because of the block copying during the structure construction. But in the end it keeps the type system simple and the algorithms backend-agnostic.

Besides, in this case it turns out that we also can just keep the $\mathbf{Y}$ structure (7.3) around (which means the block stitching happens only once), and we can just update labels ς_i and minimal squared distance $d^2 \left(\boldsymbol{x}_i, \mathcal{C} \right)$ values in-place during multiple distributed passes over the memory-cached structure $\mathbf{Y}$ without incurring any actual reallocation of this distributed structure.

These observations give rise to the multiple-pass implementation of step (3):

(1) Compute $\phi_D(\mathcal{C})$
(2) Sample $\mathcal{C}'$
(3) $\mathcal{C} \leftarrow \mathcal{C} \cup \mathcal{C}'$
(4) Update columns ς_i, $d^2(x_i, \mathcal{C})$ of $\mathbf{Y}$

This collocated construction also allows for the embarrassingly parallel computation of the probability p_x during the sampling pass.

Next, for simplicity, we will assume a predefined number of iterations I.

We also will set the parameter ℓ automatically such that we end up with about 2x points before the reclustering step: $\ell \leftarrow 2k/I$.

We simplify the very first iteration by making it completely *non-informative* sampling. We will not waste an entire task to retrieve just a single-point initial sample.

Finally, we are going to make yet another observation which will however lead us to a somewhat nontrivial algorithm runtime improvement. We observe that if we keep the matrix $\mathbf{Y}$ around, then the columns ς and $d^2(\cdot)$ already contain values for the closest sampled points in $\mathcal{C}$ of the previous iteration. So for any given x_i we actually do not have to find the closest point in $\mathcal{C}$; instead, we just can find the closest point in a quite smaller set $\mathcal{C}'$, and then compare the closest distance with $\mathcal{C}'$ to the previously found closest distance in the second column of $\mathbf{Y}$.

All these observations lead us to Alg. 7.2.

The inner loops over $\mathbf{Y}$ are of course in fact parallel loops over the distributed row matrix vertical blocks. We intend to implement the collection of samples with the help of the `allreduceBlock` operation, where the reduction operation is a simple vertical concatenation of the blocks containing partial samples. For the sake of clarity, the pass of updating the matrix $\mathbf{Y}$ is factored out into a separate Alg. 7.3 *updateY*.

The *updateY* algorithm's outer loop is of course also a parallel loop over matrix blocks. For every point of a $\mathbf{Y}$-block we are trying to figure out the closest point in $\mathcal{C}'$. This is a typical "nearest neighbor" problem.

There are many ways to implement a nearest-neighbor (NN) query here. For the purposes of illustration and simplicity, we employ one of the triangle inequality optimizations here, although this is far from being the fastest approach. For details of triangle inequality accelerations, see, for example, [Elkan, 2003].

This triangle inequality optimization uses lemma 1 from [Elkan, 2003], which states that for any two centroids c_1 and c_2, and a point x, if $d(c_1, c_2) \geq 2d(x, c_1)$, then it follows $d(x, c_1) \leq d(x, c_2)$.[1]

In other words, if we already know the distance from x to some point c_1, and consider another one c_2, and the distance between c_1 and c_2 is more than twice the distance x to c_1, then we can ignore c_2 for the purposes of finding the closest one – its lower bound is greater than our current best.

Going a little bit ahead, in the actual implementation (example 7.3) it is easier to operate with squared distances, so with respect to the squared distances this lemma

---

[1] The notation $d(a, b)$ for the purposes of this lemma means the Euclidean distance between a and b.

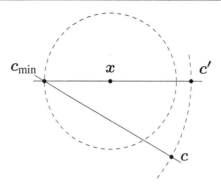

Figure 7.1: An illustration for formula (7.4).

condition transforms into

$$\frac{1}{4} d^2 (c_1, c_2) \geq d^2 (x, c_1).$$

(7.4)

A quick geometric proof. This is a direct consequence of the triangle inequality, and can be demonstrated algebraically. But a simple geometrical illustration is also possible, such as given in Fig. 7.1.

Suppose we are looking at all the sample points of C', sequentially, with the purpose of finding the closest one to some point $x : x \in \mathcal{D}$. Let the current closest sample point be c_{min}, which is initially initialized as $c_{min} = c_1'$. We are about to check the next sample point c. We have previously precomputed pairwise distances between all samples, so they are readily available without any additional computational effort. The distance between the new and the current closest point $d(c, c_{min})$ is therefore already known.

The candidate point c can be found anywhere on the circle (hypersphere) with radius $d(c, c_{min})$ and centered at c_{min}. This is the outer circle in the picture.

The inner circle(hypersphere) has its center at x and radius $d(x, c_{min})$. That is, any point that is closer to x than c_{min} must be found *inside* this "inner" circle. That means that the outer circle must actually intersect with the inner circle in order for c to have any chance of becoming the new closest point.

Of all positions on the outer circle position c' is the closest c can get to x. That is, when all three points are on the same line and x and c are on the same side of c_{min}. In order for $d(c_{min}, x) < d(c, x)$ to hold, we need to have $d(c_{min}, c')$ greater than twice the current minimal distance $d(c_{min}, x)$. If this holds, we can safely reject the candidate point c without computing any new distances beyond those we already know. But $d(c_{min}, c') = d(c_{min}, c)$ by construction. Therefore, if $d(c_{min}, c) \geq 2d(x, c_{min})$, then $d(x, c) \geq d(x, c_{min})$. ∎

This optimization works because of the assumption that the number of newly sampled points is much less than the number of the input data points:

$$|C'| \ll |\mathcal{D}|;$$

and even less than the number of the data points in a single distributed partition of $\mathcal{D}$. Therefore, when the assumption holds, the cost of precomputing the sampled point pairwise distances is much less than the cost of of distance computations it allows to avoid, subsequently.

A much faster solution would be to use one of the ANN (Approximate Nearest Neighbor) methods. There are quite a few of such methods, and we will not analyze them here. These methods are fairly simple and are easily found in the literature. We will just say that since the sketch is an approximate technique already, relaxing the accuracy of subordinate techniques makes sense, and in practice this trade-off turns out to be well worth it.

Spatial indices may also be efficient; however, to the best of our knowledge, any exact spatial indexing technique known today is said to have a NN query efficiency prerequisite which requires the number of input points to be much greater than 2^n, where n is dimensionality of the input. This pragmatically limits the spatial indexing methods with the exact nearest neighbor search to problems with only a handful of dimensions (even assuming "Big Data" applications).

The implementation of the sampling algorithm 7.2.

The implementation of Alg. 7.2 is given in example 7.2. The code follows the algorithm almost verbatim. The inner loop iteration thus contains three passes over the cache-pinned data $\mathbf{Y}$ (7.3).

First, we compute $\phi_D(\mathcal{C})$, which is just a sum of the second column in $\mathbf{Y}$ (line 17).

The second pass is the sampling pass (lines 20 to 44). It represents a typical use of the `allreduceBlock()` operation. The map operation (lines 22 to 41) performs the individual sampling of points out of $\mathbf{Y}$, and the reduce operation vertically concatenates the partial samples (line 43).

The third pass is conducted only if more iterations are expected. This pass is to update the closest point indices ς and the squared distance columns in the $\mathbf{Y}$ (line 45).

 All variables that are used inside remote closures (map and reduce parameters of the `allreduceBlock()` in this case) need to be declared *inside* the for-comprehension, not outside of it. This is a quirk with serializing Scala closures.

In Scala, a *for comprehension* is a construct that forms yet another closure. All variables outside of its scope become attributes of the *for-comprehension* closure. When we refer to them inside the *map closure*, it causes the entire *for-comprehension* closure to become an attribute of the map closure. When all things are running in a local JVM process, this does not cause any problems.

However, when Spark is about to serialize and ship the map closure to a remote worker, it will attempt to serialize the *for-comprehension* closure as well along with all its attributes (`drmY` including). Obviously, not all the attributes declared inside the *for-comprehension* closure are serializable.

This note is the reason why we have re-declared the values `innerN` and `innerL` (lines 14 and 15). Had we not done so and continued using n and l directly from the outside scope, the allreduceBlock closures would have failed to deploy to Spark workers with the `NotSerializableException` thrown.

This algorithm of course requires the implementation of $\mathbf{Y}$ construction per (7.3).

▪ Example 7.2 Implementation of sampling algorithm 7.2.

```scala
def dSample[K: ClassTag](drmA: DrmLike[K],
                         sketchSize: Int,
                         iterations: Int,
                         seed: Int = Random.nextInt())
: (Matrix, DrmLike[K]) = {
  implicit val ctx = drmA.context
  val l = sketchSize * 2 / iterations + 1 max 1
  val n = drmA.ncol
  var drmY = drmAtoY(drmA).checkpoint()
  var mxC = drmSampleKRows(drmY, 1)
  mxC = mxC(::, 2 until n + 2)
  drmY = updateY(drmY, mxC, cStart = 0).checkpoint()
  for (iter ← 0 until (iterations - 1 max 0)) {
    val innerN = n
    val innerL = l
    // Compute phi
    val phi = drmY(::, 1 to 1).colSums()(0)
    val subseed = seed + iter
    // Resample C'
    val mxCPrime = drmY.allreduceBlock(
    // Map
    { case (keys, yblock) ⇒
      if (yblock.nrow > 0) {
        val vDSq = yblock(::, 1)
        val ablock = yblock(::, 2 until innerN + 2)
        val rnd = new Random(subseed * keys(0).hashCode())
        // Perform draws
        val selected = new mutable.ArrayBuffer[Int](200)
        for (r ← 0 until ablock.nrow) {
          val p = innerL * vDSq(r) / phi
          if (rnd.nextDouble <= p) selected += r
        }
        val cPrimeBlock:Matrix = yblock.like(selected.size, innerN)
        selected.zipWithIndex.foreach { case (idx, i) ⇒
          cPrimeBlock(i, ::) = ablock(idx, ::)
        }
        cPrimeBlock
      } else { // Empty
        new DenseMatrix(0, innerN) :Matrix
      }
    },
    // Reduce
    _ rbind _
    )
    drmY = updateY(drmY, mxCPrime, mxC.nrow).checkpoint()
    mxC = mxC rbind mxCPrime
  }
  mxC → drmY
}
```

■ **Example 7.3 Implementation of Alg. 7.3 'updateY()'.**

```
private def updateY[K: ClassTag](drmY: DrmLike[K], mxC: Matrix,
    cStart: Int): DrmLike[K] = {

  implicit val ctx = drmY.context
  val mxCBcast = drmBroadcast(mxC)
  drmY.mapBlock() { case (keys, yblock) ⇒
    updateYBlock(yblock, mxCBcast, cStart)
    keys → yblock
  }
}

private def updateYBlock(mxY: Matrix,
                         mxC: Matrix,
                         cStart: Int): Unit = {

  val n = mxY.ncol - 2
  val k = mxC.nrow
  val mxA = mxY(::, 2 until n + 2)
  val vLabels = mxY(::, 0)
  val vSqD = mxY(::, 1)

  // We assume that mxC.nrow is small, << mxA.nrow.
  val mxCDsq = dist(mxC) /= 4

  for (row ← mxA) {
    var minC = 0
    var minCDsq = (row - mxC(minC, ::)) ^= 2 sum

    for (c ← 1 until k) {
      // Inverse of condition (7.4).
      if (mxCDsq(minC, c) <= minCDsq &&
          sqr(mxC(c, ::).norm(2) - row.norm(2)) <= minCDsq) {
        val dSq = (row - mxC(c, ::)) ^= 2 sum
        if (dSq < minCDsq) {
          minC = c
          minCDsq = dSq
        }
      }
    }

    if (cStart == 0 || minCDsq < vSqD(row.index)) {
      vLabels(row.index) = minC + cStart
      vSqD(row.index) = minCDsq
    }
  }
}
```

■ **Example 7.4 Computing sample point weights.**

```
// nC is |C| after sampling iterations.
def computePointWeights[K: ClassTag](drmY: DrmLike[K],
nC:Int): Vector = {

    // Single-row weight matrix with counts
    val vWeights = drmY.allreduceBlock(

    { case (keys, yblock) ⇒
      val wvec = new DenseVector(nC)
      val labels = yblock(::, 0).all
        .foreach(sgm ⇒ wvec(sgm.toInt) += 1)
      dense(wvec)
    })(0, ::)

    val s = vWeights.sum
    vWeights /= s
}
```

This implementation is given in example 7.1.

Updates of matrix **Y** are factored out into the separate procedure *updateY,* which is given in example 7.3.

There, line 23 precomputes a squared distance matrix of the sample set C', divided by 4, i.e., all the pair-wise distances in C', divided by 4. The applicability of the condition (7.4) to the next candidate point from C' is checked in the line 31.

Any squared distance computations (lines 27, 33) between any a and b follow the Mahout algebra DSL per

```
(a - b) ^= 2 sum
```

The algorithm *updateY* only needs the information about the cardinality of C rather than the entire set. This cardinality is passed as the `cStart` parameter (that is, the 0-based index of the first C' element in the ordered concatenation $(C \cup C')$). Therefore, there is no need to actually pass the entire set C in.

These algorithms of course could be further enhanced. For example, points in C' could be cached instead of sliced on-demand in *updateY*. Note that the Mahout vectors already cache the norms. We already mentioned the speed advantage of approximate nearest neighbor methods. Also, since there is a non-zero probability that the sampling procedure will fall short of the minimum required number of samples, the iterations could be extended to cover these corner case situations accurately. There are a few other possible tweaks.

Computing the sample weights.

The next (and final) task in this chapter is step (5) of Alg. 7.1. We need to compile the sample weights according to the number of closest points. This is where the ς values of the matrix $\mathbf{Y}$ are going to be quite handy. If as a result of sampling round we were able to sample at least one point, we then invoke the procedure `computePointWeights`, which is given in example 7.4.

This procedure takes two parameters – $\mathbf{Y}$ and $|\mathcal{C}|$ (number of samples). There, the `allreduceBlock()` operation comes to the rescue again. In the map part, we compute a one-row matrix containing the weight vector $w \in \mathbb{R}^{|\mathcal{C}|}$. For each ς_i found in the matrix $\mathbf{Y}$, we simply perform the update $w_{\varsigma_i} \leftarrow w_{\varsigma_i} + 1$. The default reducer performs the summing up of the partial weight counts, so we do not have to specify any reducer.

The vector w is then assumed as the answer to the problem set by the step (5) of the original Alg. 7.1.

After that, we just need to do an in-core weighted clustering of the sample $\mathcal{C}$ based on the computed weights w as was previously discussed – and the problem of the Bahmani sketch is solved.

IV

Samsara Tutorials

In part IV we present a tutorial on the training of a Samsara Naive Bayes model, demonstrating the ease with which it may be deployed to a simple text classification server.

We hope to continue with more tutorials in future editions or subsequent books in this series.

8

Naive Bayes Example

The purpose of this chapter is to provide an end-to-end example of Mahout's "Samsara" Naive Bayes classification algorithms following those presented in [Rennie et al., 2003]. While Samsara has fully engine neutral Naive Bayes implementations, elements of the algorithms can be optimized for specific back-ends. This chapter will focus on Samsara's Spark-optimized Naive Bayes implementations.

We will take a look at Samsara Naive Bayes, and give an end-to-end tutorial doing the following: acquiring and vectorizing a dataset; training and testing a Naive Bayes model; prototyping helper functions to classify out-of-sample text using the Mahout Spark-shell; and finally, deploying that model and those functions to a simple servlet, which, when some simple text is posted to, will respond with a classification for that text.

Our model will be trained on the text of a set of English-language Wikipedia pages for a binary classification problem. We will download an XML dump of English language Wikipedia documents, parse and extract their class labels, and tokenize and vectorize them for use as training and testing sets. We will then train, test, and deploy a model to a simple text classification server.

At the time of this writing, Mahout is still dependent on *MapReduce* for the XML parsing and vectorization sections of this pipeline. We will be able to see the Samsara DRM API's ability to read data from Hadoop sequence files, as well as its interoperability with native Spark data structures and functionality.

This chapter is meant as a practical demonstration of Samsara usage and will not dig deeply into the probabilistic theory behind the Naive Bayes classifier itself.

8.1　Naive Bayes for text classification

Problem 8.1 Given a corpus of m documents of ℓ classes, vectorize the documents into a dataset, $\mathcal{D} \triangleq \left\{ d^{(i)} : i = 1, 2, \ldots m \right\}$ each labeled with a class, $c : c \in \mathcal{C}$ where $\mathcal{C} \triangleq \left\{ 1, 2, \ldots \ell \right\}$. Use $\mathcal{D}$ or a subset of $\mathcal{D}$ to train a model which can be used to predict the class $k : k \in \mathcal{C}$ of out of sample text.

Samsara Naive Bayes Algorithms.

Samsara currently has two flavors of Naive Bayes implemented in its distribution. The first is standard Multinomial Naive Bayes. The second is a variation on "Transformed Weight-normalized Complement Naive Bayes" as introduced in [Rennie et al., 2003]. We may refer to the former as "MNB" or "*Bayes*" and the latter as "TWCNB" or "*CBayes*."

Where MNB has long been a standard in text classification, TWCNB is an extension of MNB that performs particularly well on datasets with multiple skewed classes and has been shown to be competitive with algorithms of higher complexity such as Support Vector Machines [Rennie et al., 2003].

Before we get to Mahout's canned classification algorithms, lets take a look at how easily we may implement a fully distributed Naive Bayes training algorithm given just a sequential procedure as outlined in the original research paper. Algorithm 8.1 outlines the steps of TWCNB[1].

As previously noted, when building an algorithm with Samsara, we will want to look for an algebraic expression of the problem. We can see that the sequential pseudocode for TWCNB as laid out in algorithm 8.1 actually maps quite easily to a fully distributed matrix algebra representation in as shown in algorithm 8.2[2].

We can see from algorithm 8.2 that the fully distributed, engine-neutral TWCNB algorithm as represented in Samsara Matrix algebraic notation can be expressed quite simply with only three more steps than the sequential algorithm as laid out in algorithm 8.1. What's more, it is implemented in a fully engine-neutral way, and the same code will run on Spark, H2O, or Flink.

Let's take a closer look at the actual implementation of algorithm 8.2.

Let us assume that we are beginning with a document set, $\mathcal{D}$, of L_2 length normalized *TF-IDF* vectors. As we see later, Mahout uses a *MapReduce* process, `seq2sparse`, for the vectorization of documents. During this process the transformation steps (1), (2) and (3) are completed. We have m document vectors representing a vocabulary of size n, and we have ℓ classes.

Step (4): we can now induce the matrix $\mathbf{D} : \mathbf{D} \in \mathbb{R}^{m \times n}$ from the transformed *TF-IDF* dataset $\mathcal{D} : \mathbf{D}_{i*} \triangleq d^{(i)}$. Let us assume that we have the class vector $y \triangleq \left(y_1 \; y_2 \; \cdots \; y_m \right)^{\top}$: $y \in \mathcal{C}^m$; y_i is the class label of the vectorized document, $\mathbf{D}_{i*}$. From these values, we have

---

[1]We have adapted the notation of algorithm 8.1 from the original paper to fit with the notation as we've defined in § A.2.

[2]Note that Mahout's `seq2sparse` text vectorization pipeline uses slightly different *TF* and *IDF* transformations than those shown in the original paper. These can be seen by comparing algorithm 8.1 and algorithm 8.2 steps (1) and (2).

■ **Algorithm 8.1 TWCNB as introduced in (Rennie et al., 2003) § 4.3.**

Let $\mathcal{D} \triangleq \left\{ d^{(i)} : i = 1, 2, \ldots m \right\}$ be a dataset of term frequency vectors; $d_j^{(i)}$ is the count of term j in document i.

Let $y \in \{1, 2, \ldots \ell\}^m$ be a vector of ordinal document class labels; y_i is the label of document $d^{(i)}$.

Let $c \in \{1, 2, \ldots \ell\}$ be the classes.

Let α be a smoothing parameter for all terms in the vocabulary.

Unless defined otherwise, the following steps are assumed to be calculated for all values of all indices.

Training:

(1) $d_j^{(i)} \leftarrow \log\left(d_j^{(i)} + 1 \right)$ 　　　　　　　　　　　　　　　　　　(*TF* transformation).

(2) $d_j^{(i)} \leftarrow d_j^{(i)} \left(\log \frac{\sum_k 1}{\sum_k \delta_{kj}} \right) ; \delta_{kj} \triangleq \begin{cases} 1, & \text{if } d_j^{(k)} > 0; \\ 0, & \text{otherwise.} \end{cases}$ 　　(*IDF* transformation).

(3) $d_j^{(i)} \leftarrow \dfrac{d_j^{(i)}}{\sqrt{\sum_k \left(d_k^{(i)} \right)^2}}$ 　　　　　　　　　　　　　　　　(L_2 length normalization).

(4) $\hat{\theta}_{cj} = \dfrac{\sum_i^{y_i \neq c} d_j^{(i)} + \alpha}{\sum_i^{y_i \neq c} \sum_k d_k^{(i)} + m\alpha}$ 　　　　　　　　　　　　(complement θ estimate).

(5) $\hat{w}_{cj} = \log \hat{\theta}_{cj}$

(6) $\hat{w}_{cj} \leftarrow \dfrac{\hat{w}_{cj}}{\sum_{j'} |\hat{w}_{cj'}|}$ 　　　　　　　　　　　　　　　　(weight normalization).

Label Assignment:

(1) Let $t \triangleq \begin{pmatrix} t_1 & t_2 & \cdots & t_n \end{pmatrix}$ be a test document; let t_j be the count of the term j in document t.

(2) Label the document: $l(t) \triangleq \underset{c}{\arg\min} \sum_j t_j \hat{w}_{cj}$

■ **Algorithm 8.2 Distributed TWCNB in matrix form.**

Let $\mathcal{D} \triangleq \left\{ d^{(i)} : i = 0, 1, \dots m - 1 \right\}$ be a dataset of term frequency vectors; $d_j^{(i)}$ is the count of term j in document i.

Let $f \triangleq \begin{pmatrix} f_1 & f_2 & \cdots & f_n \end{pmatrix}$ be a vector of "document frequency" counts for each term j. f_j is the count of documents that in which the term j occurs:

$f_j \triangleq \left| \left\{ d^{(i)} \in \mathcal{D} : d_j^{(i)} > 0 \right\} \right|.$

Let $y \in \left\{ 0, 1, \dots \ell - 1 \right\}^m$ be a vector of document class labels; y_i is the label of document $d^{(i)}$.

Let $c \in \left\{ 0, 1, \dots \ell - 1 \right\}$ be the classes.

Let α be a smoothing parameter for all terms in the vocabulary.

Unless defined otherwise, all the following steps are assumed to be calculated for all values of all indices.

Training:

(1) $d_j^{(i)} \leftarrow \sqrt{d_j^{(i)}}$ (*TF* transformation via `seq2sparse`).

(2) $d_j^{(i)} \leftarrow d_j^{(i)} \left(1 + \log \frac{m}{f_j + 1} \right)$ (*IDF* transformation via `seq2sparse`).

(3) $d^{(i)} \leftarrow \frac{d^{(i)}}{\|d^{(i)}\|_2}$ (L_2 length normalization via `seq2sparse`).

(4) $\mathbf{D}_{i*} \triangleq d^{(i)} : \mathbf{D} \in \mathbb{R}^{m \times n}$ (induce the Matrix $\mathbf{D}$ from the document set).

(5) $\mathbf{N}_{c*} \triangleq \sum_{i:y_i = c} \mathbf{D}_{i*} : \mathbf{N} \in \mathbb{R}^{\ell \times n}$ (aggregate $\mathbf{D}$ by class).

(6) $\tilde{\mathbf{N}}^{\top} = \mathbf{N}^{\top} \mathbf{1} \mathbf{1}^{\top} - \mathbf{N}^{\top}$ (take the complement of $\mathbf{N}$).

(7) $\hat{\Theta} = \left[\tilde{\mathbf{N}} + (\alpha) \right] \circ \left[\left(\tilde{\mathbf{N}} \mathbf{1} + n\alpha \mathbf{1} \right) \mathbf{1}^{\top} \right]^{\circ -1}$ (maximum likelihood estimate of Θ).

(8) $\hat{\mathbf{W}} = \log \left(\hat{\Theta} \right)$

(9) $\hat{\mathbf{W}} \leftarrow \hat{\mathbf{W}} \circ \left[\text{abs} \left(\hat{\mathbf{W}} \right) \mathbf{1} \mathbf{1}^{\top} \right]^{\circ -1}$ (weight normalization update).

Label Assignment:

(1) Let $t \triangleq \begin{pmatrix} t_1 & t_2 & \cdots & t_n \end{pmatrix}$ be a test document; let t_j be the count of the term j in document t.

(2) Label the document: $l(t) \triangleq \underset{c}{\text{argmin}} \left[t \hat{\mathbf{W}}^{\top} \right]_c$

the tuple, $\left(\boldsymbol{y}, \mathbf{D}\right)$, a DRM which we will assume as our input, drmD.

Step (5): aggregate the vectors by summing each vector, $\mathbf{D}_{i*}$ where $y_i = c$ the result being the vector $\mathbf{N}_{c*}$ for all $c \in C$. Note that we are using the DRM *transpose and aggregate* functionality per § 4.10 so we will actually end up with $\mathbf{N}^\top$. We have some extra work to do in stripping off empty rows so that we have an aggregated matrix of the correct geometry for matrix $\mathbf{N} : \mathbf{N} \in \mathbb{R}^{\ell \times n}$; this is achieved quite easily using the allreduceBlock operator.

$$\mathbf{N}_{c*} \triangleq \sum_{i:y_i=c} \mathbf{D}_{i*} \ : \ \mathbf{N} \in \mathbb{R}^{\ell \times n}$$

```
// Aggregate N by forcing a transposition
// that possesses the aggregate properties.
val drmNt = drmD.t.checkpoint()

// Remove empty rows from drmNt
// the result will be a (class x term) in-core matrix
val mxNNonEmpty = drmNt.t.allreduceBlock( {
        case(keys, block) ⇒
          val nonEmptyRows = ArrayBuffer[(Vector, Int)]()

          // Keep only the aggregated rows
          for (i ← 0 until block.nrow) {
            if (block(i, ::).getNumNondefaultElements() > 0) {

              // get the class label (the key) for the row
              nonEmptyRows += ((block(i, ::), keys(i)))
            }
          }

          // Now that we know the number of aggregated rows
          // in this partition create a new matrix for those
          // rows and their class labels.
          val blockB = new SparseRowMatrix(
                          nonEmptyRows.size,
                          block.ncol + 1)

          for (i ← 0 until nonEmptyRows.size) {
            blockB(i, ::) := nonEmptyRows(i)._1

            // Append the class label to the last column
            blockB(i, block.ncol) = nonEmptyRows(i)._2
          }

          blockB: Matrix
```

```
        },


        // Reduce by stacking the aggregated rows
        _ rbind _
)


// Parallelize the aggregated mxNNonEmpty and set the
// keys to the correct class label. the result will be
// N-transpose, a (class x term) drm matrix
val drmNtNonEmpty = drmParallelize(mxNNonEmpty)
        .mapBlock(ncol = mxNNonEmpty.ncol - 1) {
            case (keys, block) ⇒

                // Strip the classes off the matrix
                val classes = block(::, block.ncol - 1)
                for (i ← 0 until keys.size) {
                    // Set the keys as the class for that row
                    keys.update(i, classes(i).toInt)
                }
            (keys → block(::, 0 until block.ncol - 1))
        }
            .t
```

Step (6): calculate $\tilde{\mathbf{N}}$, the complement of $\mathbf{N}$. Each row, $\tilde{\mathbf{N}}_{c*}$, the column-wise sums of $\mathbf{N}$, a vector with each element being the sum of each term weight across all classes, subtracted from $\mathbf{N}_{c*}$. Remember though that we are already working on $\mathbf{N}^\top$ so terms are actually represented row-wise and thus in the following code block, we subtract row sums from each row.

$$\tilde{\mathbf{N}}^\top = \mathbf{N}^\top \mathbf{1}\mathbf{1}^\top - \mathbf{N}^\top$$

```
// Complement N
val drmNc = drmNtNonEmpty.mapBlock() {
    case (keys, block) ⇒
        val termTotals = block.rowSums()
        block ::= { (r, _, v) ⇒ termTotals(r) - v }
    keys → block
}
    .checkpoint()
```

Steps (7), (8): implement our Maximum Likelihood Estimator for the Multinomial parameter matrix Θ and take the element-wise natural logarithm of the estimates, $\hat{\Theta}$, as $\hat{\mathbf{W}}^\top$.

$$\hat{\Theta} = \left[\tilde{\mathbf{N}} + (\boldsymbol{\alpha})\right] \circ \left[\left(\tilde{\mathbf{N}}\mathbf{1} + n\alpha\mathbf{1}\right)\mathbf{1}^\top\right]^{\circ-1}$$
$$\hat{\mathbf{W}} = \log\hat{\Theta}$$

```
// Total number of terms in our dataset
val nTerm = drmD.ncol

// alpha_i -- fixed parameter of a Dirichlet prior.
val alpha_i = 1.0
val alpha = alpha_i * nTerm

// Nc*1 + alpha*1: denominator for the computation of Theta.
val ncSum = drmNc.colSums() += alpha
val ncSumBcast = drmBroadcast(ncSum)

// Calculate Theta and its element wise log, W:
val drmWtUnweighted = drmNc.mapBlock() {
  case (keys, block) =>
      // Pin to the task memory
      val ncSum: Vector = ncSumBcast

      // Compute theta and its log.
      (block += alpha_i) := { (_, c, v) => log(v / ncSum(c)) }
      keys -> block
}
```

And finally, step (9): weight normalization of $\hat{\mathbf{W}}$.

$$\hat{\mathbf{W}} \leftarrow \hat{\mathbf{W}} \circ \left[\mathrm{abs}\left(\hat{\mathbf{W}}\right)\mathbf{1}\mathbf{1}^\top\right]^{\circ-1}$$

```
// Sum up the absolute value of each term weight
// per term per class
val cTotals = dabs(drmWtUnweighted).colSums()
val cTotalsBcast = drmBroadcast(cTotals)

// Normalize Wt by term weight totals.
drmWtUnweighted.mapBlock() {
  case (keys, block) =>
      // Pin to the task memory
      val cTotals: Vector = cTotalsBcast
      // normalize
      block ::= { (_, c, v) => v / cTotals(c) }
      keys -> block
}
```

That is it; fully distributed, TWCNB training, which can be run on Spark, H2O or

Flink in less than 50 lines of code.

Naive Bayes as implemented in the Mahout Distribution.

So now that we've seen how easy it is to implement our own algorithm, what is the use of Mahout's Naive Bayes implementation?

First, the above algorithm requires an Int-keyed DRM as our document vector input. Mahout's current vectorization pipeline uses String keys. This complicates things slightly. While the Mahout distribution does have fully engine neutral implementations of both previously mentioned Naive Bayes flavors, the introduction of String keys makes the engine neutral implementation sub-optimal, and therefore leaves us an opportunity to optimize it in each back-end package. At the time of this writing, Mahout Naive Bayes only ships with a Spark optimized implementation, which we will discuss later.

Second, sometimes it is nice to have canned algorithms with a familiar API. The Mahout implementation of *Bayes* and *CBayes* have `train(...)` method, which returns a model object that can be easily persisted to HDFS and deployed, and a `test(...)` method which returns classification statistics, including a confusion matrix on a hold out set. These methods are examined later in this chapter.

To better understand Mahout's Naive Bayes implementations, let us consider a corpus of m documents. We assign an ordinal unique index to every document, i. Therefore, we identify documents by i, where $i \in \{1, 2, \ldots m\}$.

Let the number of unique lemmatized terms in all the documents be n. We assign an unique ordinal index j to every term in the vocabulary of the corpus. Therefore, we can identify every term by its ordinal index j, where $j \in \{1, 2, \ldots n\}$; i.e., the dictionary.

Vectorization and pre-processing.

We express our corpus as $\mathcal{D}$, an ordered set of document "term frequency" (*TF*) vectors. $\mathcal{D} \triangleq \left\{ d^{(i)} \in \mathbb{R}^n : i = 1, 2, \ldots m \right\}$, where $d_j^{(i)}$ is the number of occurrences of term j in document i.

Let $\mathcal{K} \triangleq \left\{ k_i : i = 1, 2 \ldots m \right\}$ be an ordered set of strings. Each $k_i \in \mathcal{K}$ is a unique string identifier of of the correspondingly indexed document $d^{(i)}$. What's more, each $k_i \in \mathcal{K}$ contains the class label of the correspondingly indexed document, $d^{(i)}$.

Let $f \triangleq \left(\begin{array}{cccc} f_1 & f_2 & \cdots & f_n \end{array} \right)$ be a vector of "document frequency" counts for each term j. f_j is the count of documents in which the term j occurs:

$$f_j \triangleq \left| \left\{ d^{(i)} \in \mathcal{D} : d_j^{(i)} > 0 \right\} \right|$$

It would be possible to use the matrix $\mathbf{D} : \mathbf{D}_{i*} \triangleq d^{(i)}$, induced from $\mathcal{D}$ in its current state as our training set. However as noted in [Rennie et al., 2003], *TF* and "inverse document frequency" (*IDF*) transformations [Sparck Jones, 1972], have been shown to boost performance in Naive Bayes classification.

Commonly known together as *TF-IDF*, the *TF* transformation serves to dampen the weight that a repeated term has on a has on a given document; the *IDF* transformation of a term frequency with respect to a given corpus gives less weight to a term the more often

> ■ **Algorithm 8.3 Distributed Naive Bayes: Mahout Implementation.**
> Given a set of m documents and a vocabulary of size n; each term in the vocabulary is indexed by j.
> Let $\mathcal{D} \triangleq \left\{ \boldsymbol{d}^{(i)} : i = 1, 2, \ldots m \right\}$ be a dataset of term frequency vectors; $d_j^{(i)}$ is the count of term j in document i.
> Let $\boldsymbol{f} \triangleq \begin{pmatrix} f_1 & f_2 & \cdots & f_n \end{pmatrix}$ be a vector of "document frequency" counts for each term j. f_j is the count of documents in which the term j occurs:
> $$f_j \triangleq \left| \left\{ \boldsymbol{d}^{(i)} \in \mathcal{D} : d_j^{(i)} > 0 \right\} \right|.$$
> Let $\boldsymbol{y} \in \{1, 2, \ldots \ell\}^m$ be a vector of ordinal document class labels; y_i is the label of the vectorized document $\boldsymbol{d}^{(i)}$.
> Let $c \in \{1, 2, \ldots \ell\}$ be the classes.
> Let α be a smoothing parameter for all terms in the vocabulary.
> Unless defined otherwise, the following steps are assumed to be calculated for all values of all indices.
>
> **Transformations:**
> (1) $d_j^{(i)} \leftarrow \sqrt{d_j^{(i)}} \left(1 + \log \frac{m}{f_j + 1} \right)$ (*TF-IDF* transformation via `seq2sparse`).
> (2) **if** (*CBayes*)
> $\boldsymbol{d}^{(i)} \leftarrow \frac{\boldsymbol{d}^{(i)}}{\| \boldsymbol{d}^{(i)} \|_2}$ (L_2 length normalization via `seq2sparse`).
>
> **Training:**
> (1) $\mathbf{D}_{i*} \triangleq \boldsymbol{d}^{(i)} : \mathbf{D} \in \mathbb{R}^{m \times n}$ (induce the matrix $\mathbf{D}$ from the document set).
> (2) $\mathbf{N}_{c*} \triangleq \sum_{i : y_i = c} \mathbf{D}_{i*} : \mathbf{N} \in \mathbb{R}^{\ell \times n}$ (aggregate $\mathbf{D}$ by class).
> (3) $\boldsymbol{s} \triangleq \mathbf{N}\boldsymbol{1} : \boldsymbol{s} \in \mathbb{R}^{\ell}$ (calculate class aggregate sum *TF-IDF* vector).
> (4) **if** (**Bayes**) Calculate term weights $\hat{w}_{cj}$ as:
>   (a) $\hat{\theta}_{cj} = \frac{\mathbf{N}_{cj} + \alpha}{s_c + n\alpha}$ (maximum likelihood estimate of θ_{cj}).
>   (b) $\hat{w}_{cj} = \log \hat{\theta}_{cj}$
> (5) **if** (*CBayes*) Calculate normalized term weights $\hat{w}_{cj}$ as:
>   (a) $\hat{\theta}_{cj} = \frac{\sum_k^{k \neq c} \mathbf{N}_{kj} + \alpha}{\sum_k^{k \neq c} \sum_{j'} \mathbf{N}_{kj'} + n\alpha}$ (complementary maximum likelihood estimate of θ_{cj}).
>   (b) $\hat{w}_{cj} = -\log \hat{\theta}_{cj}$ (take each weight, w_{cj} as the negative natural log of θ_{cj}).
>   (c) $\hat{w}_{cj} \leftarrow \frac{\hat{w}_{cj}}{\sum_{j'} |\hat{w}_{cj'}|}$ (weight normalization).
>
> **Label Assignment:**
> (1) Let $\boldsymbol{t} \triangleq \begin{pmatrix} t_1 & t_2 & \cdots & t_n \end{pmatrix}$ be a test document; let t_j be the count of the term j in document $\boldsymbol{t}$.
> (2) Apply the *TF-IDF* transformation using document frequencies from the training set
> $\mathcal{D}: t_j \leftarrow \sqrt{t_j} \left(1 + \log \frac{m}{f_j + 1} \right)$.
> (3) **if** (*CBayes*) Length normalize each document vector: $\boldsymbol{t} \leftarrow \frac{\boldsymbol{t}}{\| \boldsymbol{t} \|_2}$
> (4) Label the document: $l(\boldsymbol{t}) \triangleq \underset{c}{\arg\max} \sum_j t_j \hat{w}_{cj}$

it appears in other documents in that corpus. Conversely, the fewer documents in which a term appears, the more weight it is given after the transformation.

Mahout term weighting formulas deviate slightly from those in TWCNB as presented in [Rennie et al., 2003]. Mahout performs the transformation on our *TF* vectorized corpus using *TF-IDF* calculation as follows in 8.1.

For each $d^{(i)} \in \mathcal{D}$ we compute the *TF-IDF* transformation as:

$$d_j'^{(i)} = \sqrt{d_j^{(i)}} \left(1 + \log \frac{m}{f_j + 1} \right) \tag{8.1}$$

giving us the document set $\mathcal{D}'$. If we are training a *CBayes* model, we length-normalize each document in the set, using the L_2 norm for all $d'^{(i)} \in \mathcal{D}'$:

$$d''^{(i)} = \frac{d'^{(i)}}{\|d'^{(i)}\|_2}. \tag{8.2}$$

For a *Bayes* model, we now represent our *TF-IDF* vectorized corpus as a matrix, $\mathbf{D} \in \mathbb{R}^{m \times n}$ induced from $\mathcal{D}' : \mathbf{D}_{i*} \triangleq d'^{(i)}$. If we are training a *CBayes* model, we'll induce our matrix from $\mathcal{D}'' : \mathbf{D}_{i*} \triangleq d''^{(i)}$.

Document i is represented as the *TF-IDF* vector $\mathbf{D}_{i*}$.

The steps up to here are performed by a *MapReduce* process, `seq2sparse`. After this point the vectorized corpus can be read from HDFS into the Samsara environment as a `DrmLike[String]`, `drmD`.

Per § 4.2 we can think of this this DRM as a tuple: $\left(k, \mathbf{D} \right)$ where $k \in \mathcal{K}^m$ is a sequence of the String keys of the DRM mapped to the correspondingly indexed document vector rows $\mathbf{D}_{i*}$.

Extracting the class labels.

Let us briefly discuss the class labels of our corpus. In supervised training algorithms we must know the class label of each data point in the training set. Mahout *Bayes* and *CBayes* provide for the extraction of the class labels from the training set's keys. We will briefly touch on the class label extraction here and go into slightly more depth later as it is a good example of engine-specific optimization.

Where $\mathcal{C} \triangleq \left\{ 1, 2, \dots \ell \right\}$ is a set of ordinal class labels, the cardinality of $\mathcal{C}$ will be ℓ, the number of unique class labels extracted from $\mathcal{K}$; each $c \in \mathcal{C}$ is a class.

We have the class label of each vectorized document stored in the row keys. However, as the String keys also contain a unique document identifier for each document, we must extract all possible document labels from the row key set, $\mathcal{K}$. For now let us assume an implicit mapping with the function $\text{cParser}(\cdot) : \mathcal{K} \to \mathcal{C}$ on each element of the key sequence, k, to extract the class labels from the String keys of `drmD`[3]. Thus we may now consider `drmD` as the Int-keyed tuple $\left(y \in \mathcal{C}^m, \mathbf{D} \in \mathbb{R}^{m \times n} \right)$.

---

[3] In reality, the cParser $(\cdot)$ function actually is implemented in the Mahout distribution as a String $\Rightarrow$ String function from each String key to a String class which is then mapped to an ordinal index. For simplicity here we will consider it a direct String $\to$ Int mapping. See examples 8.1 and 8.3 for its actual usage.

We define the matrix $\mathbf{N} \in \mathbb{R}^{\ell \times n}$ as the aggregate sum per class of each document vector $d^{(i)} \in \mathbf{D}$ for each class $c \in \mathcal{C}$. $\mathbf{N}_{cj}$ is the sum of the (*TF-IDF* transformed) frequencies of term j, in all documents i, labeled as class c in the training set:

$$\mathbf{N}_{c*} \triangleq \sum_{i}^{y_i=c} \mathbf{D}_{i*}, \forall c. \tag{8.3}$$

Let $s \in \mathbb{R}^{\ell}$ be the total sum of the (*IDF* transformed) frequencies of all terms used in all documents of each class:

$$s_c \triangleq \sum_{j=1}^{n} \mathbf{N}_{cj}. \tag{8.4}$$

In matrix form the equation (8.4) is $s = \mathbf{N}\mathbf{1}$; that is, s is the row-wise sums of $\mathbf{N}$.

Training (Bayes).

Multinomial Naive Bayes classification algorithm has the goal of classifying a document into one of ℓ classes, c, where $c \in \mathcal{C}$.

To that end, the algorithm estimates the uncertainty parameters θ_{cj}, one for every class-term combination c, j. Each parameter estimate, $\hat{\theta}_{cj}$, is calculated using a smoothed version of the Maximum Likelihood estimator:

$$\hat{\theta}_{cj} = \frac{\mathbf{N}_{cj} + \alpha}{s_c + n\alpha} \tag{8.5}$$

where α is the smoothing factor. The default α is the Laplace smoothing factor where $\alpha = 1$.

Decision weights are then taken as log parameter estimates for each term, j, for each class $c \in \mathcal{C}$.

$$\hat{w}_{cj} = \log(\hat{\theta}_{cj}). \tag{8.6}$$

Per algorithm 8.3 *Training* (4)(a),(b), the weight calculation, $\hat{w}_{cj}$ for each term, j, for each class, c, is is calculated as shown in example 8.2.

Label Assignment.

Finally we can assign a label to a vectorized document, $t \in \mathbb{R}^n$, using a classifier function: $l(\cdot)$. Using the minimum-error classification rule [Duda et al., 1973] and ignoring any prior class probabilities, we define our classifier, as:

$$l(t) \triangleq \operatorname*{argmax}_{c} \sum_{j=1}^{n} t_j \hat{w}_{cj}. \tag{8.7}$$

Simply put, standard Multinomial Naive Bayes predicts a document's classification by assigning a class, $k : k \in \mathcal{C}$, the class to which the document has the largest posterior probability of belonging.

Training (*CBayes*)

CBayes estimates each parameter vector, $\hat{\theta}_{c*}$, for each class, $c \in \mathcal{C}$, seeking to minimize the likelihood that a document belongs to *any other class* than c:

$$\hat{\theta}_{cj} = \frac{\tilde{\mathbf{N}}_{cj} + \alpha}{\tilde{s}_c + n\alpha}$$

$\tilde{\mathbf{N}}_{cj}$ is the sum of (*TF-IDF* transformed) frequencies of term j occurring in all documents labeled *other than* class c in the training set. $\tilde{s}_c$ is the total summation of the (*TF-IDF* transformed) frequency of all terms used in documents labeled with a class *other than* c. Again α is the Laplace smoothing parameter, $\alpha = 1$. In more detail, we can see that the calculation of $\hat{\theta}_{cj}$ is:

$$\hat{\theta}_{cj} = \frac{\sum_k^{k \neq c} \mathbf{N}_{kj} + \alpha}{\sum_k^{k \neq c} \sum_{j'} \mathbf{N}_{kj'} + n\alpha}. \tag{8.8}$$

Simply put, for *CBayes*, we are looking to assign a document to a class by *minimizing* the likelihood that it belongs to any of the other classes. Finally we set out term weights:

$$\hat{w}_{cj} = -\log(\hat{\theta}_{cj}). \tag{8.9}$$

Note that in contrast to the *Bayes* model (8.6), the final *CBayes* weight calculation (8.9) for a term class pair, $\hat{w}_{cj}$ is taken as the negative of the natural logarithm of the $\hat{\theta}_{cj}$ parameter estimate. Again, this is because we are seeking to label our documents class which *most poorly* matches our complementary model estimates.

The final transformation of *CBayes* is the weight normalization step. Per [Rennie et al., 2003] § 3.2, in order to lessen the bias of weights towards classes with a larger number of training documents in skewed datasets we normalize each weight per term j for each class $c \in \mathcal{C}$:

$$\hat{w}'_{cj} = \frac{\hat{w}_{cj}}{\sum_{j'} |\hat{w}_{cj'}|}. \tag{8.10}$$

Label assignment for *CBayes* is the same as for *Bayes*:

$$l(t) \triangleq \operatorname*{argmax}_c \sum_{j=1}^n t_j \hat{w}'_{cj}. \tag{8.11}$$

■ **Example 8.1 NaiveBayes.scala**

```scala
trait NaiveBayes extends java.io.Serializable {
    /** Laplace smoothing parameter */
    def defaultAlphaI = 1.0f

    // function to extract categories from string keys
    type CategoryParser = String ⇒ String

    /** Default: seqdirectory/seq2Sparse Categories are
        Stored in Drm Keys as: /Category/document_id */
```

```
def seq2SparseCategoryParser:
  CategoryParser = x ⟹ x.split("/")(1)

def train(observationsPerLabel: DrmLike[Int],
          labelIndex: Map[String, Integer],
          trainComplementary: Boolean = true,
          alphaI: Float = defaultAlphaI): NBModel = {

  // Summation of all weights per feature
  val weightsPerFeature = observationsPerLabel.colSums


  // Distributed summation of all weights per label

  val weightsPerLabel = observationsPerLabel.rowSums

  // Collect a matrix to pass to the NaiveBayesModel
  val inCoreTFIDF = observationsPerLabel.collect

  // thetaNormalizer is only used in TWCNB
  var thetaNormalizer = weightsPerFeature.like()

  /** thetaNormalizer would be trained here in the
    case of a Complementary model */


  new NBModel(inCoreTFIDF,
              weightsPerFeature,
              weightsPerLabel,
              thetaNormalizer,
              labelIndex,
              alphaI,
              trainComplementary)
  }


  // Algorithm 8.3, Training, (2)
  def extractLabelsAndAggregateObservations(
      stringKeyedObservations: DrmLike[String],
      cParser: CategoryParser = seq2SparseCategoryParser)
    (implicit ctx: DistributedContext):
      (mutable.HashMap[String, Integer], DrmLike[Int]) = {

    {.../** Engine neutral implementation */ ...}

  {...}
}
```

■ **Example 8.2 computeWeight.**

```
// Algorithm 8.3, Training (4)(a,b)
def computeWeight(featureLabelWeight: Double,
                  labelWeight: Double,
                  alphaI: Double,
                  numFeatures: Double): Double = {
  val numerator: Double = featureLabelWeight + alphaI
  val denominator: Double =
    labelWeight + alphaI * numFeatures

  Math.log(numerator / denominator)
}
```

8.2 Spark-optimized implementation

As is sometimes the case, a 100% algebraic engine-neutral implementation of an algorithm is not optimal. Samsara algorithms can easily overcome this problem by optimizing certain parts of these algorithms for specific backends. Naive Bayes label extraction and observation summation is one of these cases.

The label extraction and and summation of *TF-IDF* observations per label require some shuffling, and therefore are not particularly well suited to the blockified parallel matrix computation paths used by Samsara DRMs. While a full Naive Bayes label extraction and aggregation method is implemented in the engine-neutral *math-scala* module, it is a case where we can benefit greatly from the native methods of Spark (or other back-ends).

In order to optimize Naive Bayes for Spark, certain classes have been extended in the *spark* module and methods overridden to make use of Spark's native methods. The package structure for the Naive Bayes classes in the *math-scala* module is mirrored into the *spark* module.

Since the *spark* module is dependent on the *math-scala* module, everything in *math-scala* is available to us in *spark*. In this case the NaiveBayes object, implemented in *math-scala* has been extended into the *spark* module, overriding the preparation function, extractLabelsAndAggregateObservations(...) and the test(...) function; this way it is possible to make use of the Spark RDD.reduceByKey(...) method. See example 8.3 for the Spark optimized implementation of extractLabelsAndAggregateObservations(...). Similarly, we can make use of Spark's SparkContext.broadcast(...) method in order to simplify distributed batch testing of our test set in the test(...) function. We will revisit this concept in § 8.5.

■ **Example 8.3 SparkNaiveBayes.scala.**
```
object SparkNaiveBayes extends NaiveBayes {

  override def extractLabelsAndAggregateObservations(
      stringKeyedObservations: DrmLike[String],
      cParser: CategoryParser = seq2SparseCategoryParser)
      (implicit ctx: DistributedContext):
        (mutable.HashMap[String, Integer],
         DrmLike[Int]) = {
  val stringKeyedRdd = stringKeyedObservations.rdd
  // Algorithm 8.3 (2),(3)
  val aggregatedRdd = stringKeyedRdd
        .map(x ⇒ (cParser(x._1), x._2))
        .reduceByKey(_ + _)
  {.../* extract a map of keys → idx as labelIndexMap */...}


  val aggregatedRdd =
    drmWrap(aggregetedObservationByLabelDrm)
  (labelIndexMap, aggregetedObservationByLabelDrm)
}
```

8.3 Command line usage

The Wikipedia document classification example takes a recent XML dump of the English language Wikipedia dataset and parses the XML, extracting a document from the <text> element of each page and labeling it with a category given in the document itself. After vectorizing the text, we can train a Naive Bayes model and classify new out-of-sample documents using that model.

The first part of this section uses the legacy Mahout-MapReduce tools, `mahout seqwiki`, `mahout seq2sparse`, and `mahout split` respectively to parse and label, to vectorize, and to split the raw XML text into training and testing sets of sparse vectors. Later we'll look at the command line usage of Samsara's `mahout spark-trainnb` and `mahout spark-testnb` which train and test Naive Bayes models from the command line.

We will see from this process the interoperability of Mahout "Samsara" algorithms with Mahout-MapReduce and other Hadoop sequence-file-based algorithms.

For our example, we classify documents into two classes: "united states" and "united kingdom". To keep things simple, we'll tokenize the documents into unigrams; however using bigrams, trigrams, etc., is a trivial extension of the process.

Available in the `$MAHOUT_HOME/examples/bin` directory is an example bash script which will download the latest English language Wikipedia XML dump into the `/tmp/mahout/mahout-work-wiki/` directory, put the data into HDFS, vectorize it using `seq2sparse`, split it into training and testing sets, and build a legacy *MapReduce* model. This section will step through much of that script.

For our purposes, we need only the vectorized documents and their class labels. We take the following steps from the command line to download the data, parse the XML files into sequence files, vectorize the those files. Optionally we may build a Spark Naive Bayes model from the command line.

First we must create a working directory, we'll use /tmp/mahout-work-wiki/ throughout this example. To simplify, we'll export an environment variable, WORK_DIR, which will point to our base working directory. Next we'll download a partial XML dump of all current English Wikipedia pages, unzip it, and put it into HDFS.

Step (1): Setup working directories and acquire data.

```
export WORK_DIR=/tmp/mahout-work-wiki
mkdir -p $WORK_DIR/wikixml
curl http://dumps.wikimedia.org/enwiki/latest/
enwiki-latest-pages-articles10.xml-p002336425p003046511.bz2

 -o $WORK_DIR/wikixml/enwiki-latest-pages-articles.xml.bz2

cd $WORK_DIR/wikixml/
bunzip2 $WORK_DIR/wikixml/enwiki-latest-pages-articles.xml.bz2
cd $WORK_DIR
hdfs dfs -mkdir -p $WORK_DIR
hdfs dfs -put $WORK_DIR/wikixml $WORK_DIR/wikixml
```

 It is possible to use the full English language Wikipedia XML dump by downloading http://dumps.wikimedia.org/enwiki/latest/enwiki-latest-pages-articles.xml.bz. Please note though that this dataset is rather large, ~10G zipped, and tokenizing it into anything more than unigrams will require significant resources.

Next we copy the $MAHOUT_HOME/examples/bin/resources/country2.txt file into our working directory as country.txt. This file contains, by row, in plain text, the class labels which we will be using for our classification[4].

Step (2): Copy country2.txt to country.txt.

```
cp $MAHOUT_HOME/examples/bin/resources/country2.txt

 $WORK_DIR/country.txt
```

Taking a look at our country.txt category file we can see the two classes that we'll be classifying our documents into:

---

[4]Note that when we use the terms "class" and "label" we are referring to the classes upon which we are building our model. When we use the term "category" we are referring to a Wikipedia document's category tag, from which the document's class label is ultimately derived. See Fig. 8.1 for an example.

cat /tmp/mahout-work-wiki/country.txt

```
United States
United Kingdom
```

The categories in our category file do not need to be case-sensitive in order to match with the categories given in the page text in the XML dump.

 We could easily work with different classes by changing the categories in the category file. E.g., if we wanted to classify our documents into the classes "math," "science," and "literature" we could create a `category.txt` file and append those class labels to it:

```
echo math >> category.txt

echo science >> category.txt

echo literature >> category.txt
```

and use `category.txt` in place of `country.txt` when calling `mahout seqwiki`.

We are now ready to launch `mahout seqwiki`. This *MapReduce* process will seek to extract documents with a Wikipedia category tag which contains a String matching a line in the category file. If no match is found and the `--all` option is set, the document will be labeled as "unknown." The documents will then be written out as a `<Text, Text>` sequence file of the form (Key: /class_label/document_title, Value: {document's `<text>` element}).

Step (3): Parse the Wikipedia XML dump.

```
mahout seqwiki
    -c $WORK_DIR/country.txt
    -i $WORK_DIR/wikixml/enwiki-latest-pages-articles.xml
    -o $WORK_DIR/wikipediainput
```

The above command parses the `<text>` element of each page of the English language Wikipedia dump. Each Wikipedia page contains (multiple) category tags towards the bottom of the page. With the options provided above, a document will be assigned a label if it has a category which contains a string matching a line in the classification file; in this case `country.txt`.   If no match is found, with these options, the document is not included in the output. In the case that more than one match is found, the document will be labeled as belonging to the class of the first matching category.

For example, an arbitrarily selected page, the page for the United States Army Reserve, https://en.wikipedia.org/wiki/United_States_Army_Reserve (Fig. 8.1) will be labeled as "united states". We can see that Fig. 8.1 has been tagged with two categories: "United States Army Direct Reporting Units" and "United States Army Reserve". Since we have not set the `--exactMatch` option, "United States Army Direct Reporting Units"

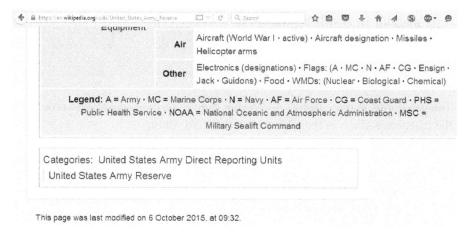

Figure 8.1: United States Army Reserve Wikipedia page categories.

will be enough to label this page as "united states" since it contains (after conversion to lowercase) "united states". The <text> element of this page will be written to a <Text, Text> sequence file with Key = "/united states/United_States_Army_Reserve" and Value = {page <text> element}.

We can take a look at the sequence file entry for the United States Army Reserve page using the mahout seqdumper tool:

Sequenced United States Army Reserve Wikipedia page.

```
mahout seqdumper -i $WORK_DIR/wikipediainput
  | grep -A 60 United_States_Army_Reserve

{...}
Key:
  /united states/United_States_Army_Reserve:
Value:
  {...}
  ==History== On 23 April 1908 <ref>
  [http://www.almc.army.mil/alog/issues/NovDec08/
  army_reserve100.html]</ref> Congresscreated the Medical
  Reserve Corps, the official predecessor of the Army
  Reserve.<ref>United States Army Reserve, Army Reserve: A
  Concise History, 2012, p.4. Exact date for OR-ORC from Army
  Lineage and Honors.</ref> After the [[First World War]],
  under the National Defense Act on 4 June 1920, Congress
  reorganized the U.S. land forces by authorizing a [[Regular
  Army (United States)|Regular Army]], a National Guard, and
  an Organized Reserve (Officers Reserve Corps and Enlisted
  Reserve Corps) of unrestricted size, which later became the
  Army Reserve. <ref>[http://www.history.army.mil/books
```

```
/Lineage/M-F/chapter4.htm#b3 Chapter IV: The Aftermath
of World War I]</ref> This organization provided a peacetime
pool of trained Reserve officers and enlisted men for use in
war. The ORC included the Officers' Reserve Corps, Enlisted
Reserve Corps and [[Reserve Officers' Training Corps]]. The
Organized Reserves were redesignated 25 March 1948 as the
Organized Reserve Corps. Recognizing the importance of the
Organized Reserve to the World War II effort, Congress
authorized retirement and drill pay for the first time
in 1948
{...}
```

Next we'll vectorize the document using `mahout seq2sparse`. The output will be a sequence file of form `<Text, VectorWritable>` corresponding to the transformed term frequency matrix, $\mathbf{D}$, with rows bound to elements of the key set $\mathcal{K}$. This output can be viewed as the tuple $\left(k, \mathbf{D}\right)$ and can easily be read into a `DrmLike[String]` using `drmDfsRead(...)` and thus can be used in any Samsara-based algorithm.

With the following options, `seq2sparse` will tokenize each document into unigrams (`-ng 1`), accept only terms which appear in less than 30% of documents into the dictionary (`-x 30`), perform the *TF-IDF* transformation on term frequencies, $\mathbf{D}$, step (1) of algorithm 8.3 (`-wt tfidf`). Since we will be training a *Bayes* model, there is no need to length-normalize the document vectors.

The vectorized documents will be written to `$WORK_DIR/wikipediaVecs/tfidf-vectors` directory. `mahout seq2sparse` is the last required Mahout-MapReduce tool in our pipeline.

Step (4): Vectorize the documents into TF-IDF vectors.

```
mahout seq2sparse
    -i $WORK_DIR/wikipediainput
    -o $WORK_DIR/wikipediaVecs
    -wt tfidf
    -nv
    -ow
    -ng 1
    -x 30
```

Also in the `$WORK_DIR/wikipediaVecs` directory will be a dictionary file, `dictionary.file-0` and a document frequency file, `df-count` which we will use later in § 8.4 to vectorize out of sample text.

Let's take a look at our vectorized example document, "United States Army Reserve".

Example vectorized document.

```
mahout seqdumper -i $WORK_DIR/wikipediaVecs/tfidf-vectors/ | grep
United_States_Army_Reserve
{...}
Key:
  /united states/United_States_Army_Reserve:

Value:
  /united states/United_States_Army_Reserve:{32641:4.14562
498626709,60281:5.945291996002197,61823:5.703279972076416,
158658:3.230912923812866,25071:9.00680923461914,133342:2.9
1446852684021,28192:10.530653953552246,148259:5.8013978004
45557,58287:5.493307113647461,169147:8.147268295288086,673
23:3.455472469329834,62484:5.288512706756592,152229:5.1465
23952484131,72644:4.060750961303711,155982:4.3727116584777
83,78762:6.820760726928711,38895:10.31032657623291,169739:
5.731718063354492,7159:17.466283798217773,91828:4.91227722
16796875,153032:9.290599822998047,161327:4.23622465133667,
57855:4.665681838989258,14905:12.140103340148926,121165:2.
983461380004883,128862:6.638439178466797,27283:10.89045238
494873,14234:11.922101020812988,56331:8.340564727783203,78
356:6.1864542961120605,149277:2.9030399322509766,106361:10
.969178199768066,43906:4.962836265563965,39854:4.379656791
687012,140502:2.2042269706726074,85716:8.27925968170166,13
0221:5.631176948547363,60433:4.335854530334473,60855:2.903
0399322509766,27577:5.339156627655029,160387:4.21490192413
3301,152874:2.8833487033843994,34838:5.313723564147949,300
43:3.9808473587036133,155766:11.425339698791504,185426:4.0
901384353637695,65537:2.7335848808288574,13019:2.227374315
261841,23166:9.277496337890625,33769:10.678313255310059,44
858:11.303296089172363,161782:3.5637638568878174,80969:4.6
65681838989258,67522:3.8376681804656982,3544:12.7135181427
00195,7404:15.184319496154785,24126:9.259517669677734,...

{...}
```

Now, optionally, we can split the dataset into training and testing sets. The following will create a randomly sampled training set containing 60% of the vectorized Wikipedia documents and testing set with the remaining 40%.

Step (6): Split the data set into 60/40 training and testing sets.

```
mahout split
```

```
-i $WORK_DIR/wikipediaVecs/tfidf-vectors
--trainingOutput $WORK_DIR/training
--testOutput $WORK_DIR/testing
-rp 40
-ow
-seq
-xm sequential
```

We can now train our model simply by calling `mahout spark-trainnb`. The `-i` option specifies a path to our Wikipedia *TF-IDF* vectors, the the training set. The `-o` option specifies the directory in which we'll write the model. The `-ow` option allows the `mahout spark-trainnb` to overwrite any existing data in the output directory, and `-ma` is the URL of the Spark master. Since we've set up our environment per § 2.2, we may just supply the MASTER environment variable.

Step (7): Train a model from the command line.

```
mahout spark-trainnb
    -i $WORK_DIR/training
    -o $WORK_DIR/model
    -ow
    -ma $MASTER
```

We can test the model on our holdout set by calling `mahout spark-testnnb`. Similarly to training, `mahout spark-testnnb` has a `-i` option which specifies a path to our *TF-IDF* testing vectors; the testing set. Again, the the `-ma` option points to the Spark master. Upon completion of `spark-testnb` a confusion matrix will be displayed to the standard output.

Step (8): Test a model from the command line.

```
mahout spark-testnb
    -i $WORK_DIR/testing
    -m $WORK_DIR/model
    -ma $MASTER
```

8.4 Using Samsara Naive Bayes from the shell

Having completed steps (1) through (4) in § 8.3, we have a vectorized set of Wikipedia documents with observable class labels: "united states" or "united kingdom." We can see that our model, trained and tested via the command line, performs quite well on our holdout set. However, if we want to use the model in a practical situation, on data unseen during the initial vectorization of the training and testing sets, we must define some additional functions. The Mahout Spark-shell is quite useful in this type of situation.

We can launch the shell, read in our data (and our previously trained model if we wish) and define functions to tokenize, vectorize and classify unseen text.

To begin, we launch the Mahout Spark-shell with a few given Spark options. We may need to tweak some of the JVM options as well; e.g., increase the maxPermSize of the JVM.

Step (1): Launch the Mahout Spark-shell.

```
MAHOUT_OPTS="-Dspark.kryoserializer.buffer.mb=200

 -Dspark.executor.memory=1g" mahout spark-shell
```

An *.mscala* script is available in the Mahout distribution: $MAHOUT_HOME/examples/ bin/spark-document-classifier.mscala. In the rest of this section, we will walk through that script and add a few steps.

However, if we'd like to skip the following tutorial steps in this section, we can simply run the script by entering:

```
:load <MAHOUT_HOME>/examples/bin/spark-document-classifier.mscala
```

at the mahout> command prompt. With the exception of saving our model to HDFS, this script will complete all of the necessary steps below and leave us with a classifyText(txt: String): String function as seen in example 8.6 which accepts a string and classifies it, in our example, as either "united states" or "united kingdom."

However, walking through the script will give a much better idea of what is going on, and of some of the possibilities provided by the Mahout Spark-shell.

Note that we do leave some fields in the global scope in order to shorten the example.

We begin with the necessary Mahout imports to build and test a Naive Bayes model.

Step (2): Samsara Naive Bayes imports.

```
import org.apache.mahout.classifier.naivebayes._
import org.apache.mahout.classifier.stats._
import org.apache.mahout.nlp.tfidf._
```

Remember that the Mahout Spark-shell automatically imported all of the base Samsara classes per §§ B.1, C.1, and C.13.1 on start up.

Next we must add a few Hadoop imports which will be used to read in the dictionary and document frequency files created by mahout seq2sparse.

Step (3): Hadoop imports.

```
import org.apache.hadoop.io.Text
import org.apache.hadoop.io.IntWritable
```

```
import org.apache.hadoop.io.LongWritable
```

Now we are ready to read our full dataset from HDFS as vectorized by seq2sparse. We'll set our base path, pathToData, to point to the same path as our WORK_DIR environment variable in the previous section, /tmp/mahout-work-wiki/.

Step (4): Read the full dataset into a DRM.

```
val pathToData = "/tmp/mahout-work-wiki/"
val fullData = drmDfsRead(pathToData +
                 "wikipediaVecs/tfidf-vectors")
```

We now have a String-keyed DRM, fullData, with keys: /class_label/document_id bound to sparse row vectors with each element the value of the *TF-IDF* transformation of a term frequency, for that document and columns indexed by our dictionary. Note that by reading a Hadoop sequence file of form <String, VectorWritable>, using drmDfsRead(...), we automatically get a String-keyed DRM. This is algorithm 8.3, *Training* (1).

We must now extract the the class labels from our training set. First let's work with the entire dataset. As discussed in § 8.2, the NaiveBayes object has a helper function, extractLabelsAndAggregateObservations(...) to prep the data for training. This function will return a map of labels extracted by the CategoryParser: String ⇒ String typed function, cParser(...), supplied as a parameter. This function will strip everything but the class label from the keys of the DrmLike[String] where the keys, as prepared by seqwiki will be of the form /class_label/document_Id as is the convention for legacy Mahout text classification pipelines. The default CategoryParser is seq2SparseCategoryParser.

```
type CategoryParser = String ⇒ String
def seq2SparseCategoryParser: CategoryParser =
  x ⇒ x.split("/")(1)
```

We can see that our example document, with key /united states/United_States_Army_Reserve document will be parsed into "united states" by the default category parser. The category parser will be applied to each key in the document and each unique key will be added to the labelIndex map; a map of class → index. After all keys have been extracted by the category parser, the dataset will be aggregated by key and each *TF-IDF* value will be summed per algorithm 8.3, *Training* (2),(3).

Step (5): Extract categories and sum TF-IDF values for each category.

```
val (labelIndex, aggregatedObservations) =
  SparkNaiveBayes.extractLabelsAndAggregateObservations(
          fullData,
          cParser = NaiveBayes.seq2SparseCategoryParser)
```

In our case, for this binary classification problem, we will be left with an aggregated two row DrmLike[Int], aggregatedObservations, with keys: $\left\{0,1\right\}$ and a (String → Int) map, labelIndex, which is a simple index map from each String class label to its corresponding ordinal class.

We are now ready to build a model. First let's train a *Bayes* model[5] on the full set, self testing on the training set.

Step (6): Build a Multinomial Naive Bayes model and self test on the training set.

```
val model = SparkNaiveBayes.train(aggregatedObservations,
                                  labelIndex,
                                  false)

val resAnalyzer = SparkNaiveBayes.test(model, fullData, false)
println(resAnalyzer)
```

The printout of resAnalyzer will be a confusion matrix and should look something like example 8.4.

We can see from the confusion matrix that the model performs quite well when self-testing on the full set with an accuracy of 98.924%.

But what if we want a better idea of how a given Naive Bayes model will perform on a holdout set? We have a couple of alternatives. One, we can load the training and testing sets created by mahout split from § 8.3. Two, since we are in a Spark backed environment, we can take advantage of Spark's native functions on the backing RDD of our DRM. We can see here how we can easily extract the backing RDD from our fullData DRM to use the RDD.randomSplit(...) function:

Step (7): Split the data into 60/40 training/testing sets.

```
// use the RDD randomSplit API to split train/test sets
val sets = fullData.rdd.randomSplit(Array(0.6, 0.4),
                                    seed = 1234L)

val trainingSet = drmWrap(sets(0))

val testingSet = drmWrap(sets(1))
```

As you can see we simply pull the backing RDD out of our DRM, in this case, fullData.rdd. We can then apply any applicable functions from the native Spark RDD API on it. And of course, when working with Samsara algorithms, we must then convert it back to a DRM using drmWrap(...).

---

[5]We choose to use a *Bayes* (MNB) model for this binary classification tutorial as the many of the real performance gains in a *CBayes* (TWCNB) model are seen in multi-class classification problems.

■ **Example 8.4 Confusion Matrix: self testing.**

```
============================================================
Summary
------------------------------------------------------------
Correctly Classified Instances: 11676 98.924%
Incorrectly Classified Instances: 127 1.076%
Total Classified Instances: 11803
============================================================
Confusion Matrix
------------------------------------------------------------
b        a       <--Classified as
9141     107      |  9248   b      = united states
20       2535     |  2555   a      = united kingdom
============================================================
Statistics
------------------------------------------------------------
Kappa:                    0.9677
Accuracy:                 98.924%
Reliability:              66.0201%
Reliability (std dev):    0.5718
Weighted precision:       0.9895
Weighted recall:          0.9892
Weighted F1 score:        0.9893
```

We are now ready to build our model on a training set, 60% of the Wikipedia vectors, and test it on a holdout set[6] of 40%.

Step (8): Train and test our model on respective sets.

```
val (labelIndex, aggregatedObservations) =
  SparkNaiveBayes.extractLabelsAndAggregateObservations(
    trainingSet)

val model = NaiveBayes.train(aggregatedObservations,
  labelIndex, false)

val resAnalyzer =
  SparkNaiveBayes.test(model, testingSet, false)

println(resAnalyzer)
```

We can see from the confusion matrix displayed in example 8.5 that the model still performs quite well, with 95.2159% accuracy.

Now that we have our model, we can move on to defining the functions to classify new, out of sample text. In order to vectorize our new text we'll need to work with the same dictionary and document frequency count that we used to vectorize our training data. We can easily read these in from our seq2sparse output.

Step (9): Read and create our dictionary and document frequency maps.

```
val dictionary = sdc.sequenceFile(pathToData +
                    "wikipediaVecs/dictionary.file-0",
                    classOf[Text],
                    classOf[IntWritable])

val documentFrequencyCount = sdc.sequenceFile(pathToData +
                    "wikipediaVecs/df-count",
                    classOf[IntWritable],
                    classOf[LongWritable])

// get dictionary and document frequency count as RDDs
val dictionaryRDD = dictionary.map {
    case (wKey, wVal) ⇒ wKey.asInstanceOf[Text]
      .toString() → wVal.get()
```

---

[6]Note that because our *IDF* transformation has been performed using document frequencies calculated for each term across the entire dataset before it was split, the *TF-IDF* values in our training set actually contain a large amount of information on our testing set.

■ **Example 8.5 Confusion matrix: test set.**

```
============================================================
Summary
------------------------------------------------------------
Correctly Classified Instances: 4498 95.2159%
Incorrectly Classified Instances: 226 4.7841%
Total Classified Instances: 4724
============================================================
Confusion Matrix
------------------------------------------------------------
b        a        <--Classified as
3522     175      |  3697    b     = united states
51       976      |  1027    a     = united kingdom
============================================================
Statistics
------------------------------------------------------------
Kappa:                      0.8634
Accuracy:                   95.2159%
Reliability:                63.4335%
Reliability (std dev):      0.5494
Weighted precision:         0.9558
Weighted recall:            0.9522
Weighted F1 score:          0.9531
```

```
}

val documentFrequencyCountRDD =
  documentFrequencyCount.map {
    case (wKey, wVal) ⇒
      wKey.asInstanceOf[IntWritable]
        .get() → wVal.get()
}

// convert our dictionary and document frequency RDDs
// to maps
val dictionaryMap = dictionaryRDD.collect.map(
                    x ⇒ x._1.toString → x._2.toInt).toMap

val dfCountMap = documentFrequencyCountRDD.collect.map(
                    x ⇒ x._1.toInt → x._2.toLong).toMap


// set up our label maps and other values we my need
// from our model
val labelMap = model.labelIndex
val numLabels = model.numLabels
val reverseLabelMap = labelMap.map(x ⇒ x._2 → x._1)
```

Next, per algorithm 8.3, *Label Assignment* (1), (2), (3) we must define a function to tokenize and vectorize and transform new text using our current dictionary.

For this simple example, our function, vectorizeDocument(...) will tokenize a new document into unigrams using native Java String methods and vectorize it into *TF-IDF* values. It is important to remember that we must use our already loaded dictionary and document frequencies; the same that were used to vectorize the training set of the model that we will be basing our classification on.

 Tip

> You could use a Lucene Analyzer for bigrams, trigrams, etc., and integrate Apache Tika to extract text from different document types (PDF, PPT, XLS, etc.).

Step (10): Define a function to tokenize and vectorize new incoming text.

```
def vectorizeDocument(document: String,
                      dictionaryMap: Map[String,Int],
                      dfMap: Map[Int,Long],
```

```
                        lengthNormalize: Boolean = false):
                   Vector = {

  val wordCounts = document.replaceAll("[^\\p{L}\\p{Nd}]+", " ")
                          .toLowerCase
                          .split(" ")
                          .groupBy(identity)
                          .mapValues(_.length)
  val vec = new RandomAccessSparseVector(dictionaryMap.size)
  val totalDFSize = dfMap(-1)
  val docSize = wordCounts.size
  val tfidf: TermWeight = new TFIDF()
  for (word ← wordCounts) {
    val term = word._1
    if (dictionaryMap.contains(term)) {
      val termFreq = word._2
      val dictIndex = dictionaryMap(term)
      val docFreq = dfMap(dictIndex)
      val currentTfIdf = tfidf.calculate(termFreq,
                                docFreq.toInt,
                                docSize,
                                totalDFSize.toInt)
      vec(dictIndex) = currentTfIdf
    }
  }
  if (lengthNormalize) {
    vec / vec.norm(2)
  }
  else {
    vec
  }

}
```

We now choose the appropriate classifier based on the model type. The classifier's `classifyFull(...)` method will return a vector of size ℓ, with each element a score for class $c : c \in C$ where $C \triangleq \left\{0, \ldots \ell - 1\right\}$ and each $c \in C$ serves as a vector index. In this case the vector will contain two elements.

Step (11): Instantiate the correct classifier for the trained model.

```
// instantiate the correct type of classifier
val classifier = model.isComplementary match {
  case true ⇒ new ComplementaryNBClassifier(model)
  case _ ⇒ new StandardNBClassifier(model)
```

```
}
```

Per algorithm 8.3, *Label Assignment*, (4) we will be assigning a label to the document with the category with the highest score, so we must define an *argmax* function which will return the index and value of the element of a vector with the highest value.

Step (12) Define an argmax function for a vector.

```
def argmax(v: Vector): (Int, Double) = {
  var bestIdx: Int = Int.MinValue
  var bestScore: Double = Double.MinValue
  for(i ← 0 until v.size) {
    if(v(i) > bestScore){
      bestScore = v(i)
      bestIdx = i
    }
  }
  (bestIdx, bestScore)
}
```

Taking a look at our reversed label index map, we can see the index of each class $c : c \in C$ where in our binary classification example, $C \triangleq \{0, 1\}$.

```
mahout> reverseLabelMap
res17: scala.collection.Map[Integer,String] =
  Map(1 -> united states, 0 -> united kingdom)
```

We can see that "united kingdom" is index (class) 0 and and "united states" index (class) 1.

By algorithm 8.3, *Label Assignment*, (4), we can now classify a vectorized document by looking at all scores given by `classifier.classifyFull(...)`, finding the index with the max score using `argmax(...)` and looking up the index in our `reverseLabelMap`.

Step (13): Defnie a vector classification function.

```
def classifyDocument(dVec: Vector) : String = {
  val cVec = classifier.classifyFull(dVec)
  val (bestIdx, bestScore) = argmax(cVec)
  reverseLabelMap(bestIdx)
}
```

Finally, we can tie everything together, and define a function to tokenize, vectorize and classify raw text, according to our trained model.

> ■ **Example 8.6 Final text classifier.**
> ```
> mahout> classifyText("Hello world from Queens")
> res15: String = united states
> mahout> classifyText("Hello world from London")
> res16: String = united kingdom
> ```

Step (14): Tie it all together and defnie a text classification function.

```
def classifyText(txt: String): String = {
  val v = vectorizeDocument(txt, dictionaryMap, dfCountMap)
  classifyDocument(v)
}
```

We can now classify some simple text: see example 8.6.

We are now ready to save this model to HDFS.

Step(15): Save our model to HDFS.

```
model.dfsWrite("/tmp/mahout-work-wiki/model")
```

Be sure to save this model as we will be using it in § 8.6. Note that this command will fail if the path being written to is not empty, so if you've run step (6) of § 8.3 you'll need to remove "/tmp/mahout-work-wiki/model" if you want to save it again.

We can now retrieve our trained model from HDFS and embed it into an application.

Read our model from HDFS.

```
NBModel.dfsRead("/tmp/mahout-work-wiki/model")
```

8.5 Distributed batch classification

Since we can only broadcast native Mahout and Scala objects (e.g., `o.a.m.Vector`, `o.a.m.Matrix` to a `mapBlock(...)` closure, if we then want to classify a large batch of Vectors in a distributed fashion, we must drop down into engine-specific code to do so. This is simple to do in Spark:

```
val classifier = model.isComplementary
  match {
    case true ⇒
      new ComplementaryNBClassifier(model)
    case _ ⇒
```

```
              new StandardNBClassifier(model)
  }
val bCastClassifier = ctx.broadcast(classifier)

val scoredDocSet = docSet.mapBlock(ncol = numLabels) {
  case (keys, block) ⇒
    val classifier =  bCastClassifier.value
    val numInstances = keys.size
    val blockB = block.like(numInstances, numLabels)
    for(i ← 0 until numInstances){
      blockB(i, ::) :=
        classifier.classifyFull(block(i, ::) )
    }
  keys → blockB
}
```

We simply choose the correct classifier for the already trained model, and broadcast it via Spark's SparkContext.broadcast(...) API. The above code block will return a CheckpointedDrmSpark[Int], with columns corresponding to the class label indices extracted previously and rows corresponding to each vectorized document to be classified. Therefore in each row i each column $c : c \in C$ value is a score for class c.

For example, for a matrix **D** representing m vectorized, transformed documents on a vocabulary of n terms, $\mathbf{D} \in \mathbb{R}^{m \times n}$ (docSet in the above code block), we want to calculate a score matrix, $\mathbf{S} \in \mathbb{R}^{m \times \ell}$ (scoredDocSet in the above code block). For each row $\mathbf{S}_{i*}$ of the scoredDocSet DRM, $\mathbf{S}_{i*} = $ scoredDocSet$(i, ::)$; a vector of size ℓ of scores for each class $c \in C$ for document i. A higher score in column c represents a higher likelihood that the the document in row i belongs to the class c. Per algorithm 8.3, *Label Assignment*, (4) we classify our document rows, i , with labels as $k : k \in C$ where $k = \underset{c}{\operatorname{argmax}} \, \mathbf{S}_{ic}$. We can then use our label index map to determine the String class label for the ordinal class prediction, k.

8.6 Deploying a trained model to a server

In the final step of our example, we'll create a simple servlet class which can be used to classify posted text using our trained model. Of course there is some configuration needed to launch our server, but that is beyond the scope of this example. We will limit this tutorial to the development of a Naive Bayes text classification servlet, along with the necessary dependencies. We have provided a simple standalone Tomcat server maven project example with the following code in the GitHub repository for this book.

First let's take a look at the maven artifacts needed when building our webapp.

pom.xml for Naive Bayes classification servlet: Samsara dependencies.

```
<dependencies>
```

```
      <dependency>
        <groupId>org.scala-lang</groupId>
        <artifactId>scala-library</artifactId>
        <version>2.10.4</version>
      </dependency>
      <dependency>
        <groupId>org.apache.mahout</groupId>
        <artifactId>mahout-math-scala_2.10</artifactId>
        <version>0.10.2</version>
      </dependency>
      <dependency>
        <groupId>org.apache.mahout</groupId>
        <artifactId>mahout-spark_2.10</artifactId>
      <version>0.10.2</version>
      </dependency>
  {...}
</dependencies>
```

Of course we'll need to add any dependencies necessary to the servlet container that we choose to use, e.g., Tomcat or Jetty. These should contain the base `HttpServlet` class which we will be extending into our `NaiveBayesServlet` class in example 8.7.

We'll need add our Samsara imports per §§ B.1, C.1, and C.13.1 along with the Hadoop and Naive Bayes imports that we used in § 8.4.

Naive Bayes servlet imports.

```
import org.apache.mahout.math._
import scalabindings._
import RLikeOps._
import org.apache.mahout.sparkbindings._
import org.apache.spark.SparkConf

import org.apache.mahout.classifier.naivebayes._
import org.apache.mahout.nlp.tfidf._
import org.apache.hadoop.io.Text
import org.apache.hadoop.io.IntWritable
import org.apache.hadoop.io.LongWritable

import javax.servlet.http.HttpServlet
import javax.servlet.http.HttpServletRequest
import javax.servlet.http.HttpServletResponse
```

We can now test our classification service. Launching the servlet in example 8.7 on the localhost, we can post some text to it and see that we'll get the same response as we did in the shell when developing our classification functions. Compare the below results

■ Example 8.7 NaiveBayesServlet.scala.

```scala
{...}
class NaiveBayesServlet extends HttpServlet {
  val master = System.getenv("MASTER")
  val conf = new SparkConf()
    .set("spark.executor.extraClassPath",
        "/path/to/project/" +
        "/target/mvnArtifactId-1.0-SNAPSHOT.jar")
  implicit val sdc = mahoutSparkContext(
    masterUrl = master,
    appName = "NaiveBayesExample",
    sparkConf = conf )
  val pathToData = "/tmp/mahout-work-wiki/"
  /** read our model from HDFS */
  val model = NBModel.dfsRead(pathToData + "model")
  val labelMap = model.labelIndex
  val numLabels = model.numLabels
  val reverseLabelMap = labelMap.map(x => x._2 -> x._1)

  def classifyText(txt: String): String = {
    val v = vectorizeDocument(txt,
            dictionaryMap,
            dfCountMap)
    classifyDocument(v)
  }
  /* define values and methods as in sec 8.4 */
  val dictionary = {...}
  val documentFrequencyCount = {...}
  val dictionaryRDD = {...}
  val documentFrequencyCountRDD = {...}
  val dictionaryMap = {...}
  val dfCountMap = {...}
  val classifier = {...}
  def vectorizeDocument(document: String,
                dictionaryMap: Map[String,Int],
                dfMap: Map[Int,Long]): Vector = {...}
  def classifyDocument(clvec: Vector): String = {...}

  def argmax(v: Vector): (Int, Double) = {...}

  /** respond to posted text with a classification */
  override def doPost(request: HttpServletRequest,
                response: HttpServletResponse) {
    val txt = request.getReader().readLine()
    response.getWriter().append(classifyText(txt))
  }
}
```

with the shell classification results seen in example 8.6.

```
curl -d "hello world from queens" localhost:7000/app/country
united states


curl -d "hello world from london" localhost:7000/app/country
united kingdom
```

And finally let's look at a use case with some real world text. We'll take two excerpts from SEC filings from the EDGAR database. The first is from a filing by an American company, The Madison Square Garden Company [EDGAR, 2014], which refers to American football and the company's television network viewership.

Naive Bayes classification servlet: Text from an SEC filing for The Madison Square Garden Company refering to American football.

```
curl -d "MSG Network is also the official regional sports
    network of the New York Giants, delivering exclusive, special
    non-gamecoverage of the National Football League team,
    including Head Coach Tom Coughlin's live weekly press
    conference.  Additional programming on MSG+ includes a
    lineup of select NCAA college football and basketball games,
    the New York Racing Association horse racing, and international
    sports content such as Union of European Football Association
    league soccer, as well as original programming related
    to the network's professional teams.  The average of the
    combined reach of MSG Network and MSG+ is approximately
    7.8 million viewing subscribers, primarily in New York,
    New Jersey, and Connecticut." localhost:7000/app/country

united states
```

When we post the data from the The Madison Square Garden Company's filing to our server, we can see that it responds as we would expect, with a classification of "united states".

The second is an excerpt from an SEC filing for Manchester United, plc [EDGAR, 2013], an English Football club.

Naive Bayes classification servlet: Text from an SEC filing for Manchester United plc, an English football club.

```
curl -d "References to our 659 million followers are based on a
```

Naive Bayes classification servlet: Text from an SEC filing for Manchester United plc, an English football club.

```
survey conducted by Kantar Media a division of WPP plc and
paid for by us.  As in the survey conducted by Kantar Media,
we define the term followers as those individuals who answered
survey questions, unprompted, with the answer that Manchester
United was either their favorite football team in the world or
a football team that they enjoyed following in addition to
their favorite football team.  For example, we and Kantar Media
includedin the definition of follower a respondent who either
watched live Manchester United matches, followed highlights
coverage or read or talked about Manchester United regularly.
Although the survey solicited unprompted responses, we do not
distinguish between those respondents who answered that
Manchester United was their favorite football team in the
world and those who enjoy following Manchester United in
addition to their favorite football team.  Since we
believe that each of our followers engage with our brand in
some capacity, including through watching matches on
television, attending matches live, buying retail merchandise
or monitoring the team's highlights on the internet, we
believe identifying our followers in this manner provides us
with the best data to use for purposes of developing our
business strategy and measuring the penetration of our brand."
localhost:7000/app/country
```

```
united kingdom
```

Again when the text is posted to the server, the response is what we would expect to be a correct classification: "united kingdom".

Appendix

Mahout Book Conventions

A.1 Coding conventions for names in Mahout

Mahout Scala Bindings employ a few coding conventions. Throughout this book, we try to follow them in the examples.

In-core matrix variables (of `org.apache.mahout.math.Matrix` type) start with the prefix 'mx', e.g.: mxA.

Variables for distributed row matrices (DRM) use the prefix 'drm', e.g.: drmA.

Vectors use names with no prefixes, e.g.: a, b, c ...

Algorithms are initiated via a top-level package function with a short usually abbreviated method name, rather than an object method or a class construction, e.g., `chol()` but not `new CholeskyDecomposition(...)`. This is to follow an R style of brevity.

Routines for distributed algorithms start with 'd', e.g.: dssvd. Algorithms for in-core procedures do not have any special prefix. If there are both in-core and distributed implementation of a fundamentally equivalent method, then the names match as in dssvd ⇔ ssvd.

A.2 Math notations

x	a non-vector variable.
x or $\mathbf{x}$	(bold) a vector.
x_i	(regular) the i-th element of a vector x.
$\mathcal{D}$	(calligraphic, capital) a set of points or values; a dataset.
x_i or $x^{(i)}$	the i-th vector in a dataset.

X   (bold) a matrix.

$\mathbf{X} \in \mathbb{R}^{m \times n}$ a matrix **X** which has m rows and n columns, populated with real values.

$\mathbf{X}_{ij}$ the element of matrix **X** in row i and column j.

$\mathbf{X}_{i*}, \mathbf{X}_{*j}$ the i-th row and j-th column of matrix **X**.

$\triangleq$ "defined as".

$\forall x$ forall x.

1   (bold) a vector of context-implied dimensionality with all entries equal to 1. E.g., **X1** means the row sums of **X**

(α) a matrix with all elements equal to some scalar α. For example, the expression $\mathbf{A} + (\alpha)$ means "add value α to all elements of a matrix **A**".

$\mathbf{X} \circ \mathbf{Y}$ the Hadamard product of **X** and **Y**.

$\mathbf{X}^{\circ \text{-}1}$ the Hadamard inverse:

$$\mathbf{X}^{\circ \text{-}1} \triangleq \begin{pmatrix} \frac{1}{x_{11}} & \frac{1}{x_{12}} & \cdots & \frac{1}{x_{1n}} \\ \frac{1}{x_{21}} & \frac{1}{x_{22}} & & \frac{1}{x_{2n}} \\ \vdots & \vdots & \ddots & \vdots \\ \frac{1}{x_{m1}} & \frac{1}{x_{m2}} & \cdots & \frac{1}{x_{mn}} \end{pmatrix}.$$

In a more general case, the Hadamard power is

$$\mathbf{X}^{\circ a} \triangleq \begin{pmatrix} x_{11}^a & x_{12}^a & \cdots & x_{1n}^a \\ x_{21}^a & x_{22}^a & \cdots & x_{2n}^a \\ \vdots & \vdots & \ddots & \vdots \\ x_{m1}^a & x_{m2}^a & \cdots & x_{mn}^a \end{pmatrix}.$$

As special cases, there are also the Hadamard square $\mathbf{X}^{\circ 2}$ and the Hadamard square root $\mathbf{X}^{\circ 0.5}$.

$\mathbf{X} \circ \mathbf{Y}^{\circ \text{-}1}$ element-wise division of **X** and **Y**.

$\langle \mathbf{x}, \mathbf{y} \rangle$ dot product – same as $\mathbf{x}^\top \mathbf{y}$.

$\log \mathbf{X}$ element-wise application of the natural logarithm to every element of matrix **X**.

$\text{abs}\left(\mathbf{X}\right)$ the element-wise absolute value of every element of matrix **X**.

For vectors, we assume a vertical orientation as the default:

$$\mathbf{x} = \begin{pmatrix} x_1 \\ x_2 \\ \vdots \\ x_n \end{pmatrix}.$$

Therefore, whenever we introduce a vector inline, we use transposition, e.g.: $\mathbf{x} = \begin{pmatrix} x_1 & x_2 & \cdots & x_n \end{pmatrix}^\top$.

For sets, we use capital letters of the calligraphic typeset, and we use braces in a definition: $\mathcal{C} \triangleq \{a, b, c\}$. Whenever we use subscript ordinals for labeling the elements, we imply that it is an *ordered* set by default:

$$\mathcal{C} \triangleq \{c_i : i = 1, 2, \ldots, n\}.$$

We use standard numeric sets: $\mathbb{R}$, the set of all real numbers, $\mathbb{C}$, the set of complex numbers, $\mathbb{N}_0$ and $\mathbb{N}_1$, the sets of all natural numbers, starting with 0 and 1 respectively.

Tensor sets include superscripts to denote their cardinalities. For example, $\mathbf{x} \in \mathbb{R}^k$ denotes a vector with k real numbers elements; $\mathbf{X} \in \{0, 1\}^{m \times n}$ denotes a matrix of m rows and n columns, with elements being only 0 or 1.

We use parenthesis for sequences:

$$\mathcal{A} \triangleq (a_1, a_2, \ldots, a_n).$$

We often consider datasets consisting of m multi-dimensional data points, i.e., vectors:

$$\mathcal{D} \triangleq \{\boldsymbol{x}_i : i = 1, 2, \ldots, m\}.$$

For the sake of an algebraic representation of these points, we often form a matrix $\mathbf{X}$ such that the data points form *rows* of the new matrix in the order of the corresponding data points in the ordered set $\mathcal{D}$:

$$\mathbf{X} \triangleq \begin{pmatrix} \boldsymbol{x}_1^\top \\ \boldsymbol{x}_2^\top \\ \vdots \\ \boldsymbol{x}_m^\top \end{pmatrix}.$$

We say that the matrix $\mathbf{X}$ is *induced* by the dataset $\mathcal{D}$, and sometimes also denote this construction as $\mathbf{X} \hookleftarrow \mathcal{D}$. As a convention, in this book $\mathbf{X} \hookleftarrow \mathcal{D}$ always means *row-wise* matrix construction from the points in the dataset.

The use of row-wise matrix formation mostly due to the fact that our main distributed type, the distributed row matrix (DRM), is serialized and partitioned by rows. Therefore, formulations for which the inputs are formed row-wise are more natural to think about when mapping to actual program code.

The Hadamard inverse and root notation (or the Hadamard power in the most general case) are not very common in literature. Instead, the conventional literature tends to use element-wise notation to define such operations, for example:

$$a_{ij} = x_{ij}/y_{ij}, \ \forall i, j.$$

In matrix form this is an application of the Hadamard inverse:

$$\mathbf{A} = \mathbf{X} \circ \mathbf{Y}^{\circ -1}.$$

The Mahout distributed algebra expression for these two equivalent notations is simply `drmA = drmX / drmY`. Since we do not explicitly manipulate every individual element when using such an expression in practice, we usually prefer matrix form notation to element-wise.

B

In-core Algebra Reference

In this appendix we consider the Samsara DSL related to in-core math only. That means that the operator arguments are either numeric value types, vectors (o.a.m.math. Vector), or matrices (o.a.m.math.Matrix).

The in-core DSL acts over org.apache.mahout.math.Matrix(Vector) trait implementations. These are actually Java interfaces, so Java methods are available along with the Scala DSL; however the Scala DSL is intended to use R-like semantics so one should prefer, eg., mxA.nrow to the Java interface's mxA.numRows() when writing code. As well, the DSL is not always a simple Java redirect; for example, the Scala matrix multiplication operator %*% is not the same as the Java times(), and is optimized quite differently when compared with the Java version. Some capabilities are thus unique to Scala DSL operations.

From here on out we assume a pure Scala environment and will consider the Scala DSL only.

B.1 Imports

The following two Scala imports are used to enable the Mahout Scala DSL bindings for Linear Algebra

```
import org.apache.mahout.math._
import scalabindings._
import RLikeOps._
```

Another option is to use the "MATLAB-like" dialect

```
import MatlabLikeOps._
```

However, Mahout's MATLAB-like dialect is significantly limited and for this reason the Mahout standard is its R-like dialect.

B.2 Inline initialization

Dense vectors

```
val denseVec1: Vector = (1.0, 1.1, 1.2)
val denseVec2 = dvec(1, 0, 1.1, 1.2)
```

Sparse vectors can be created from sequences of tuples (index, value)

```
val sparseVec = svec(5 → 1 :: 10 → 2.0 :: Nil)
val sparseVec2: Vector = 5 → 1.0 :: 10 → 2.0 :: Nil
```

Matrix inline initialization, either dense or sparse, is always row-wise:

dense matrices

```
val A = dense((1, 2, 3), (3, 4, 5))
```

sparse matrices

```
val A = sparse(
 (1 , 3),
 (0, 2) :: (1, 2.5) :: Nil
)
```

B.3 Diagonals and diagonal matrices

Diagonal matrix with constant diagonal elements.

```
diag(3.5, 10)
```

Diagonal matrix with its main diagonal backed by a vector.

```
diagv((1, 2, 3, 4, 5))
```

Obtaining a matrix's diagonal.

```
val dvec = mxA.diagv
```

Assigning values to a matrix's diagonal.

```
mxA.diagv = 3.0
```

Identity matrix.

```
eye(10)
```

B.4 Slicing and Assigning

General blocking/element access.

Getting a vector element

```
val d = vec(5)
```

Setting a vector element

```
vec(5) = 3.0
```

Getting a matrix element

```
val d = mxA(3, 5)
```

Setting a matrix element (setQuick() behind the scenes)

```
mxA(3, 5) = 3.0
```

Getting a matrix row or column

```
val rowVec = mxM(3, ::)
val colVec = mxM(::, 3)
```

Setting a matrix row or column

```
mxM(3, ::) = (1, 2, 3)
mxM(::, 3) = (1, 2, 3)
```

It also works via vector assignment

```
mxM(3, ::)  := (1, 2, 3)
mxM(::, 3)  := (1, 2, 3)
```

Sub-slices of a row or vector work too

```
a(0, 0 to 1) = (3, 5)
```

Or with vector assignment

```
a(0, 0 to 1) := (3, 5)
```

Assignment to the contiguous blocks of a matrix, as matrix assignment

```
// block
val mxB = A(2 to 3, 3 to 4)
// assignment to a block
mxA(0 to 1, 1 to 2) = dense((3, 2), (2, 3))
```

Or via the matrix assignment operator

```
A(0 to 1, 1 to 2) := dense((3, 2), (2, 3))
```

The assignment operator, used to copy between vectors or matrices

```
vec1 := vec2
M1  := M2
```

This also works in cases where the left hand side operand uses matrix or vector slicing.

Assignment thru a function literal (matrix).

```
mxA := { (row, col, x) ⇒ if (row == col) 1 else 0 }
// matrix functional in-place assignments
mxA := { x ⇒ x + 1.0 }
mxA ::= { x ⇒ x + 1.0 }
mxA := { (row, col, x) ⇒ x + 1.0 }
mxA ::= { (row, col, x) ⇒ x + 1.0 }
```

For a vector, the same

```
// Short functional literal
vec := sqrt _
// Vector functional in-place assignments
aVec := { x ⇒ x + 1.0 }
aVec ::= { x ⇒ x + 1.0 }
aVec := { (idx, x) ⇒ x + 1.0 }
aVec ::= { (idx, x) ⇒ x + 1.0 }
```

B.5 Element-wise operations

Plus/minus: vector, matrix, or numeric, with assignment or not

```
a + b
a - b
a + 5.0
a - 5.0
```

Hadamard (element-wise) product:vector, matrix, or numeric operands

```
a * b  // a∘b
a * 5  // 5∘a
5 * a
5 - a  // 5−a
5 / a  // 5∘a^{∘-1}
5 + a
```

Element-wise operators with in-place assignment (computation is performed on one of the operands)

```
a += b // a ← a+b
a -= b
a += 5.0
a -= 5.0
a *= b
a *= 5
1 / mxX // Hadamard inverse X^{∘-1}
```

Assignment with right-association below means "compute 5-a , in-place, and assign to a"

```
5 -=: a // a ← 5−a
```

Element-wise (Hadamard) power operator

```
a ^ 2  // Hadamard square, a^∘2
b ^= 2 // element-wise in-place b ← b^∘2
mxA ^ a  // Hadamard power A^∘a
```

B.6 Concatenation

B.6.1 Vector concatenation

```
a.c(b) // compare: c() operator in R
1.c(a) // we can also concatenate numeric values on right or left
a.c(5.0)
```

B.6.2 Matrix vertical and horizontal concatenation

Horizontal and vertical matrix concatenation

```
val mxC = mxA cbind mxB // horizontal, C ← (A | B)
```

$$\text{val mxC = mxA rbind mxB // vertical, } C \leftarrow \left(\frac{A}{B}\right)$$

```
// or infix
val mxC = mxA.cbind(mxB)


// concatenations involving scalar-expanded vectors:
val mxC = mxA.cbind(5.0) // C ← (A | 5)
val mxC = 3.0 cbind mxA  // C ← (3 | A)
```

$$\text{val mxC = mxA rbind 5.0 // } C \leftarrow \left(\frac{A}{5^\top}\right)$$

$$\text{val mxC = 5.0 rbind mxA // } C \leftarrow \left(\frac{5^\top}{A}\right)$$

B.7 Dot product

```
a dot b
```

B.8 Matrix /vector equivalence

Note that this is dangerous, the exact equivalence is rarely useful. It is better use norm comparisons with the admission of small errors

```
a === b
a !== b
```

B.9 Matrix multiplication (matrix operands)

```
mxA %*% mxB
```

B.10 Matrix-vector multiplication

Mahout directly supports matrix times vector operation

```
val a = dvec(1, 2, 3)
val mxB = dense((1, 2, 3), (3, 4, 5))
val mxC = mxB %*% aVec // C ← Ba
```

At the time of this writing, there is no a vector times matrix operation. Part of the reason is interpretation: $a\mathbf{B}$ really means that $\mathbf{B}$ must be a single-row matrix, which is usually denoted as $ab^\top$, which is 'a cross b'.

It is also possible to transform vectors to single-column matrices and do a functionally equivalent operation

```
mxC = aVec.toColMatrix %*% mxB // c ← aB
```

Something that might make sense is $a^\top\mathbf{B}$, but Mahout consciously does not support the notion of a vector orientation or transposition. All vectors in Mahout are assumed to be column-vectors (as they are in general math notations).

B.11 Transpose

```
val mxAt = mxA.t
```

 Transposition currently is handled via a *view*

B.12 Means and sums

```
mxA.colSums
mxA.colMeans
mxA.rowSums
mxA.rowMeans
v.mean
v.sum
```

B.13 First and second moments

Computing column-vise first and second moments

```
val (mu, variance) = colMeanVars(mxA)
val (mu, sigma) = colMeanStdevs(mxA)
```

B.14 Distance and squared distance matrices

Distance and square distance matrices (equivalent to the dist() routine in R)

```
val mxD = dist(mxA)
val mxDsq = sqDist(mxA)
```

Pairwise distance and pairwise squared distance matrices.

If $\mathbf{A} \in \mathbb{R}^{m \times d}$ and $\mathbf{B} \in \mathbb{R}^{n \times d}$ then these procedures compute a (square) distance matrix $\mathbf{D} \in \mathbb{R}^{m \times n}$ ($\mathbf{D}^{(2)} \in \mathbb{R}^{m \times n}$) such that $\mathbf{D}_{ij} \triangleq \left\| \mathbf{A}_{i*} - \mathbf{B}_{j*} \right\|_2$ (or $\mathbf{D}_{ij}^{(2)} \triangleq \left\| \mathbf{A}_{i*} - \mathbf{B}_{j*} \right\|_2^2$).

```
val mxD = dist(mxA, mxB)
val mxDsq = sqDist(mxA, mxB)
```

B.15 scala.math._ element-wise analogs

There are element-wise analogs of functions in scala.math: exp(), log(), sqrt(), abs(), signum(). By convention, functions accepting a matrix argument are prefixed with 'm', and functions accepting a vector argument are prefixed with 'v'. For example, the following is equivalent to computing first norm:

```
val norm1 = mabs(mxA).sum
```

B.16 Decompositions

All arguments in the following are matrices.

B.16.1 Cholesky decomposition

(as an object of the CholeskyDecomposition class with all its operations)

```
val ch = chol(mxA)
```

this computes $\mathbf{L}$, the lower triangular matrix of the decomposition

$$\mathbf{A} = \mathbf{L}\mathbf{L}^\top.$$

$\mathbf{A}$ must be square, symmetric and positive definite.

The $\mathbf{L}$ matrix of the decomposition is then can be obtained via method getL().

If $\mathbf{A}$ is not positive definite (within rounding error), then $\mathbf{L}$ may not be truly triangular and full rank. To detect if there's rank deficiency situation, one may consult isPositive-Definite() method.

Like some other compositions producing triangular matrix, Cholesky decomposition can be used for solving linear systems of the form

$$\mathbf{A}\mathbf{x} = \mathbf{b}.$$

If $\mathbf{A}$ is positive definite, then it can be decomposed $\mathbf{A} = \mathbf{L}\mathbf{L}^{\top}$, and then solved in two passes for one or more $\mathbf{b}$ by first solving $\mathbf{L}\mathbf{y} = \mathbf{b}$ for $\mathbf{y}$ using forward substitutions and then solving $\mathbf{L}^{\top}\mathbf{x} = \mathbf{y}$ using back substitution.

This same procedure can be optimized to solve a number of systems for the same matrix $\mathbf{A}$ at the same time of the combined algebraic form

$\mathbf{AX} = \mathbf{B}$.

In this case, let $\mathbf{Y} = \mathbf{L}^{\top}\mathbf{X}$. Then we are dealing with

(1) a forward substitution solver of $\mathbf{LY} = \mathbf{B}$ (for $\mathbf{Y}$); and
(2) a back substitution solver of $\mathbf{L}^{\top}\mathbf{X} = \mathbf{Y}$ (for $\mathbf{X}$).

In other words, the forward substitution solver computes $\mathbf{L}^{-1}\mathbf{M}$ and the back substitution solver computes $\left(\mathbf{L}^{\top}\right)^{-1}\mathbf{M}$ for some argument $\mathbf{M}$ in linear time without actually doing any inversions or matrix multiplications.

The forward substitution solver is implemented by the method `solveLeft(Matrix)` and the back substitution solver is implemented by the method `solveRight(Matrix)`[1].

B.16.2 SVD

```
val (mxU, mxV, s) = svd(mxA)
```

B.16.3 EigenDecomposition

```
val (mxV, d) = eigen(mxA)
```

B.16.4 QR decomposition

```
val (mxQ, mxR) = qr(mxA)
```

B.16.5 Rank

Check for rank deficiency (runs rank-revealing QR)

```
mxA.isFullRank
```

B.16.6 In-core SSVD

```
val (mxU, mxV, s) = ssvd(mxA, k = 50, p = 15, q = 1)
```

B.16.7 Solving linear equation systems and matrix inversion

This is fully similar to R semantics. There are three forms of invocation:

---

[1]In the current implementation at the time of this writing, back substitution actually computes $\mathbf{M}\left(\mathbf{L}^{\top}\right)^{-1}$ which is actually the same as `solveLeft(M`$^{\top}$`)`, so it probably needs to be looked at.

```
solve(mxA, mxB) // solves AX = B
solve(mxA, b) // solves Ax = b
solve(mxA)      // computes inverse A⁻¹
```

B.17 Miscellaneous

Second norm, vector or matrix argument.
```
a.norm
```

Vector cardinality.
```
a.length
```

Matrix cardinality.
```
mxA.nrow
mxA.ncol
```

A copy-by-value (vector or matrix).
```
val b = a cloned
```

Distributed Algebra Reference

In this appendix we consider the Mahout distributed DSL. That means that at least one operator argument is a distributed matrix (DrmLike[K]).

C.1 Imports

Backend-agnostic imports.

```
// Import matrix, vector types, etc.
import org.apache.mahout.math._

// Import scala bindings operations
import scalabindings._

// Enable R-like dialect in scala bindings
import RLikeOps._

// Import distributed matrix apis
import drm._

// Import R-like distributed dialect
import RLikeDrmOps._

// A good idea when working with mixed
// scala/java iterators and collections
import collection.JavaConversions._
```

Backend-agnostic decompositions (ssvd, qr etc.).

```
import org.apache.mahout.math.decompositions._
```

Spark-specific operations (wrap, export rdd, create a mahout context on a Spark session, etc.)

```
import org.apache.mahout.sparkbindings._
```

Spark-specific operations on an optimizer checkpoint are enabled by implicit conversion to the `CheckpointedDrmSparkOps` decorator. This decorator effectively adds only one Spark-specific operation to the distributed matrix: `rdd`.

C.2 DRM Persistence operators

C.2.1 Loading a DRM off (H)DFS

```
val drmA = drmDfsRead(path = hdfsPath)
```

C.2.2 Parallelizing from an in-core matrix

```
val mxA = dense((1, 2, 3), (3, 4, 5))
val drmA = drmParallelize(mxA)
```

C.2.3 Empty DRM

```
val drmA = drmParallelizeEmpty(100, 50)
```

C.2.4 Collecting a DRM to the driver's JVM as an in-core matrix

```
val mxA = drmA.collect()
```

 Collection of distributed matrices happens implicitly whenever the conversion to an in-core (o.a.m.math.Matrix) type is required.

```
val mxA:Matrix = ...
val drmB:DrmLike[Int] = ..
val mxC:Matrix = mxA %*% drmB
// implied: (mxA %*% drmB).collect
```

C.2.5 Collecting to HDFS

Collect a DRM to HDFS in Mahout's DRM format files[1]

```
drmA.dfsWrite(path = hdfsPath)
```

C.3 Caching

```
drmA.checkpoint(CacheHint.MEMORY_AND_DISK)
drmA.uncache()
```

C.4 Transposition

```
drmA.t
```

C.5 Element-wise +, -, *, /

```
drmA + drmB // A + B
drmA - drmB // A − B
drmA * drmB // A ∘ B
drmA / drmB // A ∘ B∘−1
```

---

[1]If you see an error here along the lines of "no implicit view available from A => org.apache.hadoop.io.Writable" most likely you just need to import SparkContext._.

```
drmA ^ k // A^∘k
```

```
k * drmA // kA
1 / drmA // Hadamard inverse A^∘⁻¹
...
```

Binary operators involving one in-core argument (only on Int-keyed DRMs)

```
drmA + mxB
drmA - mxB
drmA * mxB
drmA / mxB
// These are the only way to invoke
// with in-core left-hand-side operands
mxA +: drmB
mxA -: drmB
mxA *: drmB
mxA /: drmB
```

C.6 Matrix-matrix multiplication %*%

$$M = AB:$$

```
drmA %*% drmB
drmA %*% mxB
drmA %*% diagv(d)
drmA :%*% mxB
mxA %*%: drmB
```

The associativity of an operation must follow the distributed argument. That is, a left-hand-side in-core operand times a distributed operand is only currently possible as right-associative 'mxA %*%: drmB'.

C.7 Matrix-vector multiplication %*%

Currently, Mahout supports a right-multiply product of a DRM and a in-core Vector ($\mathbf{Ax}$), resulting in a distributed single-column DRM, which then of course could be collected in front (usually that's the desired outcome):

```
val drmAx = drmA %*% x
val mxX = drmAx.collect(::, 0)
```

C.8 Matrix-scalar +,-,*,/,^

In this context, matrix-scalar operations mean element-wise operations of every matrix element and a scalar.

```
A + 5.0
A - 5.0
5.0 - A
A * 5.0
A / 5.0
5.0 / A
```

 From Mahout-0.10.2 on, right-associative distributed operators albeit supported, make no real difference compared to the left-associative operators.

C.9 Slicing

Slicing (read-only) is supported mostly identically to in-core slicing. A slicing row or range is of the Scala Range type, which typically can be inlined as x to y or x until y. All-range is given by ::.

General slice

```
drmA(100 to 200, 100 to 200)
```

Horizontal block

```
drmA(::, 100 to 200)
```

Vertical block

```
drmA(100 to 200, ::)
```

Note: if the row range is not all-range (::) then the DRM rows must be Int-keyed. Row slicing in the general case is not supported for key types other than Int.

C.10 Concatenation

```
val drmC = drmA cbind drmB // horizontal, C ← (A | B)

val drmC = drmA rbind drmB // vertical, C ← (A/B)

val drmC = drmA.cbind(drmB)

// concatenations involving scalar-expanded vectors:
val drmC = drmA.cbind(5.0) // C ← (A | 5)
val drmC = 3.0 cbind drmA  // C ← (3 | A)
```

$$\text{val drmC = mxA rbind 5.0 } // \ \mathbf{C} \leftarrow \left(\frac{\mathbf{A}}{\mathbf{5}^\top} \right)$$

$$\text{val drmC = 5.0 rbind drmA } // \ \mathbf{C} \leftarrow \left(\frac{\mathbf{5}^\top}{\mathbf{A}} \right)$$

C.11 Ad-hoc summaries

There are a number of operators that do not return a new distributed matrix. As such, some of them may or do trigger a computational action.

The rule of thumb is: if a method returns any in-core results, it almost always means it would trigger a computational action. Notorious exceptions are the matrix geometry properties nrow and ncol, which are usually already known via algebraic optimizer inference.

C.11.1 nrow, ncol

```
val (m, n) = (drmA.nrow, drmA.ncol)
```

C.11.2 colSums, colMeans

```
val acs = drmA.colSums
val ameans = drmA.colMeans
```

The above will *always* trigger a *computational action*. There is no lazy behavior for them (vector properties are considered to be too bulky to be a lazy property). That is, if one calls colSums n times, then the back-end will also recompute colMeans n times.

C.11.3 rowMeans, rowSums, rowSumsMap

Distributed rowMeans and rowSums operations are supported provided the distributed matrix is Int-keyed. If the matrix row keys are not of Int type, it is not possible to map such indexes into the ordinal indices of a vector result.

Regardless of the row key type, the rowSumsMap operation produces result as a map between a non-Int key and a corresponding row sum, loaded into the driver memory. See the scaladoc for details.

C.11.4 Matrix norm

The following procedure computes the second norm of a distributed matrix:

```
drmA.norm
```

C.11.5 Column-wise variances, standard deviations and covariance matrix

Column-wise means, variances and standard deviations

```
val (mu, sigmaSq) = dcolMeanVars(drmA)
val (mu, sigma) = dcolMeanStdevs(drmA)
```

Computing a covariance matrix has two variations: thin and wide.

Let the input geometry be $\mathbf{A} \in \mathbb{R}^{m \times n}$.

The thin procedure can run a bit faster but assumes that a single machine can hold (and serialize) an $n \times n$ dense matrix in memory, all other memory expenses are extra.

```
val (mu, mxSigma) = dcolMeanCovThin(drmA)
```

The wide procedure can compute covariances of wider matrices and the split result among different nodes (wide covariance is still an expensive procedure due to the asymptotic cost of the procedure).

```
val (mu, drmSigma) = dcolMeanCov(drmA)
```

Since the thin procedure produces an in-core matrix result, it will always trigger computation. The wide procedure will only trigger a computation of the mean; the covariance matrix result is subject to lazy evaluation.

C.12 Distance and Squared Distance

Definitions of the distributed versions of these methods follow the same definitions as the in-core versions in §B.14. As of the time of this writing, only squared distance functionality is available as a standard function.

```
val drmDistSq = dsqDist(drmA)
```

Of course, a regular distance matrix is only one step away:

```
val drmDist = dsqrt(drmDistSq)
```

C.13 Distributed Decompositions

C.13.1 Imports for decompositions package

```
import org.apache.mahout.math.decompositions._
```

Note that this package contains both in-core and distributed variants of decompositions.

C.13.2 Distributed thin QR

```
val (drmQ, mxR) = dqrThin(drmA)
```

C.13.3 Distributed Stochastic SVD (dssvd, ssvd)

The following procedure computes the reduced rank singular value decomposition of a distributed matrix.

```
val (drmU, drmV, s) = dssvd(drmA, k = 40, q = 1)
```

For more complete information about parameters and limitations, see the scaladoc. The in-core counterpart method name is `ssvd()`.

These are the same methods that are discussed at length in chapter 5.

C.13.4 Distributed regularized and non-regularized ALS (dals)

ALS (alternating least squares) is an approximate numerical procedure for computing a matrix factorization corresponding to a local minimum of ALS (squared) loss with Tikhonov regularization. The regularization parameter (not shown in the example) is used as a way to counter overfitting effects of the ALS procedure. Here is the most simple use example:

```
val (drmU, drmV, rmse) = dals(drmA, k).toTuple
```

Here, $\mathbf{A} \approx \mathbf{U}\mathbf{V}^\top$: $\mathbf{A} \in \mathbb{R}^{m \times n}$, $\mathbf{U} \in \mathbb{R}^{m \times k}$, $\mathbf{V} \in \mathbb{R}^{n \times k}$. The return parameter *rmse* is a sequence of RMSE metrics computed after each iteration, which can be subsequently used for convergence analysis. As it stands, the code computes the RMSE metric only if the conversion threshold is greater than 0 (i.e., the procedure is instructed to watch conversion based on the RMSE decrease). If the conversion threshold is not specified, the decomposition just alternates "maximum allowed iterations" number of times.

For further details, see the scaladoc.

Bibliography

Dimitris Achlioptas. Database-friendly random projections. In *Proceedings of the twentieth ACM SIGMOD-SIGACT-SIGART symposium on Principles of database systems*, pages 274–281. ACM, 2001.

David Arthur and Sergei Vassilvitskii. k-means++: The advantages of careful seeding. In *Proceedings of the eighteenth annual ACM-SIAM symposium on Discrete algorithms*, pages 1027–1035. Society for Industrial and Applied Mathematics, 2007.

Bahman Bahmani, Benjamin Moseley, Andrea Vattani, Ravi Kumar, and Sergei Vassilvitskii. Scalable k-means++. *Proceedings of the VLDB Endowment*, 5(7):622–633, 2012.

Christopher M Bishop. *Pattern recognition and machine learning*. springer, 2006.

Sanjoy Dasgupta and Anupam Gupta. An elementary proof of a theorem of johnson and lindenstrauss. *Random structures and algorithms*, 22(1):60–65, 2003.

Scott C. Deerwester, Susan T Dumais, Thomas K. Landauer, George W. Furnas, and Richard A. Harshman. Indexing by latent semantic analysis. *JAsIs*, 41(6):391–407, 1990.

James Demmel, Laura Grigori, Mark Hoemmen, and Julien Langou. Communication-optimal parallel and sequential qr and lu factorizations. *SIAM Journal on Scientific Computing*, 34(1):A206–A239, 2012.

Richard O Duda, Peter E Hart, et al. *Pattern classification and scene analysis*, volume 3. Wiley New York, 1973.

SEC EDGAR. Manchester united plc, 2013. URL `http://www.sec.gov/Archives/edgar/data/1549107/000104746913009876/a2217035z20-f.htm`. Form 20-F. Retrieved 15-January-2016 from the SEC EDGAR website.

SEC EDGAR. The madison square garden company, 2014. URL `http://www.sec.gov/Archives/edgar/data/1469372/000146937214000008/msg6302014-10k.htm`. Form 10-K. Retrieved 15-January-2016 from the SEC EDGAR website.

Charles Elkan. Using the triangle inequality to accelerate k-means. In *ICML*, volume 3, pages 147–153, 2003.

Gene H Golub and Charles F Van Loan. *Matrix computations*, volume 3. JHU Press, 2012.

Nathan Halko, Per-Gunnar Martinsson, and Joel A Tropp. Finding structure with randomness: Probabilistic algorithms for constructing approximate matrix decompositions. *SIAM review*, 53(2):217–288, 2011.

Nathan P Halko. *Randomized methods for computing low-rank approximations of matrices*. PhD thesis, University of Colorado, 2012.

David Heckerman. *A tutorial on learning with Bayesian networks*. Springer, 1998.

Gareth James, Daniela Witten, Trevor Hastie, and Robert Tibshirani. *An introduction to statistical learning*, volume 112. Springer, 2013.

Ping Li, Trevor J Hastie, and Kenneth W Church. Very sparse random projections. In *Proceedings of the 12th ACM SIGKDD international conference on Knowledge discovery and data mining*, pages 287–296. ACM, 2006.

Norman Matloff. *The art of R programming: A tour of statistical software design*. No Starch Press, 2011.

Douglas C Montgomery, Elizabeth A Peck, and G Geoffrey Vining. *Introduction to linear regression analysis*, volume 821. John Wiley & Sons, 2012.

Kevin P Murphy. *Machine learning: a probabilistic perspective*. MIT press, 2012.

Jorge Nocedal and Stephen Wright. *Numerical optimization*. Springer Science & Business Media, 2006.

Martin Odersky, Philippe Altherr, Vincent Cremet, Burak Emir, Stphane Micheloud, Nikolay Mihaylov, Michel Schinz, Erik Stenman, and Matthias Zenger. The scala language specification, 2004.

Jason D Rennie, Lawrence Shih, Jaime Teevan, David R Karger, et al. Tackling the poor assumptions of naive bayes text classifiers. In *ICML*, volume 3, pages 616–623. Washington DC), 2003.

Karen Sparck Jones. A statistical interpretation of term specificity and its application in retrieval. *Journal of documentation*, 28(1):11–21, 1972.

Gilbert Strang. The fundamental theorem of linear algebra. *The American Mathematical Monthly*, 100(9):848–855, 1993.

Gilbert Strang and Wellesley-Cambridge Press. *Introduction to linear algebra*, volume 3. Wellesley-Cambridge Press Wellesley, MA, 1993.

Wikipedia.org. Johnson-lindenstrauss lemma. 2015a. URL https://en.wikipedia.org/wiki/Johnson-Lindenstrauss_lemma.

Wikipedia.org. Memory barrier. 2015b. URL https://en.wikipedia.org/wiki/Memory_barrier.

Wikipedia.org. Principal component analysis. 2015c. URL https://en.wikipedia.org/wiki/Principal_component_analysis.

Wikipedia.org. Random projection. 2015d. URL http://en.wikipedia.org/wiki/Random_projection.

Index

About the authors

Dmitriy Lyubimov is a data scientist who focuses on solving numerical problems on shared-nothing distributed architectures. He is an Apache Mahout contributor since 2010 and a committer since 2011. His additions to the project include distributed and non-distributed variants of Stochastic SVD, Stochastic PCA, Givens and Cholesky QR, regularized ALS and others. He contributed the initial version of the platform independent algebraic optimizer that later became the core new feature of the Mahout Samsara release.

Andrew Palumbo is a consultant specializing in large scale econometric, demographic and financial database development and analysis. He contributed the Naive Bayes implementation to the new Samsara Environment and has contributed to all three backend engine bindings. Andrew maintains both the MapReduce and Samsara versions of Naive Bayes and is an active Apache Mahout committer and PMC member.

www.ingramcontent.com/pod-product-compliance
Lightning Source LLC
Chambersburg PA
CBHW080405060326
40689CB00019B/4137